The Naked Backpacker

Hazel Porteous

Copyright © Hazel Porteous, 2017

The moral right of Hazel Porteous has been asserted.

All Rights Reserved. No part of this publication may be reproduced, stored in a retrieval system, or transmitted, in any form or in any means, by electronic, mechanical, photocopying, recording or otherwise, without prior written permission of the author.

I have tried to recreate events, locales and conversations from my memories of them. In order to maintain their anonymity in some instances I have changed the names of individuals, places and order of events. I may have changed some identifying characteristics and details such as physical properties, occupations and places of residence.

National Library of Australia Cataloguing-in Publication Entry:

Porteous, Hazel, 1965-

The Naked Backpacker / Hazel Porteous

ISBN: 9781541025783 (paperback)

Porteous, Hazel – Travel / Women Travelers – Biography / Voyages and Travel / Adventure Travel / Backpacking

First Edition

Printed by Createspace

CHAPTER ONE – THE MIGHTY MUNCHER
Zimbabwe

I couldn't breathe, submerged with tiny bubbles surrounding me in my murky tomb. Disorientated, I couldn't work out which direction to go. Every crevice, dip or hollow of my body had been invaded, gripped by the frigid fingers of the raging river. The aeration held me under, the liquid crushing my bones and constricting my chest as the energy drained rapidly from my body. Closing my eyes, I could see shimmering stars amongst the darkness. Oxygen deprivation was exhausting, and I could feel the essence ebbing from my spirit, but I wasn't giving up yet.

It had all began in 1994, when I travelled through Zimbabwe with my husband Russ. He had been the one who wanted to go whitewater rafting. I was just going along for the ride.

It took two bus journeys and a matatu ride to get to the border of Zimbabwe, which we crossed on foot.

'I'm so tired,' I said as I dragged my feet, step by step.

'It's been a long day,' replied Russ, stifling a yawn.

'Can I offer you a lift?' enquired an elderly South African man.

'Oh, yes please,' we both sang out together. Inside his Mercedes, I sunk into the plush seat, which was cool against my aching limbs. The smell of leather, mixed with a hint of aftershave, teased my nostrils. 'Could you drop us at the local campsite?' I asked, wishing I could stay in the comfort of his air-conditioned vehicle.

'Thank you,' we called back to him as we headed towards reception. It was now dark, and I couldn't wait to collapse on a relaxing bed. On discovering the campsite was full, I squeezed back tears. I knew we didn't have too many options and was concerned we wouldn't find anywhere to stay.

Despondently, I urged my feet forward as my muscles complained. Walking towards the only hotel in town that was on our affordable list, a young couple pulled over in their vehicle.

'Are you looking for somewhere to stay?' the girl enquired.

'Yes, everything seems to be full though, except the five star hotels,' I replied.

'We're also looking for somewhere cheap to stay. Perhaps we can find somewhere together?'

Precious, the security guard at the hotel where we were headed, kindly advised, 'If you drive to the park ranger's home in the Victoria Falls National Park my cousin, Antony, might let you stay with him.'

Arriving at the compound, Russ got out of the car and called out, 'Antony, are you there?'

At that moment, it dawned on me that the reason for the high chain-link fence around the buildings was to keep out predators. I called out to Russ, 'Simba. Simba. Get back in the car. A lion is coming.'

He quickly scrambled back inside and laughed. There wasn't a lion in sight, not that we could see much further than a few metres in the darkness. Luckily Vincent, Antony's son, had heard him and came out to let us in.

'Any chance we could sleep on your floor for a couple of days? Precious suggested you might be able to help us, and we can pay with US dollars in cash,' Russ said.

'Sure, I will find some blankets to lay on the ground,' he replied as his eyes lit up.

I was grateful to him for being so hospitable and didn't mind roughing it for a while, because it meant we could visit Victoria Falls. The next morning, we got a lift to town and walked to the National Park.

The rainforest of tall palms, ferns and vines opened to reveal the lookout. A rainbow arched above Devil's Cataract, produced by the diffusion of sunlight on the vapour generated by the torrent cascading below.

The thundering water caused a thick mist over the Zambezi River, plunging down into a massive gorge and travelling for miles to eventually merge into the Indian Ocean.

'I can see why the locals call it the Smoke that Thunders,' Russ said.

'Me too. I'm damp,' I replied coated in the fine spray.

Back in town, we dropped in at the agency to book on what was claimed to be the wildest one day whitewater rafting trip in the world.

'It's very popular. I'm sure you will both have a fabulous time,' advised the Manager. 'Oh, and don't forget to watch out for the crocodiles.'

I laughed and paid for the trip.

'I'm still not at all sure I want to do this, Russ. It's dangerous, and I don't want to be eaten by a crocodile,' I said when we were leaving the booking office.

'He's only joking. I'm sure you'll love it,' he replied as we headed back to our room.

That night, I didn't sleep well on the floor, because I kept thinking about dying. I wasn't at my height of fitness, and I certainly couldn't fight off a reptile categorised as a serious threat to humans.

I dreamt I was a child again, trying to swim faster than my sister. It was exhilarating diving into the pool and racing as fast as I could, lap after lap, along the marked lanes. The trainer was explaining a good technique as I listened intently to him, 'Cup your hands to push harder and faster through the water.'

I woke suddenly, with the collywobbles. We were picked up early in the morning. Because we'd selected to run three extra rapids on the Zambian side, we had to go through passport control before being dropped off at the top of the gorge for a briefing.

'There's no going back now,' teased Russ.

One of the guides handed out life jackets and safety helmets, which we helped each other to do up tightly, so there would be no chance of sliding out of them. I used a piece of string to securely tie my glasses to my swimsuit strap. I applied sunscreen to my face, shoulders and arms, but not my legs as I didn't want to slip out of the raft. The guide was running through the dangers we might encounter before asking everyone to sign an indemnity form.

'Russ, I thought they were joking when they said there were crocodiles in the river. I'm also worried about my glasses. If I have to take them off before I go through each rapid, then how am I going to see if I fall out?'

'Well, it's too late now to back out. You'll just have to make the most of it.'

I started down the four hundred foot canyon.

'Be careful. It's very slippery on the rocks,' I warned Russ whilst I slid and stumbled along the hazardous steep descent.

When we finally arrived at the edge of the mighty Zambezi, the guide said, 'Grab the rope stretched around the rock face, and swing yourself across into the inflatable.'

I turned to Russ, 'I just know I'm going to fall in. I won't be able to hold on, as my arms and legs are jelly.' Russ swung himself across first.

'Look it is easy,' he said as he took my hand and helped me get in.

The air was cool, and the calm water looked inky black from the shadows cast by the steep sides of the gorge. There was an eerie stillness which made me shiver.

Once the other five passengers were all aboard, Moshe, the guide asked, 'Who would like to be at the front? It's more challenging there and slightly easier at the back.'

I immediately replied, 'I'd like to be at the back.'

'I choose the front,' Russ chimed in.

It was low water season so the best time of year for rafting. Moshe explained a few manoeuvres, one he called "high siding" and then asked us to try them out.

He shouted, 'Forward.' Everyone leant towards the front. Russ got squashed under the surface by two of the other guys next to him.

Moshe then yelled, 'Left,' shortly followed by 'Right.'

I could see Russ was enjoying himself by his smile and hoped I could get through the trip in one piece. Could I remember which was left and which was right whilst under pressure? I knew it wasn't going to be easy.

Our guide started paddling and explained what was ahead, 'The first rapid is classed as a grade five. Follow my directions quickly as it could be the difference between tipping over and staying upright.'

I was squatting in the back of the raft and holding on to the safety rope tightly with both hands. I was trying to work out how to get from one side to the other without letting go.

As we neared the first rapid, I removed my glasses and stowed them down my cleavage. I could hear, but not see, the deafening rush of water and grasped the rope even tighter. Moshe was shouting instructions. I found myself holding my breath as the back of the raft disappeared under the frothing cappuccino. Everyone was soaked. As soon as I had the chance, I took a big gulp of air before being submerged by another wall of liquid. I was being agitated like dirty laundry in a top-loader washing machine.

As we cleared the white water, I became aware my fingers had gone numb from holding on so tightly. The churning in my stomach subsided when I realized we'd made it through the first one. Only seventeen more to go, I thought.

Silently, we glided along the flat river, but just as I started to relax, Moshe explained, 'We're approaching the next rapid, and it's going to be over a big drop, so there's a good chance the vessel could flip.'

Once again, I took off my glasses as the thunder became louder. Without them I could barely see the drop, let alone the cascade below.

Moshe shouted, 'Get down.' Before I had time to inhale, massive waves were breaking over the vessel, tossing it around like a toy and the back was once again swamped. I thought I was going to suffocate as there was no time for breathing between each wave. Coming out of the rapid, I was trembling but with a wide grin because we hadn't flipped.

The next lot of fast moving water came up all too quickly. Here we go again, I thought. I was ready this time and filled my lungs with air. It was a short rapid, but the raft spun around like the teacup ride at a theme park when it reached the swirling whirlpools. I'd survived the first three and hadn't fallen out. Maybe it wasn't going to be so bad after all, I hoped insecurely. I began to understand why I'd let Russ talk me into this trip. I was shivering, a mixture of adrenalin and being cold and wet.

Strengthening my resolve, I listened as Moshe explained, 'The next is the longest stretch on the trip. In fact it's actually made up of four different rapids running consecutively.'

The force of the water through the narrow gorge had a fury I'd never seen before. It wasn't surprising considering the enormous volume cascading over Victoria Falls. It all had to go somewhere.

The angry bubbling river broke over the inflatable from all directions. It was hard to cling on to the safety line, but I wasn't going to let go under any circumstances. I would inhale another mouthful of oxygen as soon as there was a chance, however brief. The current was carrying the raft along, which Moshe skilfully manoeuvred through the series of rapids, the turbulence appearing endless. We hit a large boulder and bounced off, just a tiny speck on the surface of a wild snake, twisting and turning along a course cut long ago through the gully.

The peaceful stretch of river that followed was a wonderful contrast. The sun shone down and warmed my skin. I smiled, gently releasing my grip whilst I sat on the side of the raft and admired the scenery. Green bushes occasionally clung to the steep sides of the barren rocky ravine. The only other way out would be by helicopter.

Moshe pointed out a crocodile and advised, 'The park rangers can't remove them unless they have actually attacked a vessel.' I shuddered, feeling vulnerable to its sharp teeth puncturing the rubber dinghy. It gave new meaning to the idiom "Sitting Duck".

As we drew near another rapid, Moshe asked, 'Would anyone prefer to take the Chicken Run as one of the other rafts is going to take that route whilst I will steer the more difficult centre of the drop off.'

I decided to stay and take the main run because we hadn't tipped over so far. I also thought that I stood more chance of falling in trying to climb from our inflatable into the other. I could see the kayaks waiting nearby to help out should someone fall in, and it boosted my confidence.

This was a formidable rapid with a five metre hole. I braced myself when we moved forward. Moshe skilfully guided us around the sharp razor edges of the rocks in the centre of the river. Surfing along a wave, we plummeted down deeper and deeper into the whisked egg white, buoyantly rising back up, liquid streaming off the bloated tubes, only to be flicked by a side curler, spinning the vessel upside down and sprinkling us all into the mighty muncher like sugar in a café latte. Within seconds, I was underwater and regretting my decision. The flip happened so quickly that one second I was in the raft and the next submerged. Confused, I tried not to panic, because I needed to conserve oxygen.

A vision of my mum appeared in the gloom. Her short grey tresses revealed her smooth complexion and generous smile. Tall and slender, she bent like a reed in the harsh wind, but she was a sturdy oak when I needed her, branching out to me affectionately. She encouraged me to work hard and follow my dreams. What would she think if I drowned at such a young age?

My dad was beside her. I'd inherited his thin hair, dark eyelashes and acrophobia. Standing on the edge of a precipice, he would shake from the top of his receding hairline all the way to his neatly cut toenails. Being scared of heights neither hindered or helped me in this moment, although I could have done with his great sense of humour, because he often made me laugh with his quips.

In front of them, was my sister Diana. Her beauty won her first prize in a baby contest at the age of one. Her ebony eyes glistened as she grinned at me. She was my playmate from an early age. I'd sit in her swing, and she would push me making me laugh. Laugh, would I ever do so again?

My eyes swam into focus and slowly followed the length of my arms towards my hands which were miraculously still clinging to the taut line. Looking towards what I thought must be the surface, I thrashed, striking out with my legs towards the tunnel of light. The current carried me along silently as I reached towards the images swirling into the darkness and disappearing. No, this couldn't be the end. I longed to see them again. To touch them. To hold them.

I kicked with my feet using all the energy I could summons, desperate for air until my head finally broke the churning surface and another wave crashed over me. I gasped and gulped a mouthful of water. My knuckles turned chalky, clinging tightly whilst being tossed along the intimidating stretch of white water. I hoped there weren't any crocodiles nearby.

Moshe stirred me from my reverie. The thoughts of my family fading when he grabbed hold of the shoulders of my life jacket and pulled. He was on top of the upturned craft making sure there wasn't anyone missing whilst pulling each person to safety.

He heaved again and shouted, 'You have to help me pull you up.'

I heard myself barely murmur, 'I can't. I'm exhausted.'

I propelled my legs as I released my grip on the safety line and flopped on top of the raft like a scoop of quivering gelatine. I looked for Russ, who was already on board and smiling at me.

Establishing everyone was accounted for, Moshe advised, 'Jump back in whilst I right the inflatable.'

When he was sure everyone was unharmed, he explained, 'The next rapid is classed a grade six, so un-runnable as it's a serious risk to life. Therefore, we'll lift the rafts out and carry them around.'

I considered the last one had been a serious risk to my life already. As we pulled ashore, I appreciated the solid land under my feet. We struggled to carry the heavy boat across the rocky bank and drop it back into the river.

There was only one more before lunch and Moshe said, 'This rapid is going to be easy as it's just a class four.'

'I can't wait to stop for a break,' I confessed to Russ, because I needed time to unwind.

The food was delicious, and I talked to him whilst listening to the vervet monkeys chattering in the tree tops. Their cute little black faces peered down at me from their olive coats. I knew they disliked water as much as I was beginning to. I sipped at my drink, careful not to consume much as I was wearing a one-piece swimsuit and didn't want to strip naked to relieve myself behind a tree, and I certainly wasn't going to get back in the Zambezi voluntarily.

'It's great to dry out from the warmth of the sun,' I said.

'Are you happy to carry on? You can leave at this point if you would really like to.' Russ suggested.

'What doesn't kill you makes you stronger, but hopefully it will be easier this afternoon.'

As Moshe called everyone together, bruised and battered I was ready to face my demons. It was all going smoothly until he explained, 'We have reached the last rapid, which is made up of three massive waves, the third one being renowned for the most raft flips in the world.'

A wave of nausea overwhelmed me as we approached the last whitecap, and the front of the inflatable lifted to almost vertical. I leaned forward resting my hand on the floor of the craft, illogically trying to push it back down and inhaled deeply to prepare for the worst. Pearls of salty water decorated my forehead. I prayed, and my guardian angel must have been listening. My jaw hung slack when the vessel dropped back down, and we were safely through.

'We made it, we actually made it,' I stammered with a beaming grin.

'We haven't quite finished yet. We have this steep gorge to get out of first,' replied Russ.

When I looked up, I bit my lip. There were ladders in places it was too steep to climb. Not only was I scared of heights but not fit enough to tackle that sort of climb. Adrenalin had got me through the day, but it was running out now. I was tired and thirsty.

'It's 750 feet high. That's equivalent to about seventy storeys. It'll be a breeze,' said Russ, tying his shoelaces securely.

'Please wait for me. I'm going to be the slowest,' I pleaded.

In order for me to keep up, we would rest every fifty metres or so. My legs had become marshmallows, protesting at each new step. My hands trembled as I gripped the side of the ladder, and drops of perspiration raced down my cheeks, jumping like lemmings off the end of my chin. I swayed dizzily, my eyelids squeezed together, so I couldn't see how far the sweat had fallen. Never looking up or down, I fumbled my way cautiously upwards breathing heavily.

'Wow, look at the porters steaming ahead up the slope with the heavy rafts on their shoulders. They must be strong,' pointed out Russ.

'I can't look,' I admitted, 'I need to concentrate on not letting go.'

Just behind us, Moshe confessed, 'The climb never gets any easier, and I struggle being a smoker.'

When we finally reached the top, the bottle of icy water from the back of the truck bubbled down my throat like the Zambezi restoring life along its route. I still couldn't believe I'd survived the journey. Although the next day I could hardly move, my muscles ached, and I was sore from the grazes and bruises. Browsing the shelves of a local shop, I discovered it was too painful for me to lift my arms to pick up anything. I must have jarred them hanging on to the life line when we flipped over.

CHAPTER TWO – SWEET GYPSY BLOOD
England, Singapore, Australia

I was born in England during the sixties, a flower child, oblivious to the declining economy and high taxes whilst nurtured in a cocoon of love and peace. My eyes were a kaleidoscope of colours. The dark pupil, surrounded by shades of topaz with hints of amber, softly merged into a ring of blue haze which harmonised with my wavy long tresses. Often mistaken for my sister because many people thought we looked alike, I knew that only I had dimples when I smiled. My mother described me as being a well behaved chatterbox, who loved climbing, cuddling animals, eating chocolate buttons, listening to music and dancing. However, I also remember being shy and lacking confidence in myself.

During that decade and the first half of the next, my family holidays were spent in South England in Devon, Cornwall, Sussex, the Isle of Wight and Wales. There were enticing sites to explore, fascinating people to meet and many new places to learn about. We didn't have to wear seat belts, so often Dad would put down the back seat of his Austin Maxi, to make a larger boot, so Diana and I could sleep stretched out in the back of the car.

I suffered from travel sickness on the road, on the water and in the air. Mum often reminded me of one time we visited Wales.

She would tell everyone, 'You wouldn't believe this, but when Hazel was six years old, she was sick six times in the back of the car on the way there.'

She used to put travel sickness tablets inside a glacé cherry for me to swallow before the trip started, but they tasted disgusting and never seemed to work.

I recall visiting Beddgelert. The local legend was about a prince who left his devoted wolfhound Gelert to guard his son. When he returned from a hunting trip, there was blood everywhere, and he thought his dog had mauled his baby. Plunging his sword into his faithful hound, only moments later he realized the blood was from the wolf that Gelert had slain to protect his successor.

I was at the impressionable age of six and illogically pleaded with my father, 'Dad, please carry me on your shoulders. I'm frightened.'

The strength and stamina he had from playing regular badminton matches was useful because I wouldn't let him put me down for the rest of the day. Even though the wolf was dead, I was convinced it would attack me too. During the night I couldn't sleep, worried it might find me. Every time I closed my eyes, I could see images of it waiting to pounce on me from under the bed. I was sharing a room with Diana, and my parents were asleep in a room upstairs in the guesthouse. I was sweating, not daring to move. Eventually I gathered enough courage to get out of bed, put my feet on the floor and climb the stairs to my parent's room, all the while imaging the wolf might come.

When I got there and knocked on the door, all Mum said was, 'Hazel go back to bed. The wolf is dead.'

A yearning to travel had always been in my blood. I wasn't sure whether this was inherited from my great-grandmother who was a Romany Gypsy, or I was just born with a curiosity to see the world. I never even met my grandmother because she died of meningitis when my mum was only a year old. I didn't know exactly what I was searching for but wanted to see what was out there. I was looking for warmth, not just from sunshine but from love and happiness.

As a child, I was fascinated with my dad's collection of stamps, and sometimes he would let me help him soak them in water and peel them off the envelopes. I wondered about the pictures of mystic destinations like Zanzibar, Tanganyika, Siam and Rhodesia. They conjured up images of remote, exotic faraway places full of mystery and oriental aromas of spices and incense.

I enjoyed school and learning about different countries and cultures.

During an English class, the teacher pointed at Jane and asked, 'What do you want to do when you leave school?'

'I'd like to get married and have two children,' she replied.

'Susan, what do you want to do?'

'I want to find the perfect man and have a big white wedding, wearing a dazzling ball gown.' Many of the girls wished for the same thing.

'Deidre, what about you?'

'I'd like to be a model.'

I blushed when he called out my name.

'I'd love to travel,' I stuttered.

There must be more to life than wedlock, I thought. I was determined to travel the world before settling down. I just needed someone like-minded to travel with, but unfortunately none of my friends were interested in doing so. I read about places such as Egypt (where I longed to see the giant pyramids at Giza), Kenya (where the plains were filled with herds of zebra, wildebeest and antelope, as far as the eye could see) and Rome (where the mammoth monuments like the Colosseum and Vatican City tower above you).

In geography class, we learnt there were five continents, Europe, Africa, Asia, Australasia and America. I hoped one day I'd have the opportunity to explore each of these regions.

Two years later, I couldn't have been more excited when Mum told me, 'We're going to Australia to visit my sister.'

'Wow, does that mean we get to fly in an airplane?' I asked, my eyes shining as I hopped from one leg to the other.

'Yes, and the flight will take thirty-six hours, but we will stop in Singapore for a few days on the way there.'

I hadn't visited anywhere outside of Europe. My Aunty and her family immigrated to Australia when I was still a baby, so I'd no memories about her, my uncle or five cousins.

There was much to organize before we could leave, and because we were stopping in Asia for a few days, needed vaccinations against polio, small pox and cholera. At a young age, I'd already been given shots against whooping cough and diphtheria and had suffered from measles and chicken pox so had built an immunity. Mum had contracted tuberculosis before I was born, so I had my BCG vaccination at only six months old.

'Thanks Mum for my new lightweight clothes,' I said appreciatively.

'They're made of cotton or natural fibres for our trip because it's going to be hot,' she replied.

Immediately the plane doors opened at Singapore airport, the humidity hit me. I'd never been anywhere warm, except France where the heat was dry. The mugginess in Singapore was oppressive. I started to sweat and felt like a piece of fish steaming in a plastic bag. It was a relief to walk into our air-conditioned hotel on Orchard Road. Once more, I could breathe and slowly cooled down whilst I guzzled the jug of ice water in our room.

As part of a tour, we visited the famous Raffles Hotel, the colourful Tiger Balm Gardens and Chinatown. The afternoon monsoon rain teamed down like spilt tepid broth and dampened the washing strung out on poles from apartment windows. At the outdoor show, I floated up to the stage to hold a python around my neck. At least it was cool, its smooth dry scales soothing against my clammy skin. I posed for a photo with my new friend.

We spent an afternoon sailing on a Junk. The breeze from the Southern Islands, as we passed Malay fishing villages built on stilts, circulated the sultry air. I was sticky, and my energy was sapped until we returned to the haven of our chilled hotel room.

Not having been brought up on spicy food, I struggled to find something to eat on the dinner menu. Unusual aromas wafted from the kitchen, not entirely enticing.

'Mum, is there anything on the menu I might like to eat?' I asked.

'Look at the children's meals,' she suggested.

'I'll have fish fingers, but may I use chopsticks?' I enquired when the waitress appeared. Since my stomach was sensitive, I opted to choose something I knew I'd like.

After another day of touring, this time to Jurong Bird Park and the serene Chinese Gardens, I was pleased to leave the sauna behind. Unable to conceal the smile on my face, I boarded the plane for Australia. I hoped to find a different type of warmth there.

My sister and I decided to collect all the packets that came with our meals served on the aircraft, to put in a scrapbook when we got home. Many of the passengers heard we were saving keepsakes and gave us their sugar sachets if they didn't use them. When we arrived at my Aunts house, we weighed the sachets and discovered we'd accumulated a total of one and a half kilograms of the sweet granules.

My aunt lived in Para Hills with her husband, two sons and two dogs along with the chickens they kept in their jasmine scented garden. Her three daughters were all married with children of their own but still lived close enough to visit.

After touring the local sights in South Australia, we set off on a camping trip to Victoria. My aunt and uncle had a fold away campervan which they slept in with my parents because it had two double beds. Diana and I slept in a small tent. Three of my cousins and their children also joined us on the trip. It was cold in Victoria in winter, so we would often huddle together in the ensuite block of the caravan park and turn on the two ring cooking stove to warm up. What a contrast to Singapore.

I had a great time visiting the various sights, feeding kangaroos and cuddling koalas, but heading home in the car with my aunt and uncle, my mum said, 'Look, that car being towed looks like your cousins car.'

Unfortunately she was right. The car had rolled when avoiding a collision with a truck driving on the wrong side of the road. Further down the highway, a tall, lean man wearing fashionable spectacles, shading his twinkling eyes framed by crow's feet, waved us down. Dad no longer smoked but was drawing on a cigarette to settle his nerves.

'Can we go to the hospital? Mark has been taken there by ambulance because he has a big gash in his head and will need stitches,' explained Dad.

It wasn't until several days later that we found glass in the top of my dad's head too.

I was keen to get back to Para Hills after that, but there was still one more delay when the wheel came off the trailer we were towing and rolled off into a field like the annual cheese rolling event held in Gloucestershire. We had to await for the RAA (Royal Automobile Association) to come and tow it to a garage. By then it was dark, and we were all hungry so stopped off to have something to eat.

Mum suggested, 'It might not be wise for you to eat anything, as sitting in the back of the car, you might be sick.'

'I'm hungry. I'll be fine,' I replied but was just as amazed myself when I managed to keep everything down.

Eventually our holiday came to an end, and when the plane departed Adelaide, Diana and I cried.

The air hostess was concerned and asked, 'What's wrong? Can I get you anything?'

'Don't worry. They're fine,' my mum replied.

I'd found warmth in Australia during winter. It was the warmth of a close family, all who cared deeply for each other. I made a pact with myself that I'd return again someday.

#

It was cold and dark when I woke, and I didn't want to leave my warm cosy bed. I pulled on my corduroy dungarees and fastened them over a thick woolly jumper which made my skin itch. My waterproof jacket had a hood but stopped short above my knees. I wearily trudged through the misty rain, arriving at the newsagents damp and crumpled. My hair hung limply, the wet legs of my cords clinging to my shins and my shoes squelching as the soft wrinkled skin on my feet rubbed against the insoles causing blisters.

'Did you hear John Lennon has been shot?' asked the newsagent owner whilst he wrote the house numbers on the top of the front pages in pencil.

'Who's John Lennon?' I replied sleepily.

'One of "The Beatles".'

I knew of the band because I sometimes played their songs on my guitar, but at the time didn't know each of their names. I lifted the large satchel of newspapers onto my shoulder, which felt like it was full of granite. I had two rounds to finish before going to school.

I was frequently tired at the end of the day, but the money I earned was safely stashed away for travelling. I also sacrificed outings with my friends, to carry out cleaning work on the weekends and during school holidays, in order to save enough for another trip to Australia.

I left school at the age of sixteen, devastated to learn I had to work long hours and only got four weeks annual leave each year. However, when I'd been working full-time for eighteen months, I'd accumulated enough funds to cover my airfare and travel expenses so could escape to Adelaide and Melbourne. I worked for an organization that had a policy to let employees have extra time off to visit relatives overseas, so I applied to take almost two months over December and January.

This time, I only needed to get my tetanus and polio vaccinations updated, book my ticket and pack my bags. I was looking forward to seeing my aunt, uncle and cousins once again. My parents drove me to the airport to make sure I boarded the right plane. When the aircraft went through some turbulence, I turned pale.

'Are you feeling alright?' asked the man sitting next to me.

'Just a little nauseous,' I replied.

'I'm a doctor. Take deep breaths and you will feel much better.'

I couldn't be sure whether it was the excitement of the trip or the after effects of my farewell party, the night before, which made me air-sick, but the deep breaths worked, and after vomiting, I felt much better.

I saw many sights around Adelaide. I recall a koala being thrust into my arms whilst I laughed, hugging it close to me. It smelt of eucalyptus and happily munched on some leaves. Its fur was coarse against my arms, and its claws dug into my shoulders.

'It's so cute,' I enthused. 'Do they have a predator?'

'Only man, who is destroying their habitat,' replied the keeper.

'I'm privileged to be able to hold one,' I said, not knowing, at that time, they would ultimately become listed as vulnerable in some areas of Australia.

He gently took the koala from me and placed it on a tree branch in the centre of the enclosure.

'Would you like to pat a wombat?' he asked.

'Yes please,' I said, smiling at him.

'They have to compete with farmers' livestock for food,' he informed me.

Later, as I stroked the soft fur of the kangaroos, I thought to myself how destructive man can be and wondered why we had the need to develop so much land. The marsupials were so different to our English counterparts, and I hoped they would be cherished for centuries to come.

My aunty had warned me about the more dangerous creatures in Australia. My palms became sweaty when I stepped over a large brown snake, basking in the sun, whilst I climbed to the top of

Morialta Falls. I adored snakes but was nervous of this lithe, venomous serpent that could strike silently, bringing a slow and painful death.

I froze on my first contact with a huntsman spider. I'd just got in my aunt's car.

'Shut the door,' she chided because she was in a hurry.

'I can't,' I stuttered.

'Why not?' she asked, looking at my colourless face.

'The spider,' I stammered, pointing at the biggest arachnid I'd ever seen perched on the upholstery.

She sighed, jumped out of the car, stomped around to my side, swept the spider onto the floor and slammed the door. I wondered who I should be most afraid of, the spider or my aunt. She was amazingly capable for a small woman, and I envied her courage and practicality.

People I met were generally friendly towards me and went out of their way to be helpful. It was summer, and the weather was glorious mirroring my mood. It wasn't easy travelling alone, and at a young age, I was quite impressionable. On a train to Melbourne, I sat next to a chatty old lady called Edna, who had a blue rinse in her hair.

'Melbourne is a very dangerous place to be after dark,' she cautioned. Continuing, 'If I were you, I'd go straight to the hotel because it's not safe to be on the streets after dark.'

I started to imagine Melbourne being a perilous city. I took her advice, picking up a sandwich from the deli on my walk to the hotel, late at night, and didn't venture out until daylight.

A few days later, I was walking to the bus station in rural Victoria, carrying my suitcase whilst wearing high heeled sandals on a hot muggy day, when I made a big mistake. I should've known better. I struggled along the side of the highway when a Land Rover drove past, and a police car came by from the opposite direction. A bit further along the road, the four wheel drive turned around and came back. The driver offered me a lift. I knew it was illegal to pick up hitch-hikers, not that I was hitch-hiking, so assumed that was why he didn't stop when the police car was there. I also knew how unsafe it was to accept a lift from a stranger, but I was tired from the walk and not sure how much further I had to go.

Not thinking clearly, I stupidly climbed into the passenger seat. It wasn't until I'd shut the door, I realized what I'd done.

'Where are you headed?' the driver asked me.

'Just to the bus stop at the petrol station,' I replied.

'I hate to see a pretty young girl like you struggling with a heavy suitcase.'

Whilst we chatted, I tried to work out how I could get out if he didn't stop at the station, especially considering I didn't know where the bus stop was. I thought if he wasn't going too fast, maybe I could jump out of the moving car. Perhaps, I could say I felt sick and if he stopped the car, get out, take off my high heels and run.

He turned out to be a genuinely nice guy, wished me a good trip and helped me with my suitcase into the air-conditioned petrol station. The tension in my shoulders disappeared. I'd learned my lesson and wouldn't make that mistake again, well, at least not when I was travelling alone.

When I arrived back in England, I missed the warmth I'd experienced in Australia, so I applied to emigrate in the hope I could return permanently. I knew it could be a lengthy process and take time but hadn't realized exactly how difficult it would be. Naively I thought anyone could live in whichever country they wanted to.

My first application was refused because I needed to be over the age of eighteen to apply. Although disappointed, I didn't think it was a hurdle. I could wait and apply again after my birthday. It was only a temporary setback, and I had to be patient.

Keeping myself busy, I passed my test to get my driver's licence and bought myself a seventeen year old mini-clubman in a colour which looked like vomit. I guess it was fashionable in the sixties but not anymore. I wanted to be self-reliant so enrolled in a car maintenance class in the evenings. In those days, cars were much simpler to service. I learned to set the points and spark plugs to a fine tolerance as well as configure the timing. I even studied how to change the brake shoes but wasn't sure I wanted to rely on my own work when stopping was of such great importance. Changing a tyre was easy but needed more muscle than I had to unscrew the wheel nuts, so I struggled.

After celebrating my eighteenth birthday, I applied again to immigrate to Australia. Back then it was free to apply. I took my application to London and discussed it with the clerk at the window.

'I'll check through your application to make sure it meets the criteria,' he informed me as I handed it over. 'You need to have a profession that's in shortage in Australia to have any chance of being accepted under the points system.'

'Do you have a list to choose from?' I enquired, realizing it might not be quite as easy as I thought to get a visa.

I ran my eye down the options and decided I could study to become a stenographer. To qualify, I needed to write shorthand at one hundred words per minute and type at eighty words a minute. I was fast on the electronic typewriter but not fast enough taking shorthand so started night classes to improve my speed. In the evenings, I used to practise writing down the news when it was read on the radio or television. I studied privately for months. My heart was set on moving across to the other side of the world.

I could have celebrated when I finally got the qualifications, filled out the forms and returned to London to lodge them. I queued patiently, to be served by a different clerk behind the window. She checked over my application. This time I was confident, thinking of the saying "Third Time Lucky".

'I can't accept this,' she advised. 'You need to have at least five years' work experience as a stenographer.'

'I'm only eighteen, so how can I have five years' experience in any profession?' I queried.

Then just to make sure I didn't have any lingering hope left, she suggested, 'The professions don't stay on the shortage list forever, and a stenographer is likely to have been removed from the shortage list by the time you gain the expertise required.'

Shocked, I was momentarily lost for words. I can over overcome this setback, I thought.

'Maybe I could apply for a working holiday visa instead,' I countered.

She passed me the forms, and I left more determined than ever.

I'd heard of people being allowed to work in Australia for two years. I thought it would be a good start, and then I could come home and apply again for another visa. Over the next few days, I carefully filled out the paperwork and attached supporting information, mailing it to the embassy whilst dreaming about a new life down under.

It was several months before I was contacted for an interview. When at last the day arrived, I was as nervous as a rabbit at a greyhound track. So much depended on a good interview. I dressed carefully in my smartest suit with a crisp white blouse and highly polished shoes. Then I put together my work history and made a list of all the things I could offer to a developing country. As I was led into an interview room at the embassy, I had a foreboding but wasn't sure why.

The interviewer was an older man with a receding hairline. Dressed in an outdated corduroy jacket, gingham shirt, jeans and loafers, he pushed his glasses to the bridge of his nose as he delivered the news to me.

'I've given you a six month visa in your passport,' he advised.

'Oh, I thought I could get a two year visa?' I queried, trying desperately not to let my lip tremble.

'No, we only issue those to people with a profession that is in shortage in Australia.'

'I'm a qualified stenographer.' I fiddled with the button on my jacket.

'You don't have enough experience in that field though.'

I thought I'd gone the full circle but trying to stay positive said, 'Never mind, I can come back and apply for another one when it runs out.'

'Well no, that's not possible, because you may only ever have one working holiday visa.'

Out of options, I left the premises with my shoulders sagging and my heart aching. How times had changed since my aunt emigrated on the Ten Pound scheme. I hadn't even thought about not being able to live where I chose to.

My parents were relieved as they didn't want me to go. Be positive, there are many other countries I can explore closer to England than Australia, I told myself.

A few months later, at my cousin Ali's, engagement party, I was introduced to a young man called Russ. I'd only been back six months from my trip to Australia, and Russ had recently arrived home from a years working holiday there. Ali had asked me to mail some cassettes to him whilst I was away, and I finally got to see him in person as he was standing in the doorway, smiling at me revealing his iridescent teeth, brightening the room and tugging at my heart.

Tall and wiry, his biceps strained against the tight short sleeves of his freshly ironed shirt which was tucked into burgundy trousers beneath which his polished moccasins protruded.

He had a polite confident manner when he spoke to my uncle, who was enquiring about his travels. His eyes shone as he spoke of his experiences and desire to see more of the world.

'I'm planning to travel Europe this summer with a group of friends. Why don't you join us?' he asked me as he ran his fingers through the blonde highlights in his dark hair.

I was more than keen to go on the trip, just a little unsure of what Russ's friends might be like. I thought that we had much in common, both wanting to travel to the same places as well as having a passion for adventure.

He seemed nice enough, so I replied, 'I'll think about it and let you know.'

I thought I wouldn't hear from him again so was surprised when he phoned me and wanted to keep in touch. Over the next few months, we spent more and more time together whilst we planned the trip.

'How many of your friends are coming with us?' I asked Russ.

'All of them have now dropped out, so it will only be the two of us if you still want to go?' he replied.

'Nothing can stop me now. It will be more fun with just the two of us anyway.'

I used to visit him in my mini clubman on weekends. This particular winter, there was a thick layer of snow covering the South-East of England. I got my scraper out and hacked away at the ice that had formed across my windscreen. I belonged to the AA (Automobile Association), in case I broke down, but had heard that due to the bad weather there were long delays. My little car could be a bit temperamental, especially in cold weather, but today it started fairly easily. I popped a cassette of chart music into the player and listened to my favourite song by Stevie Wonder "I Just Called to Say I Love You" whilst I looked forward to seeing Russ again.

I drove carefully when I made my way to the M25 motorway. There was still a lot of traffic around considering the weather conditions. I was in the outside lane, travelling the maximum speed limit of seventy miles an hour. The car in front of me started to slow, so I applied the brake. Puzzled by the cars reluctance to slow, I removed my foot from the brake, and it sped up again. Sweat trickled into my eyes, making them sting when I discovered the accelerator was stuck on and fighting against the brake. My clammy hands slipped down the steering wheel. Whilst trying to decide what to do next, the speedometer started dropping rapidly. I applied the throttle but nothing happened. I'd lost power completely. I turned on my hazard lights whilst carefully manoeuvring the vehicle across three lanes to the hard shoulder where it came to a standstill about one hundred metres from an emergency phone box. I exhaled and rubbed my sleeve against the moisture condensing on the windscreen.

I could've been naked in a cold storage unit and warmer than I was at that moment. My teeth were chattering, and I was shivering. I turned the key to see whether the car would start, but it wouldn't. I'd no alternative but to get to the phone. On opening the door, a gust of cold air filled the vehicle, and I was buffeted with icy sleet. My cheeks, bright pink, were raw and burning. I pulled my scarf across the bottom of my face. The phone stand shook with me as I dialled the number for the AA, who added me to the queue and said to wait for assistance in a couple of hours. Hanging up, I turned to retrace my steps to my mini, but I couldn't see it through the thickly falling snow.

Heading towards where I thought it had broken down, I had to walk further than I remembered before I could make out the paintwork disappearing under a layer of snow. Tugging on the handle, I wrenched open the door, managing to get inside just before the frosty wind slammed it shut.

I tried the key again, but it still wouldn't start. Damn, I didn't want to sit there for hours and freeze to death. I needed to do something, but what? Think clearly, I told myself. I remembered my classes and thought maybe I should check the gaps of the spark plugs. I'd no idea what prompted me to think so, but the falling snow had eased slightly, so I popped the bonnet and with a spark plug spanner removed all four. Back inside the car, I dried them and checked the settings. They all seemed fine, so I went outside and put them back. On a whim, I turned over the ignition, and miraculously it started. I drove to the next phone and leaving the car running, cancelled my call for help. I was proud of myself.

A few weeks later, I discovered my mini's sub-frame was rotting away and needed replacing. It was a major repair and would cost more than the car was worth to get a mechanic to do it. My knowledge was basic, and it wasn't something I could attempt myself. That was when I found out how much Russ truly loved me. Not everyone would source a second hand part and spend hours outside in the freezing cold, with snow coating the ground, to replace it. Along with his sense of humour and search for fun, I couldn't wait to start travelling together.

CHAPTER THREE – LEAVING THE TRACK
Europe

This trip was going to be a little different because I'd resigned from my secure job and after two months of travelling around Europe, we planned to work in Zimbabwe. I'd have preferred Australia, but unfortunately it wasn't possible. It would be the first time I'd been away from home for more than a couple of months, and I thought to myself how great it would be having a travel companion with whom to share the experiences of all the new places. On the other hand, my mum wasn't excited. She was worried I'd settle permanently in Zimbabwe, and she'd never see me again.

The real planning now commenced. Russ and I went on a trip to London, where we purchased backpacks with a lifetime warranty and light weight sleeping bags. At the hospital of tropical diseases, I got painful vaccinations administered for yellow fever, typhoid, hepatitis, tetanus and cholera. I hadn't even heard of some of the diseases. I compiled a first aid kit, to include anti-malaria prophylactics as well as needles and syringes, because in Africa you never know what you might need. Much research was undertaken, and we became members of the Youth Hostel Association. Between us, we roughly drafted a route on the map to undertake about eighteen countries in Europe.

I told Russ what I'd read, 'Put everything out on the bed you want to take, and halve it and if need be, reduce it again.'

'My pack will be lighter than yours,' he responded but was surprised when mine weighed less at fifteen kilograms.

My mum had told me take three sets of clothes, one to wear, one in the wash and one spare, so I followed this rule and it worked well.

Russ had a soft cotton grey suit tailor made just before we left. He was to wear it as best man at Wyn's wedding, which we'd be attending in Zimbabwe. He rarely dressed up, and this was only the second suit he'd ever owned.

I wish today's compact high-zoom cameras were available then since our SLR camera and zoom lenses weighed over two kilograms, and we had to carry reels of camera film. We also took a Walkman, various music cassettes to play and two small box speakers. It's much easier these days, as we only need an ipod if we bother with music at all.

Armed with the Thomas Cook's Continental Timetable and a guidebook called "Europe by Train", we set off. My parents drove Russ and me to Dover to catch the ferry to Calais.

'Goodbye,' I said quietly, unsure when I'd see them next. I bravely hugged them, and with a lump in my throat held back the tears.

'Stay safe,' replied Mum as she clasped her hands together.

'Mum, I promise I'll phone home, now and again, and write regularly, so don't worry.' I disappeared through passport control.

On the ferry, I was quite queasy but determined not to be sick. I already had the collywobbles, anticipating the new cultures, remarkable sights and untried tastes. I put on pressure wrist bands to hold back the waves of nausea, but the crossing was quite smooth. So much so, I barely noticed the ferry moving.

It reminded me of my first visit to France, ten years earlier, in 1975. Mum, Diana and I were going camping in France with the girl guides. It was my first trip abroad, and I told everyone I bumped into where we were going. We camped in a farmer's field in Wailly Beaucamp, near Calais. The chickens were free range and often wandered through our tents pecking at food. Each guide patrol, a group of approximately six girls, slept in one tent and looked after themselves. We set a campfire and cooked over the open flames in pans, which we coated on the outside with Swarfega to make them easier to clean.

'Shoo Shoo,' I shouted at the chickens, waving my arms and running towards them. They moved off, cackling loudly before strutting back to eat cooked chicken pieces. Didn't they realize they were eating their own, I thought. I quickly pulled the frying pan off the heat as one cannibal had jumped onto it in the middle of the fire to steal the leftover spaghetti.

During the night, the horse in the next paddock got free and was charging in between the tents, up and down the paddock, mane and tail flowing like Black Beauty on a mission. I slept through the whole escapade as luckily it didn't trip on any of the guy ropes.

'We've docked,' said Russ, jolting me out of my reverie. I stood tall when I stepped off the ferry into France as I hadn't needed a sick bag.

From Calais, we caught the train to Paris, a bustling metropolis, full of unfamiliar sounds and smells. Arriving late in the afternoon, our first priority was to find somewhere cheap to stay. We wandered around the red light district of Paris, the budget end of town.

It was a warm day, and the sun was shining brightly when we traipsed through the dusty streets, carrying our heavy backpacks and stopping to check out prices of hotels. The buildings looked gloomy on such a bright day, and inside, the receptions smelt musty and stale.

'Combien coutre une chambre pour deux personnes?' I stuttered. When the receptionist quoted a price by the hour, it worked out way beyond our reach. I naively wondered why they were charging by the hour.

Eventually we found somewhere we could afford, a tiny room up numerous flights of stairs. My feet were sore, and when I took off my shoes, I discovered they were covered in blisters, but when I leaned out of the window, I could see the lights of the Moulin Rouge, and my spirits lifted.

'Why are you crying?' asked Russ as he hugged me tightly.

'Because I'm the happiest I have ever been,' I replied.

After a good night's sleep, we set out to explore the area. I found crossing the road in Paris quite difficult. All I had to do was look in the opposite direction to normal because the French drove on the right hand side of the road, not the left. However, it wasn't always easy. At a complicated junction near the Arc de Triumph, Russ pulled me back to the road island when I stepped forward right in front of an on-coming vehicle.

'You nearly lost your knee caps,' he warned me.

Knees trembling from the experience, I decided that from now on I'd follow what he did and cross the road together.

The next day, we set off to visit the Eiffel Tower, guide book in hand. I didn't know much about it other than it was one of the better known icons of Paris.

I read aloud to Russ, 'The other main sights are the Opera and, of course, the Eiffel Tower which looks at its best flood lit at night.'

After purchasing the tickets, we started to climb to the first platform. The higher we got, the better the view but the more wobbly my legs became.

'Come on get moving,' said Russ, thinking I was falling behind because I was tired from climbing several hundred steps.

I explained, 'It's not because I'm tired, but I can see through the steps how high up we are, so my legs have turned to jelly, and I'm dizzy.'

'Elderly ladies are overtaking you,' Russ teased. I persevered, pushing myself one step at a time, trying not to look down. In the end, we made it to the first platform and onto the second level, from where we caught the lift to the upper observation deck. At the top, I didn't want to leave the lift. If I thought the steps had been scary, they were nothing compared to the view from the top. Slowly, I inched out but stayed back from the edge, looking around for Russ to take my hand and give me some encouragement. The Tower gently swayed in the wind, but he had disappeared attracted by the fantastic views of Paris.

I was glad, at that time, to be unaware of the Austrian tailor, Franz Reichelt, who had died in 1912 after jumping metres from the first level of the tower to demonstrate his parachute design. I bet he wished he'd invented the special cord A J Hackett had developed for one of his first bungee jumps from the top of the Eiffel Tower in 1987. It was certainly something I didn't want to try.

From Paris, we caught the train to Lisbon, changing to a couchette at the border town of Irun. At last, we could stretch out and relax. We were allocated a four berth cabin, which we shared with two dear plump French sisters, whose crow's feet turned into laughter lines when Russ removed his socks and lifting them to his nose inhaled their odour to see whether he could recycle them in the morning.

The buildings in Lisbon appeared decayed and falling down. Paint was peeling and plaster missing, as if the city had been abandoned. So we decided to head for the coast and caught the next train to Estoril.

We found a quaint little pension, to stay in, overlooking the clean sandy beach and sparkling sapphire sea. In the afternoon, we walked down to the water to soak up the sun's rays. Being English, we wanted to get a suntan so slapped on factor three coconut oil, laid out our beach towels and basked. We could hear the radio playing "Life is Life" by Austrian Rock Pop Group, Opus, which reached number one that summer. It wasn't long before we were covered in sweat sprinkled with sand granules. Back in our room, we had a two litre bottle of water being purified by iodine tablets. Russ volunteered to go and fetch it.

He grimaced when he handed me the bottle.

'Thanks for getting the water, but is there something wrong?' I asked.

'Yes,' he replied, 'look at my feet.' I gasped at the huge blisters covering his soles.

'I forgot to take my shoes, and the tarmac is extremely hot.'

I carefully pierced each blister, cleaning them with antiseptic and covering them with a dressing. During the days it took for Russ' feet to heal, we visited the most westerly point of mainland Euroasia, Cabo da Roca.

We travelled on to Madrid and then Algerciras where we crossed the border daily into Gibraltar. Algerciras had a seedy air. Touts, moneychangers and ticket sellers were quite pushy at times, and the streets were intimidating, especially at night.

Gibraltar, an overseas territory of the United Kingdom, was pleasant to visit, and because the rock was less than seven square kilometres in size, easy to explore on foot, although some of the roads were steep. The British pound was accepted as well as the Gibraltarian pound, so we didn't need to change money. Barbary macaque monkeys, one of the best-known Old World monkey species and only remaining wild population in Europe, roamed the streets freely. They looked cute from a distance, but I didn't like them coming too close in case they bit me.

'They look strange without tails,' I mused to Russ.

'It doesn't seem to affect their balance,' he replied as they nimbly jumped from place to place.

On leaving Gibraltar, there were many journalists filming at Algerciras station, but we couldn't understand what they were saying.

'Which platform does the train to Barcelona stop at?' I asked the lady in the ticket office.

'There is a train strike in Spain,' she informed us.

Other travellers also waiting for the train suggested we each stand on different platforms because we knew what time the train was due to arrive. Then someone would be able to delay the intercity, so everyone could get on board. Great idea, but it didn't stop, continuing straight through.

'How long will the walkout last?' I asked the ticket seller. She refused to answer, putting up her closed sign.

In desperation, we caught a bus to Cadiz from where we were able to catch a train to Seville and then an overnight train to Barcelona. We arrived in the morning, on a warm sunny day, and headed in the direction of the beach. I had a map from the tourist office, but after four hours of walking whilst carrying our backpacks, we'd walked right off the map and somehow missed the beach. Exhausted, Russ hailed a taxi.

'Can you take us to the beach?' I asked wearily. He didn't seem to understand English, so I pointed to the map we had.

'No beach in Barcelona,' he replied.

'Can you take us to the train station instead?' I felt defeated. He beckoned us to get into his cab, and soon we were on a train headed for Nice in France.

In our haste to leave, we hadn't taken into account it was Saturday night, and we would be arriving in a different country on a Sunday. Banks would be closed, and we wouldn't be able to change any money into local currency. A kind pension owner agreed to let us stay the night without paying in advance, on the condition she kept our passports. Luckily we had a few French francs left over from our time in Paris but only a few.

With rumbling tummies, we found a sweet little pizza restaurant which we hoped would be cheap. The place was empty with several smartly dressed waiters standing around looking bored. When we walked through the door, all eyes turned to us.

'Bonsoir,' said the waiter.

'Good evening,' we replied in unison.

'Please be seated.' He pulled out a chair for me.

We worked out what we thought we would be able to afford, which was one plain pizza between us to share.

The waiter took our order. 'Would you like to order an entrée?'

'No thank you.' I wasn't sure we could afford one, and we didn't want to end up washing the dishes in the kitchen.

'What would you like to drink?'

'Tap water will be fine for both of us.'

'Any salads or other dishes?' He hovered near our table. Another waiter placed the mandatory basket of bread in front of us, and I explained we didn't want it. One thing we'd discovered in Paris was the bread they put on the table wasn't complimentary and the price added to the bill. He frowned and took it away.

The other waiter stood steadfastly nearby, watching our every move. The pizza arrived, and the aroma of fresh dough, hot cheese and herbs was irresistible. I savoured each mouthful, letting the mozzarella melt on my tongue. Between us every crumb was devoured.

'Merci,' I said as the waiter cleared our plates.

He recommended several desserts.

'No thank you,' I replied.

'How would you like your coffee?'

'Could you please just bring the bill?'

As he disappeared, the other waiter repositioned himself in front of the exit. Maybe they thought we would make a run for it and leave without paying.

I'd added the price of the pizza, the percentage for TVA (like our GST) and the service charge so thought we would be within budget. However, when the bill arrived, I hadn't taken into account there was an extra charge for service on a Sunday. I counted out the few notes we had, and we were still short by one franc. The blood rushed to my face.

'Russ, we don't have enough to settle the bill,' I whispered whilst frantically searching through my bag.

I found my purse, and in the side pocket were several coins. I was relieved to find they added up to more than a franc, and we could depart with our heads held high.

Whilst walking back to the pension, I told Russ about my second trip to France, in 1978, my first opportunity to travel on my own, to visit my pen friend, Jeanne.

Luckily Jeanne spoke excellent English due to my school-girl French being extremely limited. My parents had driven me to Dover to make sure I got on the right ferry. Diana was supposed to be travelling with me but unfortunately had come down with a stomach bug only a couple of days earlier.

Hugging my parent's goodbye, I bravely boarded the ferry but then had no idea what to do next whilst I struggled with my heavy suitcase. Fortunately, one of the P&O (Peninsular and Oriental Steam Navigation Company) staff took my suitcase and stored it away. I couldn't understand what he said because my French wasn't good enough. 'Merci,' I pronounced awkwardly to thank him. I hoped I'd find my suitcase still there when I arrived in France. Pleased it was no longer a burden, I found a seat and read my book.

Perspiring heavily, I made a grab for the sick bag in the seat pocket in front of me. I should've known better than to read, especially as I was excited and nervous, not just about the trip but also about meeting Jeanne, who I'd been writing to for several years. Her father worked on the ferries so was with Jeanne, to meet me, when the vessel docked in Boulogne.

I was enchanted to meet her parents and younger sister, and we communicated reasonably well with a combination of French, English and signals. They lived close to the beach, so we'd walk there each day. I gradually got to meet her friends but found it difficult to get to know them because of the language barrier.

One day, we'd been playing boules on the beach, and when Jeanne collected up the discarded balls, she turned to talk to me whilst throwing one up in the air and catching it. I stood watching the ball go up and down, like the heads turning right to left watching a tennis game, until it hit me, smashing down on top of my head and causing my legs to collapse from underneath me. She couldn't have been more apologetic, and I learnt the French word "oeuf", meaning egg, which described the souvenir lump on the top of my head.

I was more confident travelling home on the ferry and had soon cleared passport control before running towards my parents.

'Where's your suitcase?' asked my mum.

'I don't know where to find it,' I replied.

'You need to go back through passport control and retrieve it from the luggage carousel.'

I wish she'd told me about the process before I'd travelled, but now I understood how it all worked and what to do next time, because I was keen to see more of the world.

Russ laughed at my yarn and said, 'I hope you travel with more competency these days.'

'I don't think I will ever overcome motion sickness, but I will take more care of my belongings,' I replied.

The next day, I joined a long queue in the post office to collect our letters sent Post Restante. I'd been waiting some time when a young man walked straight up to the counter and pushed in. I was flabbergasted, but nobody challenged him. This seemed to be a regular occurrence during our travels. I'd been brought up to queue in a civilized manner and couldn't understand the need to push in.

When I reached the front of the line, I asked, 'Do you speak English?'

'Oui,' replied the clerk as she put on her glasses.

'Are there any letters for me?' I enquired, producing my passport as identification.

She pulled out a big box and sorted through it trying to match my name.

Presenting three letters, she enquired, 'Are these for you?'

'Oui, merci,' I replied, smiling broadly as I took them and paid a small fee. Our friends and family were mailing us at the major Post Offices on our route. It was great to hear news from them about what everyone else was doing whilst we were absorbed in travelling. Today it's so much easier to keep in touch electronically, by email or skype, but not quite so much fun.

We left France knowing we would return and travelled on to Monaco. The principality was built on a hillside, from where there was a fabulous view of the Port of Monaco which took my breath away. The sun glistened on the clear azure water in the bay and bounced off the fiberglass hulls of the million dollar yachts and motor cruisers. This was certainly the home of the rich and famous.

'Wouldn't it be wonderful to own your own boat?' I suggested to Russ.

'You never know, maybe we will one day,' he replied optimistically.

I shut my eyes and visualized myself ploughing through the water aboard a luxurious yacht whilst sipping on a cocktail.

At the top of the hill, we stopped to watch the changing of the guards at the palace. The men were dressed in crisp white uniforms, complemented by highly polished black and white shoes that appeared from a distance to have pom-poms on them. Their rifles were slung over their shoulders and held in place by their white gloved right hand. Even their helmets were white, in the style of the old English Bobbies hats. They moved in unison to complete their drill.

'Russ, don't you think it's strange that the immense responsibility of protecting the Grimaldi family lay in the hands of men dressed in pom-pom shoes,' I suggested.

'Look closer,' he replied. I realized their shoes were simple and plain, so it must be the Greek guards who wear pom-poms.

We descended the hill to the casino at Monte Carlo but were refused entry because we were inappropriately dressed in shorts and t-shirts. I didn't want to gamble anyway, just have a look at the interior décor.

Europe was unfolding in front of me, and I found it hard to keep quiet as the train pulled in at Rome. The majestic buildings were colossal, towering over the streets. The Roman Empire must have been spectacular. We wandered the streets, a mix of modern cafes, massive historic buildings and the Vatican City whilst looking for something to eat and somewhere to stay.

Two pretty young girls approached us and started walking either side of Russ. One of the girls linked her arm through his and started kissing it. I wondered what was going on and eventually figured it was supposed to be a diversion whilst her companion was trying to lift his wallet from his back pocket. This proved too difficult with a backpack sitting on top of it. Once he realized what they were trying to do, he shook them off and yelled at them as they scampered away.

'What a welcome to the Eternal City,' I said.

After finding somewhere to stay and drop our bags, we headed back out onto the streets.

On passing the Fountain of Trevi, Russ said, 'Tradition has it you will return to Rome if you throw a coin into the fountain's water basin.'

'Try it,' I replied.

He stood with his back to the fountain and without looking, tossed a coin. So far he hasn't returned, and I wondered whether he threw it over the wrong shoulder because it's said you should throw over your left side with your right hand or vice versa. Although it would be difficult to do otherwise. Perhaps the girls we'd encountered earlier, raided the fountain and took his coins.

We travelled from Rome to Brindisi to catch the ferry across to Corfu. I had a cold sore forming on my bottom lip so was keen to keep it sheltered from the sun and wind. This turned out to be difficult because our tickets on the ferry were for deck seats only. That night, once it was dark, we laid out our sleeping bags in an alcove outside one of the doorways in the hope of a little shelter. Even though there wasn't a strong wind, the forward momentum of the ferry generated its own breeze, which lapped and caressed my cold sore until it had stretched across half of my bottom lip. I had special cream, but back in the eighties the ointments available didn't stop a cold sore from multiplying.

I looked a sorry sight when we docked in Corfu. The intense sun beamed down on my lip causing it to throb. We stayed in the spare bedroom of two friendly Greek sisters whose home opened onto a small winding cobbled street. Over the next few days, my cold sore broke, and the liquid dispelled, making it dry out and relieving the pressure. Every time I smiled, my lip would split in several places, making it bleed until finally I had a large scab across my bottom lip.

Each morning, we went to a local café to have breakfast and ordered a sandwich. The French baguette was large, and when I opened my mouth to eat it, the scabs broke, and my lip started bleeding again. This happened for several days at the same café. Using hand signals, the owner worked up the courage to ask me what happened to my lip. He pointed to my lip, then to Russ, balled his hand into a tight fist and gestured to show Russ had beaten me. We could only laugh and shake our heads.

One day, we caught a local bus out to the charming town of Kassiopi, on the north-east corner of the island. We visited the harbour where the fishermen still work but were a little disappointed with the beach because it was pebbly, although the view out to sea along the Albanian coast was fabulous.

On the way back to Corfu town, we were packed like sardines into the penultimate bus for the day. All the seats were taken, and the aisle was crammed with sweaty bodies. Although the windows were open, it was like being fired in a kiln, so I couldn't breathe properly. I tried to get nearer a window, but there were too many people in the way. I took deep breaths but could see stars and then blackness. I fainted, landing on the gear stick, the only available gap. The bus driver indicated to Russ to take me off and then drove away leaving us in the middle of nowhere.

A kind young girl appeared from the hills, which were covered with olive groves, grape vines and citrus plantations, to hand me half a lemon to suck. We hoped the last bus of the day would come this way and not be too full to take us on board. Whilst waiting patiently, unsure if we would be able to get back to town, I spotted the bus first, and we stood by the roadside frantically signalling with our arms, but it passed on by. We chased after it, waving until it came to a standstill, so we could hop on board.

We returned to Italy on the Adratic Star and caught the overnight train to Venice. The train was overflowing with passengers, and the aisles outside the carriages were lined with Italian men leaning out of the windows smoking. When it became time to get off the train, a muscle bound Italian guy offered to carry my backpack. He charged off along the corridor with me following right behind. Russ tried to keep up, but his progress was severely hampered when each guy in the corridor leaned forward to look down my top and inadvertently blocked his way. He wished someone were carrying his pack too.

We were told it wasn't safe to stay overnight at the railway station, and the police would move us on, but I thought we'd have no alternative as we had terrible difficulty finding somewhere to stay. It was peak season, and our budget was low, which made it a harder challenge. Ultimately, we ended up sharing a room with two other girls in the same predicament.

Our next country was Yugoslavia, which seemed a complicated country, made up of six different republics, Bosnia-Herzegovina, Montenegro, Croatia, Macedonia, Slovenia and Serbia. These were inhabited by eight nationalities, speaking five different languages and practicing four different religions. I was amazed at how they could all get along together.

We stayed in someone's home, in the old town of Ljubljana. From the hill, Ljubljana Castle watched over the peaceful town with quaint medieval streets, a mixture of baroque and art nouveau styles. I assumed, years later, the different nationalities couldn't overcome the different religions, cultures and languages when, after a long civil war, Yugoslavia became six independent countries, Serbia, Montenegro, Slovenia, Croatia, Macedonia and Kosovo.

'Faster,' Russ yelled at me.

'I am running as fast as I can,' I puffed as we sprinted up the stairs, pushing our way through the crowd to see the electronic sign showing the train on the platform was going to Innsbruck. I thought we were going to miss it as we were late. The doors closed, and the train took off just after we'd squeezed on board. It was then that we discovered the railway staff must have been a bit enthusiastic and had changed the sign to the next train's destination before the one we were on had left. We were headed for Zagreb, in what is now Croatia but at the time was part of Yugoslavia. We checked our Thomas Cook Timetable and discovered a train to Innsbruck left from Zagreb that evening, so we only had to find a way to pass the day.

Lucky for us, Tomislav Square was located in front of the railway station, so we decided to while away our time there. Because there wasn't anywhere to leave our backpacks, we laid them beside one of the park benches on which I sat to keep a watchful eye whilst Russ wandered around the area.

It was an attractive square with an imposing statue of King Tomislav at the centre. I hadn't been sitting alone for long when a balding, podgy gentleman came and sat beside me on the bench. It seemed strange as there were many other empty seats. Initially I wasn't worried, but when he started to proposition me, I looked around for Russ, who was nowhere to be seen.

I tried to look dumb and said loudly, 'I don't speak English,' in a silly accent.

'You English,' he said.

'No, non comprende,' I lied.

'You are beautiful.' He leaned towards me.

'Non comprende, non comprende.' I vigorously shook my head, backing away.

I let out a big sigh when he got up and left because I couldn't carry two backpacks on my own. However, it wasn't long before another middle-aged gentleman sat beside me. He sidled up close and rested his arm on the back of the bench behind me. The hairs on my arms raised, and I shivered averting my eyes.

His English was extremely good, but again I tried to pretend I didn't understand when he said, 'You look like Sophia Loren. I'd like to show you my apartment which is nearby.'

By now I was spooked, as I looked nothing like Sophia Loren, so picked up my pack and started to drag Russ' across to another seat. Luckily the stranger briskly walked away.

When Russ returned, I explained what had happened and he thought it hilarious. I didn't know much about the Italian actress at the time but have since learned Sophia Loren stayed in Zagreb's Palace Hotel in the sixties along with other famous people like Elizabeth Taylor and Orsen Wells. I could finally laugh with Russ when I was sitting on the train to Innsbruck wondering if all older Yugoslav men propositioned young back-packers.

So far we'd only stayed in pensions so always had a room to ourselves where our luggage was safe. When we arrived in Austria, it was difficult to find cheap accommodation, so we checked into a local youth hostel. This was the first youth hostel I'd ever stayed at but at least meant we were, at last, using the YHA membership cards we'd purchased. I was disappointed to find out we'd be staying in different dormitories, and there were no lockers to keep our bags in. I was shown to a dormitory several floors up, and my bed was beside a large window without any glass in it, as it had recently been broken.

I said to Russ, 'I am not sure about staying here, someone might pinch our belongings, or I might rollover and fall out of the window during the night.'

'Don't worry.' he said, 'Everything will be fine.'

The showers were on the floor above and communal, so they set a certain time for women to shower and a later time for the men. I felt a little self-conscious, not having used communal showers since I was at school. I thought I can do this and got into the shower where there were a few other girls and started to wash. Only a flimsy curtain separated the showers from a large hall where some young men were kicking a ball around. Before I knew it, the ball was in the shower, and, of course, one confident adolescent boy decided to enter the shower to retrieve it. The other girls screamed, and he departed with a smirk across his face. I wondered how often he played this trick on naked backpackers. I didn't stay in another hostel for the rest of our trip.

From Austria, we took an overnight train to Switzerland, stopping in Lucerne. A persistent drizzle had extinguished the heat from the sun, which was now encased by the clouds. Donning our raincoats, we set off to explore the area. The Chapel Bridge, spanning the Reuss River, was a good place to shelter from the wet. The seventeenth century paintings kept our attention until the rain eased a little, and then we walked to the Lion of Lucerne. The sky was dark and overcast with clouds casting shadows around us. The rain was like tears falling down, causing an immense sorrow to wash over me when I looked at the sad face of the stone carving of a dying lion. The monument was to commemorate the deaths of the Swiss mercenaries at the Tuileries, in 1792, but made me think of the animals in Africa being hunted for sport. I'd never understand how people could be so cruel.

As we waited for the train to arrive, I told Russ about the first time I visited Switzerland in 1977.

Diana and I'd travelled to Adelboden with the girl guides. We had two great leaders. Lefty, our lieutenant, was deaf and had diminishing eye-sight, eventually becoming blind. She was a great lady and looked after all the kids exceptionally well, although was often grumpy.

One night in the chalet, she was helping to cook spaghetti bolognaise for dinner. She struggled pouring the hot water out of the big pan and missing the colander entirely, the spaghetti flowed into the sink and part way down the drain hole. Not in the least perturbed, she scooped it all back out and served it up for dinner. Yummy spaghetti with an aroma of blocked drains.

Several of the girls were intrigued by the vending machines set into the outside walls of buildings. On spotting brightly painted eggs in them, we purchased a batch of four which we all assumed were made of chocolate. Stowing them safely in our pockets, to eat later, we went ice-skating. My sister fell over, crashing onto the ice on top of her egg and discovering it wasn't chocolate at all. It was hard-boiled. What a disappointment that was, but I guess with all the snow around, it wasn't likely to go off. I can't imagine it catching on in Australia.

The guides borrowed some skis, and we were allowed to use the ski-lift in a local land-owners field. I was reasonably comfortable about learning to ski because one Christmas, a few years earlier, Santa left Diana and me roller skates. They were second hand but still worked as good as new. We tied them on, over the top of our normal shoes. Outside, where the pavement was smooth but with a gentle slope, we tried them out. It wasn't long before I was sitting on my rather sore and bruised bottom after my feet whooshed out from underneath me. Not only had I never tried roller skating before, but I'd never fallen so heavily or felt so much pain either. It was certainly a different way to get around, and it wasn't long before I was confidently gliding down the avenue along the incline.

The next street, however, had a much sharper gradient, and it proved challenging stopping at the kerb. Generally, I careened across the road hoping there was no traffic coming. I had to negotiate the steps spaced at various intervals along an alleyway that continued down to the main road. It was etched into the steep hill, but a handrail ran down the middle so gave me something to grab when falling over. Although, once again, it was difficult to pull up, and I'd often lurch out onto the road. Looking back, I cannot believe how lucky we were not to get hit by any vehicles.

My confidence was to be battered on the snowy mountainside in Adelboden too. I remember spending most of the time with the snow melting under my bottom and the cold seeping through to my bones. The idea was to queue up and stand in line with the ski lift. I found this challenging because everyone had been standing in the same spot. The compacted snow made it a solid glassy ice block on which I'd slither backwards whilst waiting for the ski lift to come around.

'Quick grab hold,' shouted Diana.

'I'm trying to,' I replied whilst it sailed right past me.

'Be ready for the next one.'

I grabbed tightly and hung on as if my life depended on it. My arms snapped taut and strained, overextended, dragging my clumsy body behind them. I could only hold on for a few metres up the slope before releasing my grasp and sliding backwards down the mountain, trying to avoid those coming up behind me. Even if I'd made it to the top, the journey back down wasn't appealing at increasingly fast speeds with no brakes.

I'd just finished telling Russ my story when the train arrived, so we travelled on to the tiny principality of Liechtenstein. A little smaller than Monaco, it still had its own Prince, and his residence, Vaduz Castle, stood on the hillside dominating the landscape.

From there, we boarded the international train to Luxembourg and sat in a carriage with two young Swiss guys, who were barefoot and smelt like they hadn't washed for several days. Sitting opposite them, we were horrified when they revealed their stash of marijuana in their bag on the floor. They thought it funny, but although we didn't know the guys, we were worried we'd be arrested along with them, just because we were in the same compartment. Before we departed, passport and customs officials boarded the train with their Alsatian sniffer dog.

'Passports,' the man shouted, and I gingerly handed him mine and Russ'.

I held my breath whilst the Alsatian came into the compartment. It took one sniff of the guy's smelly feet, resting on his bag, and quickly disappeared into the corridor. The lad must have done this before.

In Luxembourg, we explored the casemates, many kilometres of underground passageways tunnelled inside the rock, at Boch. Some of the staircases between levels were steep and the stone irretrievably eroded by thousands of footsteps, making it difficult to climb.

In Belgium, we visited the Bell Tower in Brugge. It was an acute climb up 366 steps to the Triumph Bell. I did well because although the staircase was narrow, it was enclosed, and I chose not to look down through the windows. However, I wasn't so confident when I got to the top of the eighty-three metre high building. As usual, I was shaking and my legs threatened to collapse. The spiral staircase was tricky to negotiate, going back down, where the steps tapered to nothing on the inside angle. I finally stopped quivering when I reached the bottom.

The days were flying by. In Amsterdam, we searched for accommodation. There were touts on the streets who usually took tourists to rooms to stay in, but on the day we arrived, there were no vacancies we could find anywhere within our price range. Therefore, we spent the afternoon finding a tolerant society. Cannabis was for sale in the coffee shops, which is allowed and regulated by the Government. In the evening, we strolled through the red light district where scantily clad women posed boldly behind windows or in doorways because prostitution is legal in the Netherlands. It was sleazy, and I was quite happy to be moving on that night.

From here, we spent about a week straight sleeping overnight on the trains because we couldn't afford to stay in expensive hotels, and it was the only available accommodation. There was an Inter-rail Centre, at the station at Copenhagen, where we were able to have a free shower, and I dried my long hair under the automatic hand dryer.

In Denmark, I was drawn towards the bronze sculpture of a Mermaid at Langlinje Pier, which is now over one hundred years old. It was commissioned by Danish brewer, Carl Jacobsen, who was inspired by Hans Christian Andersen's fairy tale. I'd read many of his tales as a child and remembered the mermaid. She gave up her family to win the heart of a handsome prince on land, but he married another. I thought that he must have stolen her heart for her to make such a sacrifice.

In northern Sweden, we crossed into the Arctic Circle at a point in Norrbotten and travelled on to Haparanda where we saw a church that had won a prize for the ugliest building in Sweden. As I listened to Abba on our walkman, I related to their song "I have a dream" and thought to myself that I was finally living my dream. I nibbled on the thick slab of dried meat we'd bought from the supermarket, which I guessed might be moose but was probably beef. It'd be a while before we could afford to eat at a restaurant or café.

In order to spend two days in Sweden, we caught the night train to Helsiniki, in Finland, but alighted at two in the morning to catch the train back. We arrived early the next day at the same spot we had left the evening before.

Before returning home, we headed back to Portugal for another dose of sunshine and a decent meal, only stopping in Gouda to sample the local dynamite cheese.

In Estoril, although completely adverse to animal cruelty, Russ thought it would be interesting to go to a bull fight as it has been part of their culture for centuries. Unsure that I really wanted to go, I queued at the kiosk. By now more experienced at stopping queue jumpers, I swung my backpack around to block their way. I did struggle to explain what we wanted, ultimately asking in French for two tickets.

Bullfighting is different in Portugal than Spain in many ways. In Spain, the matador kills the bull in the ring. However, like a book with an unconventional ending, in Portugal, it's generally killed by a butcher, in private, once the show is over and in some circumstances even healed to face yet another defeat. In both instances, they spear the bull to enrage it. I couldn't watch, closing my eyes and covering them with my hands. As the colour drained from my face, I pondered how anyone could enjoy this.

I thought of the honour bestowed upon gladiators, who fought to the death. In comparison with the picador, the true hero is the horse, which is not there voluntarily and has a passive role to play. Even though the bull's horns are blunted to protect the horse and at the same time the toreros, it's more at risk than its rider.

At the end, when the matador speared the bull, he raised his arms to cheers from the crowd. However there were also boos, which pleased me to hear as I didn't think torture should be glamorised. It's a cruel sport, and I struggle to understand how anyone could enjoy it. I wouldn't be going again.

Europe had shown me different cultures, music and diets. I'd explored historic castles, churches and palaces. Having grown stronger, I learned how to stand my ground and not let someone push in front of me. I'd flourished in its endless sunny days, becoming tanned and relaxed. I didn't relish having to sterilize tap water in Southern Europe, but although Northern Europe was much cleaner and fresher, it lacked the warmth of the south.

Back in England for a few days before flying to Zimbabwe, Russ tried on his new suit to make sure it still fitted. He'd lost several pounds whilst travelling in Europe, and the suit now hung on his lean frame like a voluminous kaftan. It was too late to do anything about it, so I could only hope he would put some of the weight back on that he had lost before the day of the wedding.

CHAPTER FOUR – LEAP OF FAITH
Zimbabwe, Spain, England, Austria, Germany

I couldn't tell which way was up and which way was down as I somersaulted through the sky at an amazing two hundred kilometres an hour. My heart was pumping, and my perspiration neutralized the bitterly cold air at such a high altitude. The force of the wind up my nose instantly blocked my ears, so I could no longer hear, and I struggled to breathe. My skin was stretched against my cheek bones by the sheer force of the atmosphere whizzing past me whilst the ground hurtled up towards me from thirteen thousand feet below.

The first part of our journey was in a DC10 to Lusaka, which was quite comfortable, although the wait in Zambia for the onward flight was tedious. However, the tedium was better than the tiny Viscount plane Air Zimbabwe flew us on to Harare. The air turbulence was like being on the Tower of Terror thrill ride. Another flight change in Harare meant a change to a Bowen 707 on to Bulawayo where I was glad to hit the runway smoothly.

The prospective groom, Wyn, met us at the airport and took us to his parent's house for dinner. I was impressed by their huge mansion. The bathrooms were bigger than our lounge room.

When his mother called out, 'Patience, where are you?' Russ thought she was calling for their dog, not realising that she was their housemaid, and they also had a gardener.

One afternoon, we went to a braai, which is Afrikaans for barbecue, where we sampled some local food and drink. The cheapest local beer, called Chibuku, is made from maize and sorghum. It came in a carton similar to our milk or orange juice. The beer was shaken and left in the sun to ferment. It was then shaken again, to mix in the sediment which had sunk to the bottom, before we got to taste it. Warm and bitter, it was more like porridge than beer, so not something I indulged in again.

The other dish was more palatable and was called sadza. It looked like porridge but was in fact mealie-meal, or ground maize, boiled in water on the stovetop. Full of carbohydrates, it tasted bland. Apparently it's usually eaten by dipping it in gravy and accompanied by meat and/or vegetables which give it some flavour. Good job the local steaks were cheap, so we could afford to eat them.

Some things were difficult to get or just not available. The locally manufactured chocolate tasted like dog chocolate so again was something we avoided. The washing powder didn't work well either.

The day of Wyn's wedding arrived. Russ put on his baggy suit, and we headed for the church. At the reception, next door to the church, when the groom stood up to make a speech, his sky-diving buddies all started to sing to drown him out. They only sang one song, but when they stopped, the church bells started ringing for mass, so he still could not speak until they ceased.

Wyn's mother, Joy, kindly took us on a trip with her younger son, who was on holiday from boarding school in England. We visited the magnificent Victoria Falls. It was the dry season, and the water levels were low, so there was almost no spray in the air, which made viewing easy. The falls were still spectacular with an immense amount of water plunging down to the gorge below like an overflowing bathtub.

A dazzling rainbow appeared over Devil's Cataract. The sun glistened on the watercourse from an unblemished sky. I was surprised to discover the chalet that we stayed in was where Richard Chamberlain had slept whilst filming King Solomon's Mines.

At the crocodile farm, I was fascinated to hold a hatchling. It was small, although its body and head were the width of two of my hands and the long skinny tail that length again. It felt smoothly polished but surprisingly cool. Tiny teeth protruded along its jawline like mini toothpicks.

'Be careful, because last week he bit someone, and it drew a lot of blood,' said the keeper. I quickly moved my fingers to behind its head and hoped it wouldn't reach around to bite me.

I'd always loved animals and was bought up with cats, rabbits and hamsters as companions. I had enjoyed watching the foxes and hedgehogs come into our garden in winter and the robins, blue tits and sparrows drink from the birdbath. However, this tiny crocodile was equally as appealing, and I was about to discover so much more.

We left Victoria Falls for Hwange National Park. Russ and I were loading the car with boxes of supplies when I stopped to take a photo. The vervet monkey was sitting on the ground, so I squatted down and crept as close as I could to get a decent photo. Just when I took the shot, the monkey reached out and grabbed the shoe lace in my sneakers. I jumped back, surprised by its actions and turned around to see Russ watching me. Behind him many more vervets were climbing on the car roof and had got into the boot and main part of the car because we'd left the doors open when we were inadvertently distracted.

The wildlife in Zimbabwe was exceptional. I was amazed to spot my first elephant crossing the road. It trod delicately, walking like a ballerina floating in the air. Russ was out of the car and following it, to take a photo, before Joy could stop him.

'You are not allowed out of your vehicle in a National Park,' she explained.

'Good job there weren't any lion around,' I teased.

Russ knew he shouldn't have done it, but I think the excitement of the moment outweighed any caution. By the time we spotted Cape buffalo and hippos, we were well aware how dangerous they could be.

'The Cape buffalo is said to have killed more big game hunters than any other animal in Africa, and the hippopotamus is one of the most unpredictable and aggressive animals in the world,' informed Joy. So this time Russ stayed in the car.

I was devastated to hear elephant were illegally being poached. Their tusks were used to make carvings and jewellery but also used in the East for medicinal purposes. From that moment, I decided I wouldn't purchase anything made from endangered animal parts, especially ivory.

I was fascinated to watch how the giraffe drank from the water hole. They spread their legs wide, so their long slender necks could reach down to the surface of the water. Nearby, zebra grazed alongside wildebeest, waterbuck, kudu and sable whilst a white rhino stood protecting her calf. The baboons called to each other, but I found them intimidating, preferring the cuter looking vervet monkeys. As the long grass stirred, I wondered what was hidden in it. When it parted to reveal something camouflaged beneath, I could just spot the tip of the warthog's aerial tails as they trotted towards the water.

Back in Bulawayo, on a visit to Matopos National Park, a group of us were standing beside the van chatting whilst watching white rhino from a distance. Suddenly, someone spotted an ostrich headed towards us. I was the first to jump back in the van, but a few of the guys, including Russ, kept talking.

I called to Russ, 'Quick get in the van. The ostrich is very close.' He just made it inside as the bird arrived and started pecking violently at the windows to try to get in.

'That was a close one,' I pointed out.

When we stopped for a barbecue lunch at Marlene Dam and found a massive python wrapped around the outdoor table leg, although I love snakes, we decided not to disturb it and find somewhere else to sit.

In Bulawayo, we often joined Wyn, on the weekends, at the local sky-diving club. One of his friends offered to teach Russ and me how to do a parachute roll. It wasn't too hard collapsing from a standing position to roll onto our backs, but once we started jumping off the wall to do so, I found myself covered in bruises.

I didn't end up needing the training for a tandem jump with a modern parachute, which is what I ended up doing, many years later, at an airfield south of Sydney with a group of friends.

I remembered the day well. There was a noisy buzz when everyone got geared up. I was given a jumpsuit to wear over my clothes and some goggles, a helmet and harness. Craig, my jumpmaster, connected to my harness because he was going to be deploying the parachute he was carrying and requested I lift my legs and hang from it.

The small, fixed-wing plane taxied along the take-off strip and stopped to pick us up. I sat in one of the two rows along the inside of the aircraft without looking out the strip of windows each side. Tension bubbled in the air while the plane climbed higher. Everyone was quiet with just the noise of the engine and the guys farting. At that stage, although scared of heights, I was feeling excited rather than apprehensive. The pilot shouted out, 'door,' and the two closest people opened it.

Still attached to Craig, I edged towards the door, and before I knew it, was standing in the opening looking out. I didn't have a chance for fear to kick in, because I was trying to remember the drill as I crossed my arms over my chest, and he dived out the plane. I was tumbling with him, head over feet, before assuming the freefall position. Wow, this was exhilarating. I was flying.

The freefall was over all too quickly. When he pulled open the chute, we jerked to almost a standstill, still dropping but much slower. I wasn't sure where we were to land, but the ground was flat offering a fabulous view, and I could see the club-house in the distance. This was much more sedate, and I was able to enjoy the surroundings.

At the last moment, Craig reminded me to lift my legs, then he gently stepped from the sky to the ground. Someone rushed towards us to deflate the chute, and it was all over. I couldn't stop smiling.

I wanted to stay in Zimbabwe. It was a great place to live. The weather was better than in England as well as the lifestyle. I adored the wildlife which had made an indelible impression on me. However, Robert Mugabe, Zimbabwe's President, had other ideas. If we wanted to stay in Zimbabwe indefinitely, we had to give up our English passports. I was too scared to work without a visa as under "state of emergency" the government could detain people without charge and without advising anyone they had done so. I didn't cherish the idea of rotting in gaol. Russ' working visa never came through, and we didn't want to give up our escape route home, because you never knew what could happen in the future.

After all the travelling around Europe and Africa, we bought a house of our own in England. It was a small terraced house that had been converted into a maisonette on the ground and first floor with a separate unit in the basement below. We only owned the building, not the land it was built on. The ninety-three year lease meant we had to pay £25 a year ground maintenance. The entrance to the property was through an enclosed porch which opened straight into the front room. Inside, it was comfortable with a gas fire surrounded by a wooden mantel piece and leadlight windows set in the cupboard doors on either side. It was well lit through the Georgian style bay window. The living room led through to the kitchen, passed an alcove underneath the stairs. The kitchen/diner was a large room and had fitted wooden cupboards. Russ installed a combined washing machine/tumble dryer under the bench top. Beyond the kitchen were two doors, one to the back balcony, which led down to a shared garden, and the other to the bathroom that was furnished with a hideous pink suite. A doorway from the other side of the kitchen led to stairs which headed up to the two bedrooms.

Friends had been disposing of furniture which we used to furnish the house. One friend gave us an old bed settee because she bought her dog a new one. Another friend's mother donated her dressing table.

Russ and I were sitting on the sofa, watching television, when the sofa moved sideways. We both had our feet up, so we looked down to see why it had moved. Between the sofa and unit against the wall was a huge Indian python with exotic markings. He was brown with gold, cream and black patterns in the shape of those on a giraffe. His heart shaped head was flat with a golden V on top of it that separated his eyes. We'd named him Sidney, after hissing Sid, because he was an impressive twelve foot long. Whilst he pushed his way between the unit and the sofa, it got tighter, so he breathed out shifting the sofa by a couple of inches.

Sid's body was solid muscle. Russ fed him the thawed dead rats we kept in the freezer. That is, in Diana's freezer which she had lent to us. However she didn't want it back once she found out, even though they were well wrapped. Sid gave us endless hours of fun, and when friends looked after him whilst we travelled overseas, they thought we'd been burgled. Having left his vivarium door ajar, he escaped. Slithering around the house, he made his way up onto the mantelpiece and pushed everything onto the floor, breaking plant pots, ornaments and speakers in his foray. Good job he didn't escape outside.

He was a great help when salesmen came door-knocking because he was clearly visible either basking in his favourite spot in the bay window or inside his huge glass vivarium. Most visitors that we didn't know were not game enough to come in.

We purchased two sofas which were damaged so a bargain price. When the burly delivery men arrived with them, trembling they refused to bring them inside, scared Sid might attack them.

The Naked Backpacker

I loved Sid, but he could test my patience at ti.. out of his tank, I had to watch him almost constantly ironing in the kitchen whilst he was climbing the st.. generally took him about half an hour, so I thought he monitoring every second. After about fifteen minutes, I him zig zagging towards the bedrooms. He lifted the end of   at a strange angle, and I thought, oh no, he is going to the toilet. However, I was wrong. He was struggling to grip the carpet and suddenly was bumping back down the stairs, heading straight for me. I tried to catch him but to no avail. He let out a loud hiss as he landed heavily on the ground. I felt so sorry for him that I lifted him up and carried him to the top. I then had to keep a watchful eye on him as he disappeared inside the drawers under the bed settee.

A couple of years later, we thought maybe Sid could do with a friend so bought home Muscles, a dehydrated looking shoelace. He was a red-tailed boa constrictor from Honduras, but after weeks of not being fed whilst he was held up in customs, he wasted away. He was still feisty though and loved to bite me when I picked him up.

As muscles was only a quarter of the size of Sid, he was fed accordingly. He loved baby mice and rats but ate them live. I know this sounds cruel, but he asphyxiated them before they knew what was happening, and they didn't have a chance to be scared. One time, a mouse fell asleep on a branch in his tank, and Muscles pounced before it even opened its eyes.

Feeding didn't always go smoothly though. Russ came home with two baby mice for him, one evening, but he wasn't hungry. Rather than risk leaving the mice in the vivarium with him, where they might harm him, Russ put them back in the cardboard shoe box overnight, planning to try again the next day. They were two lucky mice when they managed to chew their way through the box and escape. The following evening, we saw them run across the floor in the living room and disappear inside the curtains. I dubiously went to investigate because I couldn't see when I put my head between the long drape and its lining. Suddenly, the mouse jumped onto my dress. I screamed, and it jumped off and disappeared under the furniture. I searched and searched in vain, finally giving up and going to bed.

In the morning, I called out to Russ, 'Look what I have discovered, a pair of mice snuggled up together in the drawer under the oven where it's warm and cosy.'

'I think they've earned their freedom,' replied Russ. So once he had caught them, he drove them down the road and set them free.

The following year, deprived of sunshine, we rented a friends unit in Benalmadina in Malaga, Spain. We arrived without any complications, dropped off our bags and went out to explore the area. Sunshine pirouetted across the soft searing sand, sucking the moisture from the picturesque, but crowded, beach where it was difficult to find anywhere to lay down.

In the evening, we went out in search of local cuisine. We enjoyed delicious fare and had plenty to drink. Late at night, we walked back to our unit. Finding our unit number, several floors up, I inserted the key in the lock, but it wouldn't open.

'Let me try,' said Russ after I'd given it several attempts.

'It's odd. There's a tea towel hanging in the window. I don't remember one being there before.'

Whilst our minds worked overtime, thinking maybe squatters had moved in when we were out, the occupants called out, 'You are in the wrong high-rise.'

There were three buildings side by side, all identical, and we'd entered the wrong one.

During the time we spent on holiday, we were regularly approached by touts offering all sorts of gifts if we would agree to attend a timeshare seminar. They said that they provide a taxi there and once we have listened, would give us free entry tickets to Tivoli World and provide a taxi to drop us anywhere we wanted. Initially, we declined all offers because there was so much we wanted to see and do, but eventually we surrendered and agreed to go.

On arrival at the resort, we were presented with ice cold cocktails to sample and given a tour of the rooms and complex. We then sat with one of their representatives who bestowed the benefits of purchasing a timeshare.

'We think of ourselves as travellers, not holidaymakers,' I advised him.

'Yes, we have been on a few package tours,' confessed Russ, 'but mainly we backpack and certainly do not want to go back to the same place every year.'

'This isn't a problem,' explained the salesman, 'you may swap your timeshare for others we have around the world.'

'So what country would you like to travel to?' he enquired.

I said, 'We loved Africa, so do they have timeshares in Egypt?'

'No, we don't have any there. What other countries would you liked to visit?'

'How about Kenya and Uganda?'

'We don't have any there either.'

'Zaire, Tanzania or Zimbabwe?'

'No, we don't have any timeshares in Africa,' he said frowning at us. 'Choose a country that's not in Africa.'

'We'd also like to visit Asia. Perhaps Vietnam, Cambodia and Laos.'

'We don't have any in Asia either. What other countries would you like to visit in Europe?'

'We recently spent several months travelling around eighteen countries in Europe so would like to see somewhere else. Do you have timeshares in Australia?'

By now he had turned red in the face and was glaring at us.

He shouted, 'No, we don't have any in Australia. You have just come here to get free tickets and had no intention of purchasing a timeshare.' He then got up and left us sitting at the table.

We were being absolutely honest and had no idea which countries they had timeshares in, but they obviously weren't for us.

Later in the evening, we were going inside to see a show when the hypnotist arrived in a flash limousine. He got out and walked up the pathway with two vivacious women, each clinging to one of his arms. I wondered to myself whether they were with him voluntarily or he had hypnotised them.

The show started with volunteers from the audience going on stage. The ones who went under his spell stayed on stage for the rest of the night. It started tamely enough with him giving them an onion each. He told them they were apples and delicious, so they took big bites and were chewing away when he woke them. They spat out the onion quickly, gagging at the taste.

Once again hypnotised, he asked them to strip to their underwear and ride a horse when he said the words, 'Good Evening.' He repeated several times for them to leave their underwear on but still had to restrain a few from stripping naked. Tears were streaming down my face whilst I watched them pretending to gallop along whipping their imaginary horses. I was glad I hadn't volunteered.

At the end of the night, he woke them, got them to dress and return to the audience. In his closing speech, he thanked everyone for coming and said it had been a "Good Evening". They all jumped up again, galloping on their horses. I laughed uncontrollably but wondered whether it ever wore off. If not, every time someone greeted them, they were going to start galloping.

Glumly, we returned to England, work and the gloomy weather. I missed Australia and even Zimbabwe. Feeling depressed from the dark and cheerless days we spent at home, unable to plan any outdoor activities because it usually rained, we booked on a package holiday to the Grand Canary Islands. They're part of Spain and a popular tourist destination from England. We were flying from Gatwick airport, which was handy, as it was much easier to get there compared to Heathrow. The flight was scheduled for late afternoon, and we arrived at the airport with plenty of time to spare and checked in our luggage. On viewing the screens, it said the flight was delayed.

'Let's find somewhere to sit to pass the time,' I said to Russ.

'The airport is so crowded, but look, there is a couple of spots on that bench,' replied Russ. We quickly sat down and took it in turns to check the monitor. Time ticked by and still the monitor read "Flight delayed". After numerous checks, the monitor changed to "Enquire at check-in".

Russ said, 'Save our seats, and I'll go and enquire.' The time past slowly until he returned. 'The flight cannot fly out of Gatwick airport as it's now past the curfew time. We have to catch a bus to Luton airport and fly out from there,' he informed me.

'Okay,' I said, 'so what really happened? What did they really say?'

'Seriously, we have to pick up our tickets for the bus journey.'

'Very funny when will the flight take off from Gatwick?'

'Come with me to the enquiry desk,'

At the desk, we were issued with tickets and directed to a bus travelling the 113 kilometres to Luton airport. I could only apologise for not believing Russ. We arrived at Grand Canaria Island in the early hours of the following morning and enjoyed a week of glorious sunshine.

I'd recovered from my previous disappointment in being unable to immigrate to Australia, enjoyed seeing much of Europe and some of Africa. However, I felt like I was just treading water, waiting to move on and find somewhere warmer to live. Russ also wanted to relocate to fairer climates where we could spend more of our time outdoors. It would also be great if we didn't have to return to the depressing English weather after holidaying in the sunshine. Our first preference was to move to Australia, and if that didn't work out, we'd apply to work in South Africa instead. I hoped to be accepted this time and waited impatiently for a reply.

If we were going to settle overseas, after living together for several years, the time had come to make it legal. Neither of us wanted a flash wedding because we both loved each other and wanted to spend the rest of our lives travelling together.

I thought back to my English class where I'd told the teacher I wanted to travel rather than get married. However, I hadn't thought about doing both. I was lucky to have found my soul mate.

We decided to keep our plans a secret as we didn't want a fuss and just told a couple of friends as we needed two witnesses. Rather than upset one of our friends or relatives, we thought if nobody was invited, they would all understand.

A week before the wedding, one of our witnesses dropped out. I rang my sister.

'I wondered whether you would be a witness at our wedding.' I said.

'When are you getting married?' she asked.

'On Thursday.'

'Ooh, what did Mum and Dad say?'

'I haven't told them since we are only inviting two mandatory witnesses.'

'You have to invite them. They will be devastated if you don't.' In the end, she persuaded me to invite both lots of parents.

Russ rang his mum and explained about the wedding. Because she wasn't well at the time, his parents couldn't attend but were completely understanding of the situation.

We decided to break it to my parents in person. Mum answered the door as Dad was having a bath.

'To what do I owe this pleasure?' Mum asked.

'We have some news for you,' Russ started cautiously.

'Good news I hope,' replied Mum.

'We've got engaged,' I said, showing her my new ring.

'Congratulations, I am so pleased.' She grinned at us. 'Have you set a date for the wedding?'

'We are getting married on Thursday. It's just very casual. Also, we are going to apply to move to Australia,' I blurted out.

Her beaming smile faded quickly. 'You can't move overseas, I will miss you too much. Just wait, I will get your father.'

When my dad appeared, we explained the situation to him.

He was genuinely pleased when he said, 'Congratulations, I hope you have a successful life together, wherever you live.'

I thought back to the Little Mermaid in Copenhagen, who had left her family to follow her heart. I hoped it would work out for me because my prince hadn't chosen another.

Over the following week, Mum decorated the cake she had baked for her silver wedding anniversary and gave it to us for our wedding cake.

Leaving work at lunchtime, whilst in the lift, my colleague asked me what I was doing that afternoon.

'You aren't getting married, are you?' she asked perceptively.

'Why would you think that?' I blushed.

'Well, you got engaged last week and didn't tell me until I noticed your sparkling ring.'

'I confess, I am getting married this afternoon.' It didn't need to be a secret anymore.

'I'm going to have a difficult job collecting money for a present for you as nobody will believe me.' She laughed and gave me a hug.

It was a beautiful day, and although the wind was chilly, the sun poked through the clouds. Russ was wearing his grey suit which now fitted him perfectly, contrasting with his grey shoes and crisp white shirt that highlighted his red tie.

My Joan Collins designed blue taffeta suit had padded shoulders and hugged tightly to my waist where a frill projected across my hips and over the pencil skirt which hung down below my knees. My white lace stockings were the same colour as my high stiletto heels, clutch bag and the posy of flowers pinned to my jacket.

We were all smiling as photos of the six of us were hastily taken before we headed home for some champagne to celebrate. Dad shouted us all a delicious seafood dinner. I will never forget such a special day.

The application process took some time. As well as my qualifications, Russ also had a job on the labour shortage list, and he had more than five years' experience. However, after lodging our application at the Australian Embassy in London, we decided to book a holiday in case we were turned down and needed something to cheer us up.

I found a trip advertised in a local paper which looked excellent value for money because it included travel, accommodation and full board. We journeyed by coach from London to Maurach, in Austria, where we stayed in a bed and breakfast between the Karwendel and Rofan mountain ranges, on the southern bank of Achensee Lake at an elevation of 950 meters. Each night, we would walk down to the Gastehaus Lechner to have dinner, such as hamburger and mash, or fish and chips. We really didn't expect anything better considering how much the trip cost, although many people complained bitterly about the standard of food.

The only extra cost was to book on day trips or pay to go skiing. I wasn't interested in skiing after my last attempt, so we booked on a couple of day trips, one to Saltzburg as, although I'd spent time in Koln in the late seventies, Russ had not visited Germany before.

It was the same guide on every trip, and he made me giggle each time he suggested, 'If you would like to get off the coach here and look a bit round, you are welcome to.'

'Do I look round shaped?' I asked Russ as I tried to puff myself out like a weeble when we got off the coach to explore the area.

There were two older ladies on the trip who moaned constantly, complaining about the food and the extra cost of the day trips which they thought were just a way to make commission at the various shops we stopped at along the way. We couldn't understand it because we were having a great time.

We made friends with a couple of the other guests and would often stay back after dinner for a drink or three. I drank dry martini and that was where confusion arose.

Russ asked the barman, 'Please may I have a pint of lager and a dry martini?' He was taken aback when the barman served him three martinis.

'I only asked for a dry martini.'

'Ja, drei martinis.' He had taken "dry" to mean "drei", which is Austrian for three. An easy mistake and one that gave me a migraine, the following morning, having drunk all three the night before.

I'd suffered from migraines for years, especially after exercising, a lot of stress, or drinking. I vomited constantly and struggled with the intense pain that only sleep would improve.

I thought a walk around the lake might help clear my head, because we had to check out of the bed and breakfast and wait for the coach to depart in the evening. The walk didn't do anything to make me feel better, so I was pretty sorry for myself when we finally got on board the coach. The overnight trip back to London was frightening when the driver ran red lights at alarming speeds, but we made it home in one piece.

I didn't mind returning to England, this time, because we'd been accepted to live in Australia. Maybe I'd found what I was looking for, a place to live where the sun shone warmly and opportunities abounded. My one regret was leaving my family and snakes behind.

Whilst we were stopped at the traffic lights on the High Street in Croydon, people had peculiar expressions on their faces when they glanced through our car windows at the back seat. Muscles was hidden in a shoe box with air holes, but Sid had his head stuck out the hand holds of an old microwave cardboard box. His tongue flicked in and out as he eyed the passing crowds.

It was difficult to find a new home for Sid and Muscles because we wanted to ensure they would be treated well. We left them with a company that provided reptiles for films. Tears ran in rivulets down my cheeks, pooling in my dimples as I whispered farewell and kissed my darling reptiles' goodbye, trying to console myself by thinking they were likely to become movie stars.

The last task was to sell our maisonette, and unfortunately the property market had fallen into a slump. We had a reasonable offer from a young couple, so we took the house off the market. They were allowed six weeks to get their finances in order, and then we would exchange contracts. Unfortunately when the six weeks were up, they pulled out, unable to borrow enough money to go ahead with the purchase.

We were now in a quandary. We needed to sell our home to finance our travels and resettlement overseas. Our tickets were already booked, and we would lose a large part of the cost if we cancelled. Our visas were only valid for entry within a year from the date of issue, so the pressure was mounting. We'd got so close, but weren't there yet.

It wouldn't be easy managing the sale from overseas. House values continued to drop, and our date of departure drew closer. A few prospective buyers came to view the property, but nobody made an offer. I was beginning to feel desperate. Then finally, we got a bidder but for a much lower price. We had no alternative but to accept it. This time the purchasers already had finance, so exchange of contracts went ahead, but the final settlement would not take place until after we'd departed.

My dad kindly stepped in, and we organized for him to have power of attorney, so he could sign on our behalf. I was more than a little stressed, organizing for our belongings to be either sold or shipped to Australia, resigning from my job (which I loved), getting ready for a new adventure travelling through Asia and worrying whether the sale would be completed. I was also apprehensive about being separated from my family.

CHAPTER FIVE – TO A LAND DOWN UNDER
Thailand, Malaysia, Singapore, Bali, Australia,
Vanuatu, New Caledonia

In August 1989, I departed England leaving behind the solemn dark days for a brighter sunnier lifestyle. Because we were to travel through Asia, we needed the usual vaccinations. Our doctor thought it best not to mix the injections so gave us cholera in one arm and typhoid and hepatitis A in the other.

After walking home, I said, 'I'm off to bed,' even though it was the middle of the afternoon.

'I am too,' replied Russ miserably.

I lay on my back and complained, 'Both my arms are sore.'

'Ouch, that hurts,' said Russ, trying to move.

I laughed. 'What a sorry sight we must look.'

'I feel like I've got the flu and a terrible headache. Can you get me a glass of water?' he pleaded.

Feeling sorry for myself, I didn't want to move but agreed to go downstairs. 'Ow,' I wailed when I lifted both arms, one to hold the glass and the other to turn on the tap.

I tried hard to lay perfectly still, but all night the tiniest of movements Russ made, sent waves of pain through my tender limbs.

This time we used Lonely Plants guidebook "South East Asia on a Shoestring", which was nicknamed "the travel bible" along with their travel survival kit on Australia. When I'd travelled around Europe, in 1985, they had not published a guidebook for that area and wouldn't do so until 1999. We had our trusty backpacks, heavy cameras and Walkman.

Two friends travelled with us through Asia and on to Australia where we had visas to live permanently.

Julia, whom I was working with, was a compassionate young woman and close friend. She'd been wanting to travel but like myself, many years before, she didn't have anyone to travel with.

Ian, a mate of Russ' made up the group of four. His placid nature along with a good sense of humour made travelling together a pleasant experience.

Bangkok airport in Thailand, reminded me of Singapore when I alighted the plane to be greeted by a wall of humidity and burning sunshine which left me damp and sticky. The noise of the car engines, horns being tooted and people shouting was disconcerting whilst the taxi driver skilfully manoeuvred around the traffic jams, dodging other vehicles on the way to Banglamphu near the river and Chinatown. The buildings appeared dirty, covered in grime and vehicle emissions, but the streets were busy with vendors tending street stalls selling food and every imaginable souvenir. A mixture of raw sewage and oriental spices wafted in the air as I dashed from the safety of the cab into the air-conditioned hotel.

It was a mad idea to catch a kamikaze tuk tuk to the Crocodile Farm. The four of us squashed into the open back vehicle more intimately than was comfortable and clung on to avoid falling out. The exhaust fumes, from the bumper to bumper traffic, made it difficult to breathe. I wasn't sure if I'd live to find out how much damage there'd been to my lungs from the smog, because the brakes were faulty. Every time the driver tried to stop, there was a horrible grinding sound, and the whole vehicle shuddered violently trying to toss us onto the ground.

We made it to the small zoo intact where I cooed over an adorable baby elephant. The crocodiles were the main attraction though, and a courageous, or insane man, put his head in one's open mouth to much applause from the audience. I thought, it wasn't my idea of how to make a living because I'm sure he wouldn't have been covered with a decent life insurance policy.

The following day, we strolled along the bustling streets, evading the persuasive vendors on the way to the Royal Palace Complex. The resolute guard couldn't be coaxed into letting Russ and

Ian enter because they were inappropriately dressed with vest t-shirts on. Luckily it was only a fifteen minute walk back to the hotel to change and run the gauntlet once again.

The ornate complex was quite overwhelming with luxurious golden spires towering vertically above the ruby red and bottle green roofs of the various buildings. I'd expected to see a large jade carved Buddha in the serenity of a sumptuous temple. Although intricately carved, the revered Emerald Buddha stood at only sixty-six centimetres high, in a temple crowded with visitors being herded in and out of the doors like cattle, making the experience rushed and impersonal.

At midday, we caught a bus to Rayong and then a small boat, or perhaps a better description would be a large dinghy, to the island of Koh Samet. There weren't any ladders, and the drop from the rickety pier was hard to climb down without falling into the water. I don't know how the Thais managed because their legs were shorter than mine. I then clambered from one craft to another until I reached the one leaving for our destination. When each vessel rocked and moved, I was scared of getting my fingers or toes crushed between them.

It was a serene evening whilst we motored across the sea which was as smooth as royal icing. The lights on the island finally came into view, and the engine spluttered and died. The captain tried to restart it, but it was stubborn and wouldn't oblige. I sat and watched in horror whilst we drifted with the current, and it started to rain a steady drizzle. The darkness curled around us as the skipper found a torch to inspect the motor. I calculated it was too far to swim ashore and certainly not with my backpack, so there was no alternative but to wait for rescue. Eventually I heard a clatter, then the hum of the engine, and we were on our way again.

It was late when we landed, but we still found somewhere to stay. The island was secluded with shortages of electricity and water. Our hut was close to the beach, which was delightful. The sun baked the soft fine sand, but the constant sea breeze from the sapphire sea kept me cool.

I was standing with Russ, talking to the owner of the guesthouse when I had to make a quick dash to the bathroom to vomit. The hard part was using a communal toilet when I had fluids evacuating my body from both ends. The toilet paper was collected in a basket and could not be flushed. I thought maybe that was why I got sick in the first place. I dug out my first aid kit and swallowed a dose of Imodium to stop the diarrhoea. However, unfortunately this meant I'd be sick after eating instead. It wasn't a good omen because we had a two day journey ahead, back to Bangkok and on to Phuket.

It was raining when we caught the boat. Although it didn't break down, by the time we'd transferred to a bus it took the whole day to reach Bangkok. On arrival, we discovered all the overnight coaches to Phuket were fully booked, so we had to get one to Surat Thani instead. I had tea and chocolate cake in the café whilst we waited for the bus to arrive, but it didn't stay down for long. I was grateful to have been sick before boarding the bus where I promptly fell asleep.

It was noon, the following day, by the time we arrived in Surat Thani, and we took shelter in another café as the rain teemed down, bouncing off the pavement whilst we waited for the bus to Phuket. It was running late, and I decided to not to eat anything else until we arrived at our final destination.

By the time we checked into an airy bungalow near the beach, I was a bit better, although exceptionally tired. I thought it was the ideal place to relax and recuperate. I made friends with the enormous local black pig which had his address written on his side, in marker pen, in case he got lost. However, he was only interested in my company when I had food to offer him.

In this paradise, I also became host to mosquitoes and sand flies. It wasn't long before the satiated females had caused a chain of blisters to erupt around my ankles that weren't attractive like jewellery. It didn't matter if I covered myself in insect repellent, wore socks to cover my exposed skin or burned citronella candles, they still found me, silently dancing under the table, landing weightlessly on my ankles and nourishing themselves on my blood without me knowing a thing. Later, of course, the bite sites itched like crazy and as much as I tried not to scratch them, I couldn't stop myself. When asleep, I burst them open, releasing the serum and dampening my clothing.

I was glad to be taking doxycycline now that chloroquine was becoming resistant to malaria. I didn't want to get sick whilst travelling. I'd heard of others taking Lariam who were experiencing nightmares and hallucinations.

The beaches were idyllic, and we spent many hours lounging on our towels. One morning, I discovered Russ face down in the sand, his ankles held firmly with his knees bent backwards and a woman's foot on his lower back. Stuck in that position, wearing only his swimmers, he looked vulnerable. I wondered what he'd done to upset her as she appeared to be torturing him.

As I hurried closer, she shifted position, kneeling on his buttocks and pulling both his arms so far backwards that it lifted his head and chest off the ground. She moved him into various positions. Now he was laying on his back whilst she stretched his legs up over his head. I wondered whether he was conscious as he didn't seem to be resisting. When she sat and massaged the base of his spine, I realized what was happening.

Basted in a coating of oil and sand, he looked extremely uncomfortable. He'd expected his muscles to have been rubbed, not to be manipulated into different yoga positions. Now I knew what a Thai massage was and wouldn't be requesting one.

For a change, we decided to hire a couple of trail motorbikes to tour the island. Both Russ and Ian were veteran riders, and I'd ridden pillion for many years. The waterfalls in a local nature reserve looked inviting, from the heat of the midday sun, as they gushed down the hillside. There were some gibbons in a cage and when I approached, they turned around to have their backs scratched. I poked my finger through the gaps in the mesh to oblige, but if I stopped, they would turn around and stretch their arms out for more. I was coping until three of them wanted attention and then I didn't have enough hands. So Russ came to my rescue and the one whose back he was scratching returned the favour by searching through his hair for nits.

In the evening at one of the local bars, the owner had two baby gibbons, aged five and six months old. She handed me a tiny ball of fluff. All arms and legs, he wrapped tightly himself around my waist and stayed there steadfastly until after dusk. His hairless jet black face was alluring with mysterious dark pools for eyes which looked appealingly at me above his tiny nostrils. His fur was soft like velvet. I didn't want to hand him back, even though everyone else was tired and wanted to go to sleep. Although I loved holding him, he deserved better. I wished he could roam freely in the rainforests, but because most species of gibbons are endangered, mainly due to loss of habitat, he might not have survived on his own.

A few days later, across the border at Telok Chempedak, a beach resort near Kuanton in Malaysia, we decided to hire a windsurfer for an hour. Bubbles of water coated the champagne sand as the tide advanced whilst Russ carried the board along the shoreline. We took turns to try to sail the board. I managed to climb onto the base which was bobbing up and down in the choppy ocean, but as soon as I attempted to stand, I fell off, swallowing mouthfuls of salt water. I persevered and kept getting back on until I managed to stay upright. Pulling the sail up by the rope, I reached to grab the boom, but the sail kept coming towards me, knocking me backwards off the board. I did the same thing several more times until the boom crashed down onto my head when I'd fallen into the murky sea. That was enough for me to admit defeat.

The overnight bus to Singapore was a real bone shaker, and I didn't sleep all night. It was just after six in the morning when we arrived, and without any local currency, we had a long hike to find accommodation, at Hotel Bencoolen, which was the height of luxury to us. It was handy to stay somewhere decent because I still had a nagging stomach bug which made me fatigued. Julia was also unwell but never complained. I was adamant not to miss any sights though so kept pushing myself each day. That particular day, we went for a long walk to see the Merlion and Raffles Hotel, which was closed for renovations. In the end, when I could walk no further, I decided it was worthwhile seeing a doctor.

'I have been vomiting with diarrhoea for the last three weeks, have lost a lot of weight and I'm exhausted,' I explained.

'Have you been to Thailand?' she asked in perfect English. Before I could reply, she continued, 'You probably picked up a bug there, and I have just the treatment for you.'

She gave me a drink full of electrolytes to try to boost my energy and a bottle of yellow looking syrup to take three times a day. It worked wonders, and I immediately felt much better.

I was to improve even more after contacting my dad. He advised that settlement had gone through, and full payment for our house had been made. Now we could afford to buy a home in Australia.

This time when the plane touched down in Bali, I was ready for the wall of humidity to hit me after leaving the air-conditioned aircraft. I strolled across the runway to the arrivals hall and queued to get through passport control and customs. At the luggage carousel, where I waited with Russ, Julia and Ian for my backpack to appear, several touts came up to us and tried to take our bags. We politely refused the offer and headed to the money changers. Once we had some Balinese rupiah, Russ negotiated with a taxi driver to take us into Kuta. The driver recommended some cottages, to stay at, which were reasonably priced and within walking distance of the beach, so we checked in.

I strolled along the sidewalk, towards the beach, where vendors carrying goods emerged to intercept me.

Several of the vendors asked questions at the same time, 'Hello. Where are you from? I have taxi for you. You want massage? I braid your hair? You buy from me?'

I didn't know who to answer first, so replied, 'No thank you' and continued walking towards the beach.

This didn't deter the touts though, and they followed, pressing each of us to buy something from them. I thought if we can get to the beach, we'll be fine. The touts stayed with us and were joined by others.

Another tout asked, 'How long you stay? You want manicure or pedicure?'

Again I replied, 'No thank you.'

Once on the beach, it got worse. I found a place to lay my towel down and sat on it. The touts crowded around dropping their souvenirs on my towel. I felt like a crumb being devoured by a swarm of ants.

They continued saying, 'I have nice sarong. You buy sarong? I have beads, look pretty in your hair. You buy?'

I explained, 'I just want to sun bathe. Maybe I will shop later but definitely not now.'

It was probably not a good thing to say because the responses were, 'You buy from me later?' I wondered how I would know who was who.

In the end, because none of us were interested in looking at their wares, they left, and finally I could look around and take in the beautiful vista. The sky was a brilliant powder blue dotted with white cotton wool clouds casting shadows on the azure blue sea which lapped gentle waves on the white sandy beach. I laid down, put on my headphones to listen to music and closed my eyes whilst enjoying the sun's rays dancing on my skin.

As I started to relax, I heard voices, 'Hello, hello. You buy from me? I give you cheap price. I give you good massage. I get you drink. What you want?'

I pretended I couldn't hear because I had headphones on. The ruse only worked for a few moments before they started to shake me awake to listen to them.

I said, 'I really don't want to buy anything. I'm here to get a suntan, and you are casting shadows on me. Please leave me alone.'

They moved to each of us in turn. Julia made the mistake of looking at some of the sarongs and disappeared from view beneath a crowd of touts, who thought they had finally found a customer.

I'd visited Australia twice before and was lucky enough not to have encountered some of its more dangerous wildlife. I'd read about the deadly red-back and funnel-web spiders, and I knew of the venomous brown and tiger snakes as well as the taipan. In the water, we needed to watch out for the toxic blue ring octopus, box jellyfish and stone fish along with the great white sharks. The saltwater crocodile might also pose a threat.

I'd stepped over a brown snake, once before, and encountered a harmless, but large, ugly huntsman spider on the inside of my aunt's car door but none of the others. I hoped we wouldn't encounter any on this trip either.

We hired a campervan to travel the south and east coasts of Australia, so we could see some of the countryside before settling down in Sydney. The campervan company kindly upgraded us to a six berth, for the same price as a four, which meant we'd more room to move around. Russ and I took the double berth over the cab whilst Julia and Ian slept on the bench seats around two tables which converted into two single bunks. There was a three way fridge (with freezer compartment), a gas cooker with hotplates, a sink and a shower.

Russ and I travelled in the cab, taking turns to drive whilst Julia and Ian sat in the campervan on the lounge seats which had seatbelts fitted to them. I couldn't have sat in the back, because I get motion sickness if I cannot see in the direction I'm travelling.

Driving was interesting as my car in England had been a mini-clubman so much smaller than a six berth motorhome. It took some time to get the mirrors set to be of any use. It was difficult to see what traffic was coming up the outside lane so made changing lanes especially hard.

As we arrived in Brisbane, we got a puncher. The nuts on the wheel had been done up so tight none of us could shift them. The van tool box only consisted of two small spanners, a screwdriver and half a jack, which didn't help. So we found a phone box and called the RACQ (Royal Automobile Club of Queensland). At least we could have a cup of tea and wait in comfort, inside the motorhome, for the mechanic to arrive.

He eventually turned up in his truck and rather demeaningly said, 'G'day cobber. Having problems changing your tyre? I'd have thought you could manage between the four of you.'

Russ explained, 'We only have a few tools. The nuts must have been done up with an air-gun because they're not shifting.'

'Bruce will soon fix it,' replied the repairman, referring to himself. So we all crowded around to watch him undo the nuts. He was soon perspiring heavily and stomping on his cross spanner but all to no avail. We stood quietly, not daring to say a word. As Bruce removed his straw hat and mopped his brow, I thought maybe he should be eating it. In the end, the combined effort from Russ and Bruce managed to slowly shift each nut, and the spare tyre was looking much healthier than the deflated one.

We still had time to carry on to Lone Pine Koala Sanctuary where I cuddled a koala. It was cute, although much smaller than the one I held in Adelaide and its fur woolly rather than soft like a kangaroos. Its cream belly stood out from its grey back whilst its small round eyes fixed on the eucalyptus leaves nearby. It smelt a little similar to tea leaves.

By the time we reached Proserpine, the auxiliary battery wasn't charging on the motorhome, so we had to take it to a garage to get it fixed. Once it was sorted, we booked on a day cruise out to a couple of the Whitsunday Islands. It wasn't the high risk season for box jellyfish, so we entered the water keeping an eye out for stonefish, snakes, octopus and the toadfish which was sometimes called the "toe fish" because it has been known to bite off toes.

At South Molle Island, Julia and I decided to go para-flying. A speed boat took the four of us out to a pontoon in the middle of the bay. I almost slipped into the sea whilst trying to climb over the front of the boat and onto the platform as it was so smooth and wet. Once

I had a life jacket on and was hooked up to the parachute, the boat motored away, and up I went into the air. I took my camera with me after the driver promised not to dunk me in the water. The view was remarkable from such a height. The sun beamed down on the sandy beach which appeared to be sprinkled with tiny insects, but the sea was smooth like glass. However, moments before the pontoon came into sight, the boat stopped, and I descended into the sea. I started to get worried when my ankles got wet, because my camera was only a couple of weeks old, but within seconds I was high in the sky again when the vessel picked up speed. The landing went smoothly, but it was hard to stay on the platform when the wind caught my parachute, and I was nearly dragged over the side. It didn't help that I was unhooked from the parachute on one shoulder, which was now attached to Julia, but I was still attached on the other. I thought we were going to be swimming linked together.

In Melbourne, we visited Philip Island, one evening, to watch the fairy penguins come up the beach. I waited patiently for dusk to arrive and kept scanning the beach in hope of spotting something. Sometime later, one little penguin wobbled up the beach, followed by another, then another and then a whole waddle. They came in hoards, and so did the torrential rain, drenching us in seconds. We made a mad dash back to the shelter of the motorhome in the carpark.

It had been a great trip but was now time to settle down. Our first Christmas Day in Australia was spent with my in-laws. It was quite different to an English one, being so hot.

I thought back to my childhood Christmases, a nostalgic time of year, when I looked forward to the delicious wafting smell of mince pies and Christmas cake rising to perfection in the oven. Mum always made them herself, and they were delectable. She would let me help stir the pudding which smelt pungently of alcohol until it had been steamed on the stove-top.

If I was lucky, it would snow, and the house and garden would be covered in a carpet of white velvet snowflakes. Icicles would dangle from the trees, and the moon reflected the twinkling lights setting an atmosphere of anticipation.

I'd help Mum and Diana make decorations. We would stick brightly coloured hoops together, to make paper chains, to hang around the house and along the banisters up the staircase. The best part was decorating the tree. Dad set up the flashing coloured lights whilst Diana and I added glittery tinsel, vibrant baubles and small crackers.

On Christmas Eve, we would hang out our stockings above the fireplace in the living room. Mum would give us a glass of milk and some biscuits or a mince pie to leave for Santa to eat. Sometimes, we also left a carrot for the reindeer.

The next day, we woke in the early hours of the morning and were allowed to open our stockings in bed. There was always a mandarin and some walnuts in the foot of the stocking. Later, we were allowed to open our presents which were underneath the tree.

Lunch was a family affair, and we would be joined by my mum's brother, his wife and Ali (my cousin). There were bon bons (crackers) laid out on the table, and we would pull them with the person sitting next to us. Inside, were the usual corny jokes that we read out loud and a paper hat to wear along with a little souvenir.

Mum cooked up a feast for everyone, a flawlessly roasted stuffed turkey which my dad would carve, roast potatoes and vegetables, all served with gravy. This was followed by the Christmas pudding Mum had cooked earlier in the month and was garnished with a sprig of holly from the garden. It was served with butter brandy and cream. We always had to be careful when we ate it because there was a sixpence in it for one of us to find. It was supposed to bring good luck to whoever found it.

Christmases would be different from now on, especially once Russ' parents returned to England. This year, we were having seafood followed by pavlova, and the only snow in sight was sprayed inside windows. I'd miss the family tradition.

Recession hit Australia hard in the nineties when many people lost their jobs, and high interest rates meant rising mortgage payments. Coming from England, where we were paying an interest rate of 4 percent for our mortgage, we now had to pay 17.5 percent. It was likely to be a while before we could afford to travel overseas again, but there was plenty to explore in Australia until then.

Letters to family and friends took at least a week in each direction so often crossed over, and the same subject was discussed for several weeks. In time, the introduction of the internet made it much easier to keep in touch by allowing daily contact and reply.

One Sunday, we thought a day at Jenolan Caves, out past the Blue Mountains, would be interesting.

'Wow, look at all those steps,' I whispered to Russ.

'Apparently there are nine hundred to get through the Lucas Cave,' he replied as his voice echoed loudly.

'Some singers record their albums in part of the cave,' advised the guide, 'because the acoustics are so good.'

The limestone formations were quite spectacular with stalactites hanging from the ceiling and stalagmites coming up to meet them that looked like the open jaws of a crocodile.

Driving home in our old Cortina, winding our way down the mountain, the heat haze blurred our vision. When we took a particularly tight corner, Russ nudged the brakes with his foot but nothing happened. He hit them a bit harder and still no response. We started picking up speed going down-hill.

'What's wrong?' I asked.

'The brakes have failed,' he replied, reasonably calmly in the circumstances, although I could hear the strain in his voice.

He struggled with the steering wheel trying to keep us from careening over the edge. All I can remember thinking was not yet as I still have so many more places to see and things to do. In front of us was a flat safety siding coming up. He steered the car expertly into it and pulled on the handbrake whilst also stamping on the pedal. It was enough to bring us to a gentle stop.

'That was close,' gasped Russ.

'Well manoeuvred,' I replied, letting out a deep breath.

I thought that we needed a more reliable mode of transport.

#

'Ouch,' I cried out. A wave of nausea flooded through my body when I noticed my thumb was sticking out at a rather peculiar angle. I could see sparkly lights in front of my eyes and just wanted to lie on the ground whilst pretending it was only a dream.

Whilst I was taking a sharp bend in the mud, two wheels slid from underneath me, and before I knew it, I was on the ground with my bike on top of me.

I'd ridden motorbikes as a pillion passenger many times and because I was hooked on the 500cc grand prix series and superbikes, I thought I'd like to get my own bike. It would be a new way for Russ and I to tour the country, and it would make the journey to work quicker too.

Russ has been teaching me to ride my Kawasaki KLR250 around the paddock and thought I was learning quite well. I'd finally managed to master clutch control, but the bike seat was quite high, so I could only touch the ground on tip toe. This meant when I stopped, I regularly fell over as the weight of the bike tipped me. My calves and wrists were covered in bruises, but I persevered because I wanted to be able to ride my own motorbike.

'I thought you had disappeared down the dip,' said Russ, 'but then I realized there was no dip,' he continued after he had ran to see what had happened.

He kindly lifted the bike from on top of me and said, 'Come on. Get up.'

Shock had set in pretty quickly and I replied, 'Let me lie here for a minute, my head is spinning, and I want to vomit.' He hopped on the bike and rode home to get the car to take me to the medical centre.

I was ushered to the treatment room and explained what had happened. The nurse asked me, 'Please remove your leather jacket.'

'I fell on my right side, so my right arm is very sore and painful to bend, and my left thumb won't move,' I explained.

'We can cut off your jacket,' she offered.

'No, I will help her take it off,' replied Russ. When I turned around, he pulled the jacket quickly from my back, and I cried out in pain. 'It's off now and still in one piece,' he said smiling.

The doctor was called to look at my thumb.

Russ explained, 'It must be dislocated as it was sticking out at a very peculiar angle.'

'It doesn't look like it's sticking out,' replied the doctor.

'That's because it's now very swollen,' said Russ.

The doctor humoured me and sent me to get some x-rays. When I returned with the footage, he conceded and agreed my thumb was badly dislocated, so he would reset it for me. I was worried about how painful this would be as the pain was excruciating when they just twisted my wrist to take the x-ray. I was relieved when he injected a local anaesthetic before manipulating it.

'Because it's been dislocated for a few hours, the ligaments have stretched. I will have to set it in plaster, so it doesn't pop out again,' he explained.

'Take off your rings,' the nurse requested.

'My fingers are swollen, so I can't get them off.'

'I can cut your rings off your finger if you cannot remove them.'

'No, they will be ruined,' replied Russ.

A lady, sitting beside her injured husband in the next bed, explained, 'I'm a jeweller and can try to remove them for you.'

'Yes please,' I replied, hoping Russ wouldn't try.

She covered my finger in soap and millimetre by millimetre moved the rings whilst she pushed the swollen tissue underneath them.

Russ was pleased. 'Not only have we saved your jacket but also your rings.' 'Now,' he said, 'it's up to you to fix your broken motorbike.'

I did get the parts and fixed it, but I never got on it again. My boss had given me an ultimatum.

'If you fall off that bike one more time, you can kiss your job goodbye,' he told me. I'm not sure he really meant it, but he was concerned I'd do more damage next time.

Not long afterwards, I was presented with my Australian Citizenship Certificate and couldn't stop smiling.

'I have filled out the forms to apply for our Australian passports,' I informed Russ.

'Now we are fully fledged Australian citizens, we are free to travel once more,' he responded, grinning at me.

Four years after arriving in Australia, we embarked on our first cruise. With motorbike riding no longer an option for me, I thought cruising might be a different way to travel and see different countries. The ship was to stop at four islands, Mystery Island, Isle of Pines, Port Vila and Noumea.

I was likely to get seasick so purchased some plasters which contained scoplalamine. I stuck one behind my ear before leaving dry land. The plaster worked well and was supposed to last several days, so I left it on until we got to our first stop and then removed it.

This stop was at Port Vila, Vanuatu where we were greeted by a brass band marching up and down the dock, in front of souvenir stalls selling sarongs, t-shirts and brown plastic dolls in grass skirts. Seated in a horseshoe shape, the band played the song by Abba "I do, I do, I do".

The countryside was lush and green with colourful hibiscus and frangipani plants adding vibrant colour and sweet scent to the landscape. We visited a local school where the children were friendly and smiling. They set out locally grown juicy papaya slices and crispy white coconut chunks on dark green banana leaves for us to eat.

Away from the port was a serene sandy beach with clear sapphire blue seas lapping at the shore. It was great to relax in the sunshine and sip on our ice cold drinks.

I just had one other plaster, so I thought I'd try without one because it would only last a few days, and it was still many more days before we arrived home. Nevertheless, a few hours after re-embarking, I started feeling queasy. I tried pressing on my pressure points, the one in my wrist and the other between my thumb and index finger, but to no avail. I went out on deck to breathe fresh air and have the wind in my face, but it was dark and cold, so I gave in and stuck on the other patch.

The amount of food on the ship was a feast fit for an army to consume. We were offered several courses at breakfast, more for lunch and five for dinner. On top of those meals, afternoon tea was served. I never indulged, because I couldn't bear the thought of eating anything else between meals. It was a sight to see though when the smartly dressed waiters, in their red tuxedos and black bow ties, came into the dining area with large platters containing delicate cakes and pastries, and they were mobbed. I wondered if they only had a certain amount when the guests lunged at the trays as if they had been starving on a desert island for weeks.

Our second stop was to be Mystery Island, but the swell was too big, so it was cancelled. I was disappointed, but it wouldn't be much fun anyway in the bad weather.

The ship continued on to New Caledonia. It was quiet in Noumea being a public holiday and because the skies were black and rain was pouring down. A coach took us to the hilltop, by which time the sun's ray had appeared as the clouds had lifted, so we had a clear view of the harbor and out to sea.

The Botanical Gardens were verdant. It was great to stretch our legs and wander around on dry land between elegant green palms to a pond containing water lilies, which the fish darted underneath to hide. I stumbled on, intermittently struggling to balance when the land seemed to be moving.

This time, I didn't take off the plaster I was wearing and kept it on for the rest of the trip. Unfortunately we were unable to stop in the Isle of Pines, again due to rough weather.

It was a relief to be home and on dry land. I needed a hot shower, but when I closed my eyes under the steamy stream of water, I fell backwards. I'd removed the last plaster, but it now seemed like I was on a moving boat, instead of a steady terrain. During the following week, I had motion sickness whilst my body readjusted.

I decided that I preferred backpacking to cruising because there was more time to explore inland. Cruising was more about the voyage than the places we stopped at, and I could think of better journeys because I wanted to see more of Africa, its wild ecosystems and diverse creatures. Perhaps it would even be better living in South Africa. If I didn't explore it, I'd never know.

CHAPTER SIX – WALK LIKE AN EGYPTIAN
Egypt, Greece, Kenya, Uganda

'Finally we can visit Egypt,' I said because it was one of the countries we'd both always wanted to explore. I was fascinated by Ancient Egypt and dreamed about visiting the Pyramids and Tutankhamun's burial chamber. The more we talked about it, the more we mentioned other countries we also wanted to visit in Africa.

'If we are going to Egypt, we may as well visit Kenya and Tanzania as I'd love to see the animals on safari,' I enthused.

'Me too and I'd also enjoy going back to Zimbabwe to see how much it has changed since we were last there,' replied Russ smiling.

'If we're going to Zimbabwe, we may as well check out South Africa in case we wish to move there one day.'

'Zanzibar is also somewhere I'd like to go.'

'What about Zaire where we could see the mountain gorillas? There are so many great places to explore such as Madagascar, Mauritius, Botswana and Namibia.'

'The trip is growing out of control. We'll run out of time and money. Let's stick to the east coast and the cheaper countries to visit at this stage.'

There was much to prepare before we left. Certain countries required written proof of particular vaccinations. The Cholera injection was no longer recommended, so we found a travel medical centre prepared to provide the stamp to show we'd been vaccinated, even though we were not injected. We endured Yellow Fever,

Meningitis, Hepatitis A, Typhoid, Tetanus, Diphtheria and Polio vaccinations. Yellow Fever was more painful than all the others put together and, by the end, my arm felt like a pin cushion.

We arranged travel insurance to cover us for the trip from Cairo to Cape Town, and an employee of the insurance company phoned me.

'Are you aware there is trouble in Egypt, and it really isn't safe to travel there?'

Before I could reply, she continued, 'There is unrest in Zaire and South Africa which should also be avoided.'

I dubiously asked, 'Does this mean we're not covered whilst travelling in those countries?'

'Of course we will cover you for travel, but I wanted to warn you those three countries are best avoided at the moment. In Egypt, the Islamic Fundamentalists are blowing up tourist buses, boats and trains, so the only way to travel is by plane. They're also throwing stones at travellers. With Nelson Mandela being sworn-in as the new president of South Africa, a lot of tension is building there, and tourists are being taken hostage in Zaire.'

'Thank you for your advice, but we'll still be travelling to those countries,' I informed her.

I talked my boss into allowing me to take six months unpaid leave, and Russ was granted the same by his employer. Undeterred by the insurance company, we sent tickets to Russ' parents to join us in Cairo for a week. I just hoped we could keep them safe because we couldn't afford to fly everywhere. An Egyptian friend, in Australia, asked her cousin, Yasmin, to collect us from the airport when we first arrived.

It was only six in the morning when we landed in Cairo. Mohamed, a colleague of Yasmin, met us and stood next to us whilst we negotiated our way through passport control and customs. He drove us in style, in his battered old Volvo, to a hotel in Heliopolis that he'd pre-booked. During the journey, he explained to us how much the hotel would cost per person. We were pleasantly surprised when we did a conversion from Egyptian pounds to Aussie dollars because it was quite good value, even if it wasn't in the city.

The next day, when Yasmin didn't turn up to meet us as promised, we made our way to her office to pay for the airport pick up. Yasmin was busy, so her colleague, once again, stepped in offering to organize our train travel to Luxor and accommodation whilst there. This seemed all too easy compared to our normal chaotic way of travelling. However, when we were presented with a quote for an enormous amount, we nearly fell off our chairs. Russ' parents, Dee and Bill, were going to be travelling with us and so was Julia. Mohamed had worked out the cost of a double room, plus the cost of a single room and multiplied the total by five people! His unusual mathematics would have meant he could pocket over 50 percent of the amount quoted, and we would have run out of money before our trip had barely started. Kindly declining the quote, we asked to settle the bill for the airport pickup. He charged us twice the cost of a local taxi and advised the cost of the hotel was in UK pounds, not Egyptian pounds, so much more than we thought he had told us. We paid up and left before he asked for any more money.

We checked out of the hotel and found a room in the city centre for less than half the amount we'd paid the night before. The hotel was basic, rather old and run down, but it had everything we needed.

When we left the hotel, we were immediately approached by a man asking, 'What is your name? Where do you come from?' Most of the men we met on the streets claimed to have relatives living in Australia. The only time I found a chap useful was when crossing the road.

He explained, 'Just go for it, close your eyes and pray to Allah!'

Allah must have heard our prayers as we didn't get run over. We walked everywhere, constantly approached by touts wanting to show us their uncle's painting warehouse, mothers perfume shop or sisters fabric stall. It was emotionally wearing having to firmly, but politely, refuse repeatedly.

We were aware that in Egypt, like in many poorer countries, we would be hassled because we were tourists. Nevertheless, we weren't prepared for the unrelenting harassment we had to contend with.

It was interesting that not only did we have to buy tickets for ourselves to enter attractions, but also a more expensive ticket for our camera and an extortionately priced ticket for our video camera. We paid for two reasons, one we were not likely to return to Cairo, and secondly we were reluctant to leave a valuable piece of equipment in left luggage.

The elevator to the top of Cairo Tower left my stomach at the bottom. It was great not having to climb the 187 metres, but I had collywobbles when I exited onto the open air observation deck. There was a railing all the way around so no chance of falling off, but it was open metal framework which made me tremble and ooze a cold sweat when I got close to it. The views from the top were magnificent, and I could even see the pyramids at Giza far off in the distance. Below was the bustling metropolis of Cairo with congested traffic, car horns tooting and drivers shouting at each other. Decrepit high-rise buildings, in much need of repair, competed for space. Roofs were cluttered with rubbish and home to chickens whilst washing hung out to dry on a line. The smog was dense, making it difficult to breathe and coating everything in a fine layer of soot.

Locals, realizing we were tourists, would hike the value on anything we needed. Consequently, fed up with constant bartering, we thought it would be a good idea to have lunch at a local Wimpy franchise. There was a menu with prices so no argument about cost. We went inside and picked what we wanted to eat and drink before placing an order at the counter.

Our beverages arrived quite quickly and whilst sipping them, the waiter explained, 'There is nothing available on the menu, and a burger will be US$30.' We put down our drinks and got up to leave because this was obviously not true. Beaten down, we could no longer be bothered to argue.

'Please sit down, sit down,' said the man rather sheepishly.

I replied, 'We are not paying that much for lunch.'

'No, you misunderstand me, I said US$13, not US$30.'

'It's still too expensive. Look at your price list. It should only be a few Egyptian pounds.'

'Oh yes, but they're not available. I cook special food for you.'

'I don't want different food, just what is listed for the amount stated, or we will go elsewhere.' I stood up.

He backed down. 'Ah I see, then that's what I will cook for you, and the charge is as shown.'

He shook our hands whilst grinning amiably at us.

Afterwards, we went to the Egyptian museum which housed the greatest collection of Egyptian artefacts in the world. It was certainly worth paying the extra charge to take our camera and video camera with us. There were so many rooms and corridors, all crammed with history and although stuffy, it wasn't too crowded.

Antiquities from Tutankhamun's tomb were displayed including chariots, furniture, gloves, jewellery and, of course, his famous burial mask which rested over the bandages wrapped around his face. His tomb contained four gilded shrines which were originally nestled one inside the other. They were lined up in order of size, the innermost made of 110 kilograms of solid gold and had originally covered the stone sarcophagus which remains in his tomb in the Valley of the Kings.

We first met Asfar, who was to become our regular taxi driver, when he took Russ and me to the airport to pick up Julia, Dee and Bill. Whilst waiting for them to arrive, a young girl kept pointing at Russ and laughing.

I asked Asfar, 'Why is she laughing at Russ?'

'She finds his long hair, drawn back in a ponytail, funny because Egyptian men have their hair cut short,' he explained.

Just at that moment, Russ' dad, who had lost most of his hair, arrived. He was wearing a baseball cap with a long plaited ponytail attached to it. When we introduced him to Asfar, he couldn't stop laughing.

'Like father like son,' I told him.

It was great to see Dee. As usual, she wrapped me in not just a big hug but also enveloped me in her tears. It was going to be fun to travel with Julia again, and we had much catching up to do.

The following day at Giza, Omah, our guide, offered Russ 100,000 camels to buy Julia. Russ declined because he preferred horses. Instead, Omah abducted Dee, taking her for the ride of her life. I watched stunned as my mother-in-law's rubenesque figure galloped away, on horseback, across the sandy desert. Disappearing into the distance, she merged into the vision of a washed out watercolour painting where even the horses and camels blended into the background. It was something she had always wanted to do and amazing to watch.

I rode most comfortably on a horse but did ride the camel that we'd hired for a while. Getting on the camel took some technique because it got up from its back legs first, so I had to lean back to stop falling off and then counteract by leaning forward when it got on its front legs. The camel walked with a swaying motion, jarring me backwards and forwards as well as side to side, whilst I straddled the wide leather saddle with nothing to hold on to. Wearing a long patterned black sarong, I had to be careful to keep my legs covered and at the same time keep hold of my camera.

We picked our way through messy building rubble, littered with rubbish, until we arrived at the desert with scattered limestone blocks lying strewn in the sand and a fabulous view, in the distance, of the sole remaining seventh wonder of the ancient world, the Great Pyramid of Giza.

It rose from the desert, a paler shade than the sand, standing out against the cloudless powder blue sky as it had done for thousands of years. Nearby the sphinx, a human headed lion, was guarding the pyramids. Its nose was missing.

We rode to each of the three great pyramids as well as many smaller ones. The pyramid of Cheops noticeably still had the top limestone casing intact. The blocks were massive, standing waist-high, making a huge staircase. Worried about falling, I was relieved to find it illegal to climb on them. I had to pinch myself to know my dream was real, and I was finally in Egypt.

In the evening, we boarded the train to Luxor. Although the insurance company had said it was too dangerous to travel by train, it was all we could afford. We had second class tickets with air-conditioning so were quite comfortable for the overnight journey and although seated upright, slept well. We'd heard on the news that a bus load of German tourists had tragically been blown up the day before.

When we got off the train, a well-built Egyptian man approached us offering, 'I take you to a hotel.'

I explained, 'We already have one in mind.'

Undeterred, he followed us along the road.

'You try my hotel first,' he demanded.

'No thank you,' I replied.

'Yes, look at mine first. It is good hotel.'

'No thank you. We are staying at another hotel.' I hoped they had rooms available.

I was relieved to escape inside the building because he was still quite insistent we should look at another one. He waited outside whilst we checked in. The hotel owner was kind enough to ask him to leave, which was a huge relief as I didn't want to have him following us around all day.

We set out on foot to explore Luxor. The harsh scorching sun had evaporated every last drop of moisture from the ground, leaving dry fine sand to drift in the breeze. The rich Nile River ran through this ground like an aorta pumping life and providing vibrancy in a landscape almost entirely devoid of colour. The ancient stone blended with the sandy soil.

Feluccas bobbed on this blue vein, the world's longest river, revealing a bustling life and cradling ancient civilisations whilst the wind gently nibbled at the furled headsails. Dense green foliage lined the banks.

It was extremely hot by the time we entered Luxor Temple, and touts kept approaching us, offering a guided tour. I ignored them, pretending not to speak English whilst we wandered along rows of sphinxs, past grand statues, many hieroglyphics and some huge columns with the site almost to ourselves.

The following day, Dee rested in the hotel because it was still sweltering whilst the rest of us caught the ferry to the West Bank and took a taxi to the Valley of the Kings. The heat was unrelenting, at over forty degrees centigrade, from a cloudless sky.

As we walked the steep descent into Memoptah's tomb, through the entrance decorated with Isis and Nephthys worshipping the solar disc and along the corridors which were lined with text from the Book of Gates, it smelt damp and musty. The inscriptions were painted in earthy reds, yellows and blues. Now faded, they would have been vibrant in their day. The underground tomb was invitingly cool, although stuffy and silent.

Back in the burning sun, we descended two sets of steps down to the tomb door of Ramses IX that was decorated with the Pharaoh worshipping the solar disc. I followed the three corridors which took me into an antechamber that opened into a pillared hall and then navigated the passage beyond to the sarcophagus chamber. The tomb I'd really come to see was Tutankhamun's Tomb which was small and unimpressive in comparison to the other's I saw. This was probably because he died at only nineteen years of age.

Tutankhamun's sarcophagus lay in his tomb, but I knew his mummified body was in the Egyptian Museum in Cairo where I'd previously seen it. The colourful paintings inside the burial chamber, recording different aspects of his life, were on a vivid yellow background. Twelve baboons depicted the hours through the night to get to the afterlife.

As we returned to the sunshine, I looked at Bill, a cross between Indiana Jones and Crocodile Dundee, wearing his Akubra hat. Lean and fit, with fading merchant navy tattoos on his arms, he was white, except for his arms and face. His bushy eyebrows crept like a vine across his forehead towards his receding hairline. His grey beard smouldered as he puffed on a cigarette.

His eyes reflected his gentle soul as he put his arm around me and asked, 'Where to next?'

Travelling on to the Temple of Hatshepsut, our taxi stopped to pick up a passenger. The Egyptian man wore a white gallabiyah through which I could see he was solidly built with strong broad shoulders. His legs were thick like tree trunks, and his beaky nose and stony eyes were cold as he slid into the front seat alongside Bill.

Whilst he talked rapidly to the driver in Egyptian, Russ realizing our vulnerability whispered to me, 'Is the penknife still in our daypack?'

'Yes, in the side pocket,' I replied in a hushed voice.

'If they try to rob us and abandon us in the desert, I will quickly get it out whilst you divert their attention.'

We sat in silence, warily contemplating our predicament when the car stopped and the man got out. My breathing slowed and shoulders relaxed as we continued to our destination.

A lively market lined the road to the temple, selling clothes, hats, bags and souvenirs. Julia and I looked at packets of postcards. The vendor quoted a price, and we proposed under half the cost. Rather than barter, he just shook his head and walked away from us. I'd much to learn about negotiating if I was going to buy any mementos.

That evening, Dee joined us on a trip along the Nile. We covered our arms and legs from those pesky mosquitoes that would be out and sat on some floral cushions along the edge of the felucca. The temperature was cooling as the day drew to an end, and the soft breeze from the water shrouded me. Gentle waves rhythmically lapped at the hull, making me sleepy as we sailed to Banana Island where we wandered through the fertile plantation and sampled the fruit. Someone gave Dee an exotic banana flower but then wanted paying "bakeesh" for it. On the return trip, the sun set on the Nile, enveloping it in a carroty hue, silhouetting the boats against the horizon in black. After the wind had dropped, we took turns in helping to row back. Julia and I were careful to keep our sarongs covering our legs.

The local Souk or market, running behind our hotel, was humming with energy. We all stuck closely together whilst walking along the narrow lanes lined with wares. I noticed the absence of women on the streets. Strong scented spices in large wicker baskets stood next to textiles, clothing or exposed food. Flies crawled over meat hung on hooks. We entered a multi-story shop from the market and separated to look around. We were soon greeted by the shop staff, who were unusually interested in Julia and myself.

One of the shop-keepers asked Russ, 'Can I take your wife upstairs and show her around as we have much to see on the upper floors?'

'In Australia it's not my choice. You need to ask my wife whether she wants to go.'

The shop-keeper seemed annoyed, especially when I indicated I didn't wish to accompany him by shaking my head.

He changed tacks and tracked down Bill. 'I wish to take this woman upstairs to give her a present.'

Slightly confused, Bill was momentarily lost for words.

Russ intervened and explained, 'She doesn't wish to go with you.'

Bill backed him up saying, 'She wants to stay with us,' whilst he took my hand in his.

The man stood in front of Russ, pushing his face close and towering over him shouting, 'I want to take her upstairs.'

The atmosphere was tense and when the man became more demanding, we all made a hasty beeline for the door. As we made it outside, a huge breath of air escaped my lungs, and I started to laugh.

In the evening, we went to a sound and light show at the Temple of Karnack. Rows of ram and headed sphinx fringed the avenue which, at one stage, had joined with the ones at Luxor temple, lining the roadway in between. The laser light show was fantastic. Whilst relating the history of ancient Thebes, the narrator's voices boomed around us and the lights bounced off the antiquated walls.

We caught a donkey cart back to the hotel, which I will never do again. The poor donkey wasn't only undernourished but looked like it hadn't been fed for months. The driver kept it moving with a whip.

It made my heart ache to see it treated this way, and I thought the donkey should be retired somewhere green and lush to recuperate.

Our last afternoon, in Luxor, was spent at the sister hotel which was much more upmarket than where we were staying. Lounging in the sunshine on the roof, and swimming in the pool, was exceedingly relaxing. We had time for an evening meal before catching the train back to Cairo. Both Bill and I indulged in the vegetable soup for entrée and before we'd finished our main meals, were both dashing for the toilet. Just our luck to get food poisoning before commencing a long night journey with a communal rocking hole in the ground for a lavatory. I started to understand the saying I'd heard many times, "Heaven is a dry fart in Africa".

Bill and I rested when we arrived back in Cairo whilst the others went to reconfirm Dee and Bill's flights home.

They were told, 'There has been a mix up, and your original flights have been given to someone else. There are no available alternatives for another week.'

This was a bit of a shock, but on checking again the following day, their flights were confirmed straight away. I can only assume the previous girl must have been trying to get a bribe. It was sad to be parted from family again, but our trip was just beginning.

I bought three bus tickets to the Bahariya Oasis from a man in a backstreet shack in Cairo. However, I didn't think to ask the name of the station it departed from. The next morning, Russ, Julia and I showed the tickets to our taxi driver, who dropped us off at the nearest terminal, but it wasn't the right place. We then caught another taxi to a different station which was also the wrong one.

The third cab driver spoke much better English and explained, 'The bus has now left, but it also stops in Giza.' So he drove us there and hailed down the bus when we caught up with it.

It seemed longer than six hours when we travelled the 360 kilometres from Cairo, through the hot arid desert, on hard seats coated in a layer of gritty sand. People got off the bus in the middle of nowhere and walked away. I couldn't see any buildings and wondered where they were going.

Bahariya seemed deserted. There were only two guesthouses to choose from. The one we stayed at had a dubious owner who allegedly served time in prison for taking guests on a trip into the White Desert and stranding them there when they refused to pay the extra money he demanded to take them back. I'm not sure whether we were stupid, or brave, when we took a trip to the Sulphur Springs in a four wheel drive that evening, to see a natural pyramid. The light was fading quickly whilst we ate our freshly cooked soup in the eerie silence beside the pyramid before our driver returned us to our guesthouse.

The next day, three young boys found us and guided us to verdant groves where they showed us guavas, mangoes, dates and olives growing. They also showed us hot steamy water dripping from a rusting old pipe as well as cold springs which bubbled up from the ground.

We took video footage of the kids, and they were amazed when we played it back in the viewfinder. They got us to take more footage to watch over and over again. I was surprised they could speak English so well and at such an early age.

The local Wahati people, meaning "of the oasis" in Arabic, were mainly Muslims. When we were out walking one morning, one of the men yelled angrily at Julia and me. Even though we were dressed in long sleeve tops and long skirts, he was furious because we did not have our ankles covered.

Although at times the temperature was over forty degrees centigrade, I thought Egypt lacked warmth from the people. However, our last day in Cairo resurrected my faith in Egyptians when we visited Gabalaya Park and Aquarium in the heart of Zamalek. It was serenely peaceful considering it was just minutes away from busy downtown. Fish in tanks darted around, swimming in little tunnels. A friendly Egyptian family adopted us for the day, feeding us macaroni and plums whilst trying to communicate through a combination of English, Arabic and hand signals. They tried to marry off their daughter as, even though Russ already had two women with him, they thought he should have a third.

#

Our next stop, in Greece, was a time for recovery for me because I was still suffering the after effects from food poisoning in Egypt. We met my sister and her boyfriend in Athens, caught a bus to the port and travelled on the ferry to the idyllic island of Naxos. We were greeted by many touts at the port and decided to go with one who recommended we stay at "Effies" place.

Many lazy days were spent on the beaches, wandering cobbled lanes between white-washed old brick walls where freshly caught octopus was strung out on lines to dry. Carefree hours were exhausted discovering shops selling tacky souvenirs, climbing up to the ancient ruins of the old arch on the hill for a breathtaking view of the harbour or walking to the castle and watching the sunset over the sea.

One day, we hired a mini-moke and went for a spin around the island. We drove through green gorges and fertile valleys, passed windmills. After stopping to watch the goats feed in the castle grounds, we pushed on, passed the Grotto of Zeus high up on the mountain, to see the ancient Kouros statue. We explored seaside villages where donkeys roamed the streets.

I loved spending time with my sister because it'd been several years since we'd travelled together. Although I'd been exploring the world and meeting new people of different races and religions with different outlooks to my own, I'd missed that close bond only sisters have.

The time passed all too quickly, so using the Greek we'd learned, said, 'Kylienita (Goodbye),' when we boarded the ferry back to mainland.

#

At last, we were on our way back to Africa. Having skipped Sudan and Ethiopia because we were unable to get entry visas, due to the Egyptian stamps in our passport, we landed in Nairobi and headed downtown to the cheap accommodation.

Nairobi is from a Masai word meaning cool waters, but I'd heard it more commonly referred to as "Nairobbery" because it had quite a reputation for thieves. Consequently, I was pleased when we found a rest house above a chicken and chips takeaway shop, meaning we wouldn't need to venture far after dark. The doorman even nipped across the road for Russ, to get him some Tusker beer from the brewery. I'd bought a cheap plastic watch to wear and was without my usual jewellery. I secreted a money pouch under my clothes as well as a bum bag which was covered by my warm baggy cardigan. Nothing of value was on display, and I hoped the snatch and grab muggers would not target myself.

The locals were friendly and especially helpful when it came to booking on a short budget safari to the Masai Mara. Many people we passed would offer their services. I was looking forward to relaxing. It was great having someone else work out how to get from one place to the next, set up accommodation and organize food. It'd be a treat.

I was so excited when the matatu picked us up, and our driver introduced us to the other six passengers. It had a pop top that was great for game viewing because we could stand up and look out. I couldn't sit still when we embarked on the 270 kilometre drive through the Rift Valley to a campsite in the Masai Mara. It took about five hours, initially along a tarmac road to Narok, a large Masai town, where we had lunch. I got chatting to a local courteous lad who was keen to help me with some Swahili sayings.

He told me, 'Hakuna Matata means no problem.'

I asked him the names of some of the animals I hoped to see.

'Twiga is giraffe, Simba is lion, Punda Milia is zebra and Tembo is an elephant.'

I only spoke with him for a short while, but he ran after the matatu when we left, waving and calling out, 'My name is Ishrine.' Perhaps, he thought we would meet again.

Soon the tarmac turned to dirt, and although initially quite good, it eventually became rutted and bumpy. The dry dust hung to the back of my throat. I was easily distracted when the driver pulled over and pointed out a large herd of zebra, a few Thompson's gazelle with a dark brown stripe along their side, the petite dik dik and a massive herd of wildebeest that were close to the road. It was hard to take in so many different herbivores peacefully nibbling the sparse patches of grass.

A bit further along, on parched yellow parkland, we saw a wake of sinister vultures stripping a carcass under the heat of the sun. They looked menacing with their featherless heads and sharp hooked beaks. Some had engorged themselves so much that they could no longer fly from the ground.

It was dusk by the time I laid my backpack on the floor of a sturdy tent that had the luxury of an ensuite porcelain flushing toilet. The window flaps on the tent kept coming undone, so Russ safety pinned them shut because it was freezing. Only a thin sheet and blanket covered my camp bed.

After dinner, noble Masai Warriors cavorted in the light of our bonfire. Dressed in brightly coloured sarongs decorated with beads, and holding their staffs, they took turns to jump high into the air whilst the pitches of their voices were raised. They looked quite regal as the crackling flames danced beside them, casting shadows in the darkness of the night.

Back in our tent, I recoiled as I was startled when a small frog jumped out of my haversack. It must have been cold too, but I chased it outside. Fully dressed, I curled up into a tight ball under the blanket, to try to retain some warmth. I listened to the noisy baboons before drifting off to sleep. The following morning, the Masai Mara unfolded in front of my eyes. With its vast grasslands studded with the occasional acacia tree, it was spectacular. The migration of animals from the Serengeti had not yet started, but I was ecstatic to see so much wildlife, both herbivores and predators. I hadn't realized there were so many different antelope. The Thompson's gazelle, impala and springbok were the most common. The dik dik were tiny in comparison and the topi more elusive to find. The wildebeest often intermingled amongst the zebra or impala, and I could hear them grunting whilst they grazed on the grass.

The giraffe stretched their elegant necks up high, so they could reach the succulent leaves of the acacia bushes whilst the elephant silently blended into the scenery, appearing to be rocks. Once I'd spotted one, it was easier to find all the others around it. It was fun to see the springbok leap stiff-legged into the air, which is called pronking.

I hadn't expected to see such a sleek and slightly built cheetah so quickly because they're listed as vulnerable. I thought they would be elusive and wished for their population to increase, so they would thrive. I was spoilt to see four prides of majestic lion including one eating a baboon. We stopped beside one group, and several of the lionesses got up and walked over to the vehicle. The windows of the van were open wide, and I froze, expecting one to jump inside or take a swipe at one of us. Just curious, they sauntered past the bus without much interest in us at all.

I was unsure about the cackle of hyena as they were not as cute and cuddly as the cats. Built solidly, they had thick necks and powerful jaws that could easily rip a carcass apart. The jackal were more like a dog but still proficient scavengers. Warthogs were comical to watch when they ran with their tufted tails stiffly upright in the air like a dodgem car. The herds of blue wildebeest peacefully grazed the savannah.

It was decided to have lunch beside the Mara River in which a bloat of hippos and float of crocodiles sprawled with their mouths open to cool down from the heat. The cheeky vervet monkeys swung down from the trees and with great speed and agility tried to pinch anything that wasn't fixed down, including the food off my plate. I held on tightly to my hat, sunglasses and camera because I wasn't prepared to give them away.

The next morning, we saw many more antelope, timid zebra and some hefty elephant. For the first time, we watched lion mating. After lunch back at camp, a Masai warrior led us on a climb up a steep hill. He was armed with an impressive bow and arrow should we have encountered any game. His ear lobe, pierced and stretched, was adjourned with beads. I stood absorbing the fabulous view, from the top, of both the campsite and surrounding plains before making the even steeper descent back to camp where Russ removed ticks and grass seed from his undies.

It was early when we left for Lake Nakuru. On the way, we saw both lion and antelope outside the National Park. I was disappointed that Irshrine wasn't at Narock when we stopped to refuel. At the Rift Valley Lookout, there was an amazing view of the chain of lakes, most of which were tainted with soda bubbling up with the rifts hot springs.

At Hotel Penways, I opted for a hot shower whilst the others downed an ice cold beer at the bar. When I joined them, they couldn't believe how nice I smelt. I was clean, but they had not showered for days.

Just after dawn, the world's greatest concentration of fuchsia pink flamingos, on the soda lake at Lake Nakuru National Park, made a splendid sight. There was an unpleasant smell of sulphide whilst I watched them feed on the abundant algae which thrived in the warmth of the shallow alkaline waters. Our driver drove us through the surrounding area where the landscape varied from the flat lakeside to dense woodland or rocky outcrops. In the park, we spotted many baboons, vervet monkeys and even hyraxes at the lookout. Unbelievably, the hyrax is sometimes described as being the closest living relative to the elephant. This seems strange, considering it's also known as, and looks like, a rock rabbit.

We were able to get extremely close to bunches of impala, whose tails twitched from the flies. The tiny delicate dik dik was exquisite, whereas the waterbuck stood out with a white circle like target on its bottom. Warthogs knelt down to snuffle around the ground, digging for bulbs and roots whilst the buffalo had oxpeckers gleaning insects off their hides.

I was sad to leave the animals behind. They had captured my heart, and I hoped to see many more along my journey.

Back in our oasis, in Nairobi, we applied for visas to enter Zaire and did some washing in preparation for our onward trip to Uganda. The washing didn't want to dry in our room, and because I didn't have a hairdryer, used our travel iron to try to remove the moisture. It didn't work well, so we had to pack them in a plastic bag for the journey ahead.

It was late, and already dark, by the time we alighted the bus in Kampala and caught a taxi to a budget hotel. I stayed in the cab with our bags whilst Russ checked out the rooms. It was run down and dirty, especially the shared shower and toilet, but we were tired and just wanted somewhere to snooze that night. There was no lock to our meagre room, where the paint had peeled off the walls, so we dragged Russ' bed across the doorway to stop anyone getting in whilst we were sleeping. It was a good idea because, just after midnight, someone tried pushing open the door and then calling out to us in Swahili. In my semi-conscious stupor, I couldn't understand what they were saying.

Russ called out, 'We're staying in this room tonight. Please go away.'

'It is my room,' a voice called back.

'See the owner,' replied Russ, and then it was quiet again.

I hadn't been asleep long when, once again, the door was rattled and another conversation ensued. This happened several times during the night. Needless to say, the next morning, we moved on, finding a slightly more expensive guesthouse with a clean shower. Although the one in the first room we were allocated didn't have hot water, we were moved to a room with one that did before setting out for a long walk to Kasubi Tombs.

As we trudged down the dusty dirt roads, children appeared from nowhere calling out, 'Wazungu,' meaning white man. The more adventurous ones slipped their hands in ours and walked with us.

The royal tombs were an active religious place in the Buganda Kingdom and the burial ground for the previous four Kabakas (Kings). After entering a circular dome-like building, we sat on a mat on the floor and listened to the lyrical voice of the narrator, who didn't speak English. A young girl sat behind me and stroked my hair.

I was fond of the people I met in Kenya and Uganda, and although often poor, they seemed genuinely happy. I admired their remarkable generosity because they were prepared to share what little they had. Their uncluttered lifestyle held an appeal that I couldn't quite explain.

CHAPTER SEVEN – MOUNTAINS OF THE MOON
Uganda, Zaire

Instinctively, I turned and ran when the Silverback Gorilla let out a deafening roar.

Earlier, the park ranger had explained, 'If the silverback charges, you must slowly drop to the ground, keep your head down and avert your eyes submissively.'

That was easier said than done as the fight or flight reaction kicked in. My heart was thumping so loud the sounds of the rainforest were drowned out. It was hard to believe I'd been looking forward to this moment for so long, yet this wasn't quite what I'd anticipated.

It began in July 1994, when my husband Russ and I boarded the bus to Kabale. We could hear "Happy Nation", by Ace of Base, being played. I thought it an apt song because every Ugandan I'd seen had seemed so cheerful considering the poverty some lived in. They were just pleased Uganda was no longer the place of terror created by the torturous Idi Amin, who ruled until 1979.

Rwanda was experiencing the genocide this time. The Hutu and Tutsis, once friends and neighbours, were at war. Millions of refugees were fleeing Rwanda headed for Uganda and Zaire. The people were starving and needed wood from the forests to cook food to survive. Many set traps there to catch bushbuck and other animals to feed their famished families.

The bus was crowded, so we were lucky to get seats. The cacophony of sounds made talking difficult when chattering people squashed onto the bus with their crates of cackling chickens which they sat on in the aisles. There was a strong, slightly spicy aroma with a hint of clean soap exuding from the bodies surrounding us. Diesel fumes and dust from the road clung to my throat. It was an uncomfortable five hour trip, packed shoulder to shoulder, but through beautiful lush countryside, which made it worthwhile.

Kabale town was picturesque. Set on the mountain side, like the tiers on a flapper dress, the green hills were terraced and extensively cultivated with swaying crops ruffled by the breeze. The main street was a tarmac track covered in crimson earth from the side of the road and plied by bicycle taxis.

Our hotel was basic, without running water or electricity, but it was clean and gave us somewhere to rest before continuing our journey. We needed to buy food to take with us so sought out the local market. We bartered for the little food that was for sale, which was bread, pineapples, potatoes, tomatoes and carrots. This would have to sustain us for the next few days along with a couple of tins of spaghetti we'd bought with us from Nairobi.

We climbed on the back of a utility truck, early the next morning, to transport us eighty-eight kilometres to the border at Kisoro. There were so many passengers and copious amounts of luggage, making it impossible to sit down. At least sixteen people stood in the open backed tub. Each person held on to the person in front of them. I was gripping on to Russ, but when the truck rounded the first corner, I struggled to hold on when the chain of people swung precariously over the side of the truck. My arms were fully stretched like elastic bands ready to ping at any moment. I didn't know how much longer my grip would last. I dare not lift my foot from the floor because the space was instantly filled, and I'd have nowhere to put it back down.

Fortunately, the truck stopped to pick up more passengers and someone climbed in behind me, but rather than hold on to me, he held on to Russ, so I was securely sandwiched between the two of them.

Russ asked one of the passengers, 'How do you manage travelling this way?'

He replied, 'If you can't have what you like, like what you have.'

Maybe that was why all the Ugandans had beaming smiles, I thought.

After three hours along tortuous, windy roads, the truck delivered us to the Zaire border.

'Look at us.' I laughed because we were thoroughly covered in parched red soil, as if we'd been seasoned with paprika.

I was nervous about passing through immigration on the Zaire side because we'd heard bribes were normally required and bags searched thoroughly.

Having been caught short of local currency on Sunday, we'd cashed one hundred US dollars into Ugandan shillings, but at that moment, I realized we weren't allowed to take it out of the country.

'I'm going to stash this large stack of notes in my socks,' informed Russ.

Underneath his feet, it made him a couple of inches taller than previously. He hoped the border officials wouldn't body search him. I was extremely nervous.

'I hope I can keep a straight face if they ask how much money we're bringing into the country,' I said.

The Zaire passport control officer told Russ, 'I want your socks. I swap them for my t-shirt.'

'No thanks. I need my socks for the long trek ahead,' replied Russ uneasily.

I bit my bottom lip whilst unconsciously holding my breath. The colour of my cheeks turned a rosy red. The officer soon lost interest and looked through our passports to check our visas were in order.

He asked us, 'Why do you have the same surname? Are you brother and sister?'

'No, we're married, so I take Russ's surname,' I explained.

'But why take his surname? He should take yours,' said the officer. He laughed whilst he stamped our passports and handed them back, wishing us an enjoyable trip. We'd made it through.

Russ found two teenage boys to carry our backpacks, seven kilometres, up into the Virunga Mountains, a range of extinct volcanoes. An older boy tried to take our bags from us because he wanted to steal the business, and a scuffle broke out.

Russ stepped in, firmly saying, 'These two will carry our bags, not you.'

The older boy skulked away glaring at Russ as he went. We set off for the campsite in the Virunga National Park at Djomba.

Russ pulled me to one side. 'Can you take the money now because I can't walk any longer with it in my socks?'

We hung back from the boys and shielded by the towering crops of maize and banana trees, I tucked the money away.

The scenery changed when we climbed further up the mountain. We passed through charming villages with fields of crops surrounded by grazing cattle and goats.

'Muzungu, Muzungu,' shouted the scrawny barefoot children.

'Jambo (Hello),' I called back.

Dressed in grubby rags, but smiling, they ran up to us and took our hands to lead us through their village. It still amazed me how happy they could be when they had so little.

The last fifteen minutes was up a steep incline, and by now it was raining heavily. The track was slippery with mud. Dressed in only shorts and t-shirts, we were drenched by the time we reached the office, only to find it closed. We'd have to wait until morning for it to reopen.

We didn't have a tent or sleeping bags so hoped to be able to stay in the single shack that provided shelter to the trekkers. The rudimentary hut consisted of eight grubby beds, four in each room, separated by another room housing a wooden table and chairs. Unfortunately all the beds were booked, but luckily the friendly overland travellers in one room let us sleep on a spare mattress on the mouldy smelling, dirty floor. By now it was dark, and I shivered from the cold because I was still damp from the rain. A kidogo mtoto (small boy) sold us hot beans and sweet potato for dinner, which warmed us.

The following morning, we were up early, at five, to find out the office didn't open until seven.

On enquiry, the official advised us, 'I cannot fit you in until Friday because only one group of eight people are allowed to trek each a day.' After making the reservation, the shack became our home for two more days.

The only water was collected from the roof into a steel drum. It looked inky black so needed to be purified with iodine before drinking. There wasn't any water to shower, and the outside toilet was just a stinky hole in the ground. The bushes seemed an attractive alternative until we realized we weren't the first people to have that idea.

The next day, the sun shone down and whilst the mist cleared, the start of the jungle could be seen at the edge of the cultivated farmland. We walked around the area and bought sugar cane to eat from one of the enterprising youngsters. Outside the hut, we sat in the gleaming sunshine. Teenagers from the village crept up on us, and with glowing smiles and raucous giggling, poked me on the nose before running away. I laughed, surprised at what they were doing. They then found the courage to poke Russ, so he roared at them as loud as he could. They ran away, laughing, until their bravery returned, and they sneaked back to do it again and again. They were fascinated with my long golden hair and loved to stroke it, so they could feel the soft, silky texture.

At seven thirty the next morning, it was hard to make out the forest because it was blanketed in mist. Signs of poachers had been observed the previous day, but we set off led by a uniformed ranger armed with a rifle, together with a machete wielding assistant. For the first hour, we walked effortlessly along cleared tracks. Then as time progressed, the undergrowth became denser, almost impenetrable, and the razor sharp machete wielder was sweating from exertion. I found it increasingly difficult to keep balance on the spongy layers of vines under foot. Several times I grabbed for trees, to stop from sliding over but was careful as some were covered in thorns and others would sting. The slightly pungent damp smell of rotting vegetation mingled with a distant waft of smoke. Slowly, the coating of mud stretched from my ankles to my knees, making movement even more difficult.

I couldn't work out how the park ranger knew where to go. He obviously had a great sense of direction because the towering compact bush blocked out any view that helped identify the direction in which we were travelling. However, by now I was beginning to wonder if the rangers did have any idea where we were going. After months of planning and six weeks of travelling, I pondered whether we were ever going to get there.

The rangers stopped and explained, 'We're very close because this spoor is recent. The gorillas build new nests in the trees each night, at dusk, from branches and surrounding foliage. They slept here last night so can't have moved too far away.'

I was anxious about being so close to wild animals that could kill me in an instant. I'd been dreaming of this moment for so long but couldn't entirely rid myself of an uneasiness.

I saw the female gorilla first, sitting alone.

'Look, Russ, I could just pick her up and cuddle her,' I gasped. She was stunning, covered with thick dark fur. Her arms were wrapped around her body whilst she shyly appraised me with her appealing amber eyes. I was transfixed unable to break my gaze.

A meter or so further along, we saw three other female gorillas, one with a four month old baby. The infant was adorable. His coat was unruly, the black fur appearing to have been crimped like a pie crust, with delicate ears protruding at the sides. His tiny digits clung to the fleece on his mother's back whilst she ambled away, walking on the knuckles of her broad fingers.

'We've finally found Marcel's elusive band of gorillas,' said Russ.

'We must find Marcel, the Silverback, because we don't want him surprising us,' explained the ranger. 'If he charges, you must slowly drop to the ground, keep your head down and avert your eyes submissively.'

As we followed the ranger through the corridors of vines, I heard a powerful roar. Everything the ranger had told us was forgotten, and instinct cut in when I turned and ran.

Luckily Marcel wasn't even in sight. He was just letting the rangers know he was still the boss. As we rounded the corner, he was partially hidden by the vegetation with his silver tinged back turned towards us.

'What a majestic creature,' I whispered. Marcel's silvery grey coat showed his maturity and status as leader of the band. Being the protector of his family, he was massive with a broad muscular chest and arms longer than his stout legs. He emitted an impression of authority and leadership but was in no way intimidating. I relaxed. He seemed as vulnerable as I was.

Marcel was busy munching away on leaves and stems. Now quiet, he appeared a gentle giant, both shy and retiring. A metre from him, a female sat in a tree clutching her infant. She released him because she needed both hands to pull more leaves to eat. He cautiously climbed the vine, his petite hands and feet moving one at a time to grip the bush. Mum grabbed his arm and pulled him back close to her chest. Undeterred, he was off again, climbing the same branch. Marcel moved closer, and the infant quickly sprung back into her arms.

The Silverback started grooming a different female nearby. Head down, he searched microscopically through her fur for parasites, carefully picking each one out and eating it. Two more females appeared, and Marcel became the centre of attention whilst they groomed him too. In the tree above, another gorilla chewed on a stick of wild celery, meticulously removing the outside of the stem to get to the succulent core. I was completely captivated so didn't notice a juvenile gorilla with a missing hand amble towards me.

The ranger warned me, 'Please move away, and don't let her touch you.'

The resilient gorilla had lost her hand in a snare but obviously held no grudge against humans because she wasn't in the least intimidated by us being there and wanted to get close to me. How I wished I could embrace her and make up for what the poachers had done.

I was videoing Marcel when he turned and looked straight into the viewfinder of the camera. My initial instinct was to run, but then I realized he couldn't see me staring at him, because I was hidden behind the lens. We listened to the gorillas grunting, farting and belching with contentment whilst watching them eat and play.

All too soon our time was up, and we had to leave. The rangers headed back, and I thought I'd just take a few last photos before following. They had disappeared before I turned to leave, so I hurried to catch up but took a wrong turn almost bumping into another gorilla.

The walk back down the mountain seemed much easier when we followed already cut trails. With fewer than nine hundred mountain gorillas living in the wild, I was grateful to have seen any. I sparkled with radiance from an experience I'd never forget.

From the hut, it was a further two hour trek to the border. By now the elation was starting to wear off, and I was tired from all the excitement. I couldn't wait to have a hot shower and sleep on a soft mattress in a proper bed. However, when we arrived at the border, we discovered it wasn't a market day, and there were no vehicles around to give us a lift to Kabale. We weren't in the least prepared for a night under the stars, not having a tent or sleeping bags. We spotted a utility truck with someone asleep in the cab and asked whether he would take us to Kabale if we paid him for the trip. He was half asleep and not interested in making the journey.

I had the beginnings of a migraine starting which would be difficult to deal with if I was outside in the elements for the night. As we sat down feeling discouraged, a minibus pulled up. We got chatting to a couple of journalists from Melbourne. They were trying to get into Rwanda and thought they might be able to do so via Zaire. However, the immigration official declined to let them through. That was unfortunate for them but a huge relief for us because they were headed back to Kabale and offered to give us a lift.

On the way back, we stopped at a Rwandan Refugee camp, on the Zaire border, where the journalists dropped off some gifts, including footballs, for the children in the camp. Rwanda was experiencing the mass killing of hundreds of thousands of Hutu and Tutsis. Approximately two million Hutus, in anticipation of Tutsi retaliation, fled from Rwanda, headed for Uganda and Zaire. The people at the site seemed happy and cheerful considering their circumstances.

By now I was feeling pretty bad, but tried to put on a brave face. Luckily I was sitting next to the window and managed to stick my head out before vomiting.

'That's a nice mess for our driver to clean up,' said one of the journalists.

'I'm so sorry,' I replied ashen faced.

I was relieved to finally arrive at a comfortable hotel. We decided to stay there for the night, instead of our budget hotel, because I wasn't in any condition to walk anywhere. The receptionist made a comment that we must have been on the road for some time. Having been dowsed in paprika, three days ago, and then not had a shower since, I could understand his reasoning. Russ was lucky to have a hot shower and join the journalists for dinner, but I just collapsed on the bed. When I unbuttoned my cardigan, I too realized I was more than merely stinky, but I had to try to sleep to relieve the migraine.

I woke, the following day, with the headache hovering and feeling washed out. I knew a hot shower would do the trick, but there was none that morning. The cold water took me to the verge of more pain.

The next day, we relaxed and moved back into a room at our previous hotel. Then we hired a guide for the three hour walk to Lake Bunyonyi. It was a gradual uphill walk, then a steep climb over the ridge. On the other side, we hired a dug-out canoe with a couple of other guys, one of whom was a canoeist. The fellas paddled whilst I filmed the journey. We had lunch on the island and an enjoyable walk around before paddling back. It was a three hour walk to our hotel where we got a bucket of piping hot water to wash down with.

It was time to move on, so we caught a bus to Kampala and another night bus on to Nairobi where we arrived at five the following morning. It was still dark outside, and the bus driver would not allow anyone off until daylight, at six, because it was unsafe on the streets.

Several years later, I cried uncontrollably when I learned that not long after we visited Marcel and his band of mountain gorillas, he had been murdered along with another adult female. It's believed they were trying to protect an infant from being kidnapped by poachers. Luckily the infant was rescued at the Ugandan border and reunited with his family.

I felt an ache in my heart that something so tragic could have happened. Marcel was a magnificent creature, living with captivating females and such endearing infants. I thought it was so unfair and will never understand why someone has the need to own these gentle, but wild animals, and not share them with the world.

CHAPTER EIGHT – DAYLIGHT ROBBERY
Kenya, Tanzania, Zambia

'What are your plans for tomorrow?' asked the Kenyan waiter, placing a plate of steaming fragrant curry in front of me.

'We're catching the bus to Lamu,' I replied.

'You may leave all your valuables in our safe including your currency and travellers cheques,' he politely suggested.

Russ and I were staying at a budget guesthouse in Malindi which was owned by a flamboyant Italian man who used wild hand gestures to help communicate whilst he spoke loudly to us. I wasn't sure I could trust him with all our assets. I'd read about the latest scams to relieve tourists of their money but hadn't come across this one before. Often there was no running water or electricity, which was inconvenient but a regular occurrence throughout Africa. I hoped to be able to have a shower before embarking on the long journey to Lamu, but it was to come in an unexpected form.

There were many mosquitoes around, and although I'd gone to bed with long pants, long sleeved top and socks, there was nowhere to hang the protective net we carried. I woke to find a bite on my eyelid which had swollen so much, I couldn't open my eye. It wasn't an attractive look.

The weather taunted us as torrential rain fell, drenching us beneath our cheap plastic ponchos whilst we sprinted towards our transport. Perhaps I should've stood outside earlier, naked with a bar of soap, but it was too late now.

We stowed our backpacks in the hold underneath the bus. As usual, it was crowded with mainly local traders and travellers. I was slightly nauseous from the musty smell integrated with a strong diesel aroma. The bench seats were made to hold two people, but usually three or four passengers squashed up along them because many others had to stand up in the aisles amongst packages or crates of different shapes and sizes. I sat beside the window, listening as the downpour bombarded it, sounding like chips spitting in a deep fat fryer. I zoned out whilst the voices around me faded into a whisper. Russ sat beside me with an older gentleman on his other side. When they struck up a conversation, I joined in.

'You do know Somali bandits are notorious for attacking buses on this route?' queried the gentleman.

'No, we weren't aware of this,' replied Russ cautiously.

'As the border of Somalia is only a few hundred kilometres from Lamu, the vehicle is held up about once a month. They get everyone off at gunpoint and take all your jewellery and cash.'

At that moment, I realized why the waiter had suggested leaving our money in the hotel safe.

'Do they hurt anyone?' I asked, now concerned for our safety.

'Initially nobody got shot, but then the Government sent armed guards along for security. Once this happened, the robbers would shoot to kill those equipped with a rifle, so now they no longer accompany us.'

I wondered whether that was a good or bad thing.

He continued, 'However, the thieves will make you strip in case you are hiding anything on your body and take your passports and cameras. Once they took everyone's clothes as well.'

This was sounding worse by the minute. How could we get to an embassy for help without our possessions? I certainly didn't want to end up in the middle of nowhere, both naked and broke.

The journey was already underway, so we had to endure the seven hour trip in a deluge. Initially it was along a bumpy, pot holed tarmac road but petered out to a rutted muddy strip with huge craters. When the wheels dropped into the cavities, we would fly off our solid seats and crash back down with a jolt. I heard a loud crack in the distance.

'What was that?' I asked nervously. 'Was it a gunshot?'

'It's only thunder,' said Russ with a big grin.

I had the heebie jebbies for most of the trip which seemed to take forever. Damp and cold, I shivered as my thoughts drifted to what might happen. Visibility was poor through the pelting drops which formed a sheet of mist similar to driving under a waterfall. Maybe the weather would keep the bandits away.

Eventually we got off unscathed, picked up our wet muddy packs and boarded a small wooden launch, brimming over with passengers and their possessions. I resembled the stuffing in a turkey, unable to move in any direction. My muscles were sore after sitting for so long, and I was tired and hungry. The rain continued, lashing the unhurried boat whilst we negotiated the angry Indian Ocean to Lamu. The waves banged against the hull with such force that they would spurt into the air like geysers and drench me in seawater. The constant rolling motion along with the slow progress made me queasy.

Jumi met us at the dock to take us to his guesthouse. On foot, he guided us by torchlight because there was only minimal street lighting. I needed a soak in a hot bath but only cold water was available. It was late, so good to just dry off and have a warm meal to eat before finally relaxing and falling into a deep slumber.

The next morning, awoken by the local mosques call to prayer, the sun shone, and we hung out our wet clothes to dry before heading out to explore. The winding streets, back towards the dock, smelt of drying fish and the salty sea which hung in the air.

'Shela Beach, Shela Beach,' shouted a boat captain above the general hubbub of the crowds. We wanted to walk because it was less than an hour away.

I'd learnt some Swahili so greeted passers-by with "Jambo", meaning hello. Everyone seemed friendly and smiled when returning the greeting. There were no cars on the island, only donkeys, because the alleyways between houses were narrow. It was a challenge dodging the pungent manure whilst following the maze twisting and turning through a mixture of East African, Arab and Indian influences.

The doorways to the old stone houses were quite spectacular with intricately carved heavy wooden doors that were often decorated with chunky brass fittings. The plaster was peeling from the walls appearing unloved and neglected. The roofs were mainly thatched, although some were metal, which looked quaint nestled against the tropical fronds of the palm trees.

I bought a Kanga (Sarong) which says "Raha ya Dunia ni Kupendana" and was told, in Swahili, it roughly means "Love the world and the world loves everyone together". Maybe if I wore it on our return trip, it might keep me unharmed.

From the top of the white sand dunes on the beach, we could see Manda Island, an oasis in the ocean across the bay. The sand was warm underfoot, and the sea a transparent azure blue which lapped gently along the shoreline. I paddled my toes and then soaked my feet whilst watching an elderly man herd his donkeys which were laden with baskets. There was a faint smell of aromatic spices caught on the soft breeze. I was completely at ease and relaxed on this photogenic island, surrounded by friendly helpful residents.

Back in town, we chatted to a local trader.

'We found out how dangerous it was to travel here,' I mentioned. 'Do you know how long it has been since the last attack?'

'It's been more than a month this time so overdue,' he replied. 'The Somalis are displaced from the civil war, and travellers are easy targets, so I'd recommend you fly back to Malindi instead.'

I thought we should give this serious consideration, not only because of the bandits, but also I was unsure my bottom could stand another seven hours of pummelling.

That night, we treated ourselves to Lobster Thermidor in a medieval inner courtyard. Hopefully it wouldn't be our last supper. A tiny bat sucked nectar from the flower on the banana tree whilst the scent of frangipani wafted in the warm night air. There was a power cut, so our meal was served by candle light. The food melted in my mouth as I pondered whether we should splash out and book on a flight because it was much more expensive than travelling over land.

The next day, Bwana Ali and Captain Mafoote took us on a fishing trip on his dhow, a traditional Arab sailing vessel. I practised my Swahili, much to the amusement of our hosts, when Russ caught two fish, one small and one large, saying, 'Mbili samaki, moja kidogo samaki, moja kubwa samaki.' The delicious barbecued fish only tempted our taste buds when we divided it between the four of us whilst the rain drizzled on it resembling olive oil. Large chunks of freshly baked bread helped satisfy our appetites.

On the way back to our guesthouse, we stopped to feed carrots to the donkeys in the sanctuary. The sign showed it was a worldwide charity started in Devon in the UK. One looked at me with such sorrow in its eyes, I wanted to give it a hug but couldn't reach far enough over the wall. The foals were gorgeous but had some horrible scars. It was awful to see they had been badly treated. I was relieved to discover the sanctuary because it was a haven for those mistreated or ready to retire.

I thought of the poor donkey in Egypt and hoped it too could soon retreat to a sanctuary.

Luckily we didn't have much luggage so were able to book on a thirty minute flight, in a light aircraft, back to Malindi. Whilst waiting to board, I spoke to another traveller.

She told me, 'My brother took a flight last week, and the plane crash-landed into the sea, so now he's in hospital with broken ribs.'

'I wonder whether we are really safer on the plane rather than the bus,' I replied, frowning.

The pilot was from Warsaw and the majority of passengers the same nationality, so he let them take turns to steer. He motioned to Russ to enter the cockpit and gave him a headset to wear, then immediately started speaking in Polish.

Unable to understand, Russ advised, 'I can only speak English, but I have flown before.'

'Go ahead and take the controls,' replied the aviator.

With such a variety of people flying during the journey, I sighed when it landed safely on the runway.

The night bus had two cancellations, so we were able to travel on to Nairobi. I slept well, although awoke when the flat tyre had to be changed. It was still dark when we arrived, at quarter to five, so the bus driver insisted we stay on board until after six because it wasn't safe to walk the streets any earlier.

The following day, we set off on a three day safari with Savuka. We travelled to camp via the Rift Valley again, and on the way there spotted a tower of thirty-five giraffe feeding on the leaves high in the trees.

This camp was a bit more basic than the previous one. There wasn't any running water in the shower nor any electricity or even a wash basin. The toilet, in its own separate tent, had a spider in the centre of a web stretched across the bowl, and a hornet flying around it.

'Watch this,' said Russ as he urinated in the toilet. 'I'll get rid of the web.' It was strong though and didn't break from the liquid impact. It would need more than a quick wee, and I wasn't sitting on it until the spider had moved on. After dark, I used a Kerosene lantern to find my way there whilst listening to the hyena cackle. My head throbbed, and my stomach churned as I had a migraine so had retired early. Unzipping the entrance, I could hear the hornet still buzzing when I shone the light inside. Phew, I don't know what Russ had done, but the web and spider had vanished, so I could vomit in relative comfort.

The migration was now in full swing across the Masai Mara with more than a million wildebeest, zebra and gazelle moving in a mass from the Serengeti, stretching all the way to the horizon. Crocodiles would lay in wait for them to cross the river whilst the abundance of land based predators would be close by as they travelled between the gently rolling hills, through woodland, acacia trees and across open plains.

The earth vibrated as zebra broke rank, chasing each other, tossing their heads and kicking their heels whilst making a high pitched whinnying noise. Amongst the larger herds were thousands of antelope which I was now able to identify. There was the giant kudu with its vertical white stripes and long curling horns on the males, the lively springbok pronking in the air with their dark brown horizontal stripe and white belly, the plain impala, and the tiny dik dik with its long snout and diamond shaped ears.

Whenever we stopped to observe the wildlife, the noise of the engine would fill the air along with the chatter from other passengers. I tried to video but knew the sound would never be perfect. The clutch was failing, and the driver would regularly stall causing the van to jolt forward, so my footage would blur. It was difficult to keep the camera steady with others moving around the van, making it unstable. In some ways it was good as it made me stop filming to watch and enjoy the moment. I was so lucky to be here and witness the stunning wildlife.

Watching thousands of Burchell's zebra on the plains of the Masai Mara, it was difficult to understand that some zebra are endangered. I hadn't realized there are three different species of which both the Mountain Zebra and Grevy's Zebra are protected. I hoped these splendid creatures would survive and never become extinct.

A big herd of elephant crossed the road, gently placing their feet forward towards the waterhole, and two graceful cheetah casually strolled on their long lean legs along the road. There weren't many hippos, although I could still spot them yawning and grunting at each other in the Mara River. However, there were many more people on safari than the previous time.

Everyone piled out to push when our matatu got stuck in mud. I was filming and watching the tall grass for any sign of movement.

'Push,' shouted our driver. 'All together, push.'

The van wasn't moving. More passengers joined those pushing from the back but along the side. Slowly, the tyres found grip, somewhere in the soft ground, and the vehicle lurched forward.

I shouted to the Masai guide, 'Simba, Simba' and watched with a cheeky grin when he quickly jumped back in the van. Luckily he had a good sense of humour, and we all laughed because there really weren't any lion close by.

After getting a couple of tyres fixed, we saw a huge pride of lion which looked regal but at the same time powerful and ferocious, as well as a large herd of buffalo calmly grazing on the coarse grass.

When the driver stopped, all I could manage to say was, 'Wow.' Amazed to see an almost extinct Black Rhino with her baby following closely behind, I had to pinch myself to believe I was actually seeing two. It was unbelievable and a great privilege as today there are fewer than five thousand left in the wild. I watched them with admiration and wonderment at their survival, hoping they would live on for generations to come.

She almost completed our Big Five, having already seen lion, elephant and buffalo. That just left a leopard to spot. I took photos whilst the van wobbled with people moving around and noise from the running engine interrupted the natural sounds of the bush. Oxpeckers picked the ticks from her back. I was enthralled and reluctant to leave, but unfortunately we had to head back to Nairobi.

The matatu broke down on the return trip when the clutch was burnt out, so we were towed to Narock where another driver picked us up in a different vehicle to take us to Nairobi.

It wasn't long, and we were on the road again. For three hours, we sat on a rickety old bus, waiting for it to depart for Arusha, in Tanzania. I was worried about the trip because I'd an upset stomach, and although I'd taken Imodium, wasn't sure how long it would last. Crammed in, it would be impossible to move with any speed if I needed to. About halfway through the journey, we stopped at a town for a meal break, so I asked the driver if there were toilets nearby, and he kindly went to get a key for me. I was impressed, thinking they must be good. That is until I unlocked the door.

A dark flooded corridor led to two large cubicles without doors. Both had toilets without seats. I hated that because I found hovering difficult, especially as the muscles in my legs were weak from the bug I'd caught. However, I couldn't use the toilets anyway as they were filled with old soda cans and piles of rubbish. A horrible realization dawned on me as I finally noticed the smell of a used kitty litter tray. Everyone must have used the floor, and that was why it was awash. Having already walked through it, I'd no option but to do the same and gathered my skirts, so they didn't touch the ground. Relieved the Imodium was working, I hurriedly left locking the door. I was puzzled though, unable to comprehend why they had blocked up the toilets, especially as it was unusual to find western toilets in rural Africa.

A flat tyre on the way delayed us a little longer, but there was no problem crossing the border into Tanzania. Because it was still light, I was awestruck by the marvellous view of Mt Kilimanjaro capped with snow and standing out from the mopane forest on the border like a soldier on parade.

The hallway of the hotel was lit by lanterns, casting eerie shadows on the ceiling as there was no electricity or hot water. Russ borrowed one to light up our room, but there was soon a knock on the door.

'Please return the lantern,' said a firm voice.

'But we cannot see inside our room,' Russ replied.

'You must put the lantern back.'

'Okay, but could I have a bucket of hot water to wash with as it's very cold?' I asked.

'Certainly,' came the reply.

As soon as the sun disappeared each evening, the temperature plummeted, and it felt like being enveloped in a bath of liquid nitrogen.

Having put the lantern back, the only light in our room was from my small penlight torch. We waited eagerly for the water to arrive. The time ticked by, and the night air grew colder. I navigated the hallway to reception.

'Do you know when the hot water will be ready?' I asked.

'It is coming,' she replied.

'Thank you. I'll be in my room.'

I waited again, realizing it was African time and could take a while. However, it took so long to arrive that I braved an icy shower in the dark. My lips were blue and my body shivered when my wet hair dripped frosty droplets, drenching my jumper. I had no way to dry my hair, so I slept with it wrapped in a towel with all my clothes on beside Russ, in one of the single beds, covered in all the blankets and sheets in the room, stealing any warmth his body emitted. My teeth chattered uncontrollably until I fell into a fitful sleep.

This time there was only one other couple on our safari along with the driver, Dustin, and the cook, Sied. Just inside Tarangire Park was a massive herd of elephant sheltering under the acacia trees. Many babies frolicked around their parents, who stood still in the heat of the day. The sun had sucked the moisture from the landscape, leaving brittle straw and exposed dusty red earth where once had been flourishing grasslands. The baobab trees looked like they were upside down with their roots reaching to the cloudless skies, and sausage trees were laden with fruit pods.

I could see a tsetse fly settle on Russ' navy blue sweatshirt whilst it folded its wings one on top of the other like a closed pair of scissors. It looked like a large fly, but I knew it could be much more sinister as it might be carrying sleeping sickness. There's no vaccine for this disease, and although treatment is possible in the early stages, it wasn't something we wanted to catch. I was wearing cream coloured clothing, and it wasn't interested in me, but I kept the fly in my sights whilst looking out the window at the wildlife and scenery.

Near the river, I could see the unusual ossicones of the giraffe. Zebra, blue wildebeest and chestnut coloured bushbuck, with a white stripe around its neck, intermingled. The warthogs looked unattractive with their short tusks jutting from their knobbly faces, and elephant splashed playfully in the water.

At the lodge, where we stopped for a drink, I'm not sure which bought me most pleasure, the fantastic lookout, or the luxury of a clean, flushable western style toilet with toilet paper, sink, soap and a towel provided. It might sound silly, but I missed the luxury. Breathing in the sweet smell of cleanliness, I loitered, reluctant to leave. It was a pleasurable change from an odorous dirty hole in the ground.

The next morning, we left Campvision at Mto Wa Mbu, meaning river of mosquitoes, where we'd slept peacefully under the protection of a sturdy net. Ngorongoro crater, a collapsed extinct volcano, was shrouded in a thick mist. At the crater rim, I was fascinated by two young, tall, slim Masai warriors whose long braided hair was dyed ochre and smothered in animal fat. They proudly preened themselves in the wing mirror of the four wheel drive.

It was a steep descent through forests. The road wound down a gentle slope, eighteen hundred feet, to the bottom of a crater. There, the rich flat grasslands on the floor were home to impressive wildlife that had no need to migrate because they had an almost continuous supply of water.

Around the lake, muddy lion lazed in the sunshine not far from the brightly coloured flamingos. Zebra and wildebeest were abundant nearby. Whilst eating lunch at a waterhole, the bathing hippos and elephant entertained us by frolicking happily. I pondered mans greed to murder elephant, just for their tusks, but couldn't understand why.

Later, we spotted a lion feasting on a buffalo. The lionesses generally did the hunting as a group, so I didn't think it fair the male got first pick of the spoils.

As we travelled through the crater, there were so many different types of scenery, huge expanses of highland plains, scrub bush and forests. When allowed out of the jeep, we got close to the vervet monkeys which were extremely excitable. Russ peeled an egg for them to eat and explained to them about evolution, which seemed to make them angry. Or maybe, it was because he only had one egg.

Another day, we visited Lake Manyara, which stretched fifty kilometres along the base of the Rift Valley escarpment. Whilst we were driven along the winding road, through verdant forest full of acacia trees, baobabs and mahogany, we saw a hippo completely out of the water. This was unusual as they generally only searched for food on land at night because they needed to keep their skin moist and cool during the day.

Back in Arusha, the next morning, I checked we had spare camera film in our daypack and with an uneasy feeling, asked Russ, 'Should I change the video tape as this one is almost full with forty-two minutes of footage?'

'We may as well use up the last few minutes. Just carry another blank one,' he replied. I'd a strong urge to change it but thought what Russ said made sense so put a blank tape in the daypack to change later.

We were picked up early and whilst checking into a local guest house, our daypack was stolen from the jeep. It contained our video camera, camera lenses, batteries, binoculars, video tapes and guidebook. Now I really wished I'd changed the tape. Why hadn't I listened to my intuition? It was a turning point in my life, and now when I have doubts or an uneasy feeling about something, I listen to myself. Our driver reported it to the police. They arrested a couple of men standing nearby who were from out of town.

We were all taken to the police station, and the officer told us, 'We are torturing the accused.' Seeing the horrified look on my face, he then changed it to say, 'I mean we are interrogating the accused.' I hoped his English was bad and not his punishment. Whilst making a written statement, we had to advise the value of the items taken. On quoting the cost of the video camera, the sergeant was flabbergasted.

'You can buy a second hand car for that much money in Tanzania. Are you sure that's what it cost?' he asked.

'Yes, that's what we paid for it,' I replied, slightly guilty about the materialistic world I lived in.

Nothing was ever recovered, and although our film footage was a huge loss, I hoped it wasn't to the detriment of the accused.

It was late by the time we arrived at Arusha National Park. Inside the entrance gate, we spotted elegant giraffe and dainty dik dik camouflaged in the montane forest. Further north, the rolling grassy hills enclosed the tranquil beauty of Momela Lakes which were coated with thousands of pink flamingos. The delicate film of soda crunched under my feet when I trod on it. The closer I got to the acrid smelling lake, the darker and smellier the sand became as it turned to odorous guano bird droppings.

On our way out, we passed the acrobatic black and white colobus monkeys with long ebony and ivory coats' and a harsh cry as they nimbly leapt from branch to branch. Their tails were luxurious plumes of fur, longer than their bodies, and reminded me of a foxes brush. I wished I could reach out and touch them.

After a long and eventful day, I was keen for a hot shower to help me unwind, but the hotel we were staying at didn't have running water. I collected a bucket of cold water and entered a tiny shack off the courtyard with a picket door. I was self-conscious taking my clothes off and hoped the people sitting chatting in the courtyard couldn't see between the gaps of the planks on the door. As my mind returned to the showers in Austria, I blushed inwardly but nobody was playing ball. I kept my back towards them whilst I ladled cold water over my naked body. I shivered. What I'd give for a hot shower. I shampooed my hair and soaped my body before rinsing off by pouring the water over me.

The toilet was the usual hole in the ground, although this time it was porcelain and kept clean. I struggled to squat to use the toilet, especially when I had bouts of diarrhoea because my legs would lose their strength. Holding my long sarong high off the ground, I tipped water from the bucket to flush.

It was a comfortable bus trip to Dar es Salam the following day. Not only did we have reclining seats, all to ourselves, but watched a movie as well. A visit to Kariakoo Markets proved unsuccessful in finding a new camera, so we caught the afternoon ferry to Zanzibar. A tout led us around the cobbled alleyways of Stone Town, but all the cheap accommodation was taken. So, as darkness descended, we hitched a ride on a truck to Bwejuu.

At dawn, we discovered that we were sleeping on a solid lumpy coconut husk mattress in a small painted hut with a thatched roof. It was situated on a tranquil white sandy beach, edged by the transparent sapphire Indian Ocean on one side and rustling palm trees on the other. A few hours of strolling along the empty beach built up an appetite for a delicious dinner which included delicately spiced lobster, curried octopus and crab salad. Whilst relaxing beside the water, a young girl sold us coconut cakes and fresh rambutans. It was great to eat such appetizing food again.

Back in Stone Town, the heart of Zanzibar, where we'd reserved a room on the roof of a guesthouse, it was fun to explore the labyrinth of narrow streets and alleyways and discover bustling bazaars selling delectable homemade peanut brittle and grapes.

The old buildings made of coral stone rock had exquisitely carved wooden doors with brass knockers and a distinctive Arab feel. We got into the habit of eating from the food stalls at Jamituri Gardens. In the evenings, we sampled slices of octopus tentacle dipped in chilli flakes, moist potato cakes, chunky cassava chips, meat on sticks and cane juice. The tables of food lined the gardens beside a white painted bandstand. Here, we'd fatten up a little after our forced fasting in Zaire.

On a fascinating Spice Tour with "Mr Mitu", we visited the Slave Market and Palace where he showed us soap berries which we used to wash our hands, pods that burst minutes after water is poured on them, fruit which made us sneeze and another one that made us stop. He showed us a quinine plant, sandpaper leaf and a plant smelling like cloves. When he drove us in a truck, the local children ran alongside to pick up the lollies and coins he threw out of the window for them.

My mouth watered whilst tasting the custard apple which was similar to yoghurt, the star plant which was quite tart and the sugary, juicy pomelo. It was interesting to learn cocoa is a bitter seed made sweet for chocolate, whereas coffee is a sweet bean made bitter to drink. He showed how an Iodine plant can be cut and the sap used as antiseptic as well as explaining boiled ground cloves cure diarrhoea. I could do with some of those for the rest of the trip.

The next morning, I watched three elongated, rusty red tails hanging vertically, like lollypop sticks, which were camouflaged against the bark of the tree. Tiny black spindly fingers picked insects from the dark stripe along the arm and shoulders of another male. They looked like wizened old men because their black faces sported spikey white fur above inquisitive eyes and contrasting pink nose and lips.

I'd walked through the Jozani Park Forest, craning my neck to scan the lush canopies but only saw frogs and butterflies. It wasn't until we were headed back to the taxi that we spotted the endangered red colobus monkeys up high in the trees nearby.

Our driver said, 'There are only fifteen hundred Zanzibar red colobus monkeys left in the world.' I was fortunate to have seen them but concerned at the number of species getting closer to extinction. They were so cute that it was hard to believe anyone would want to harm them.

I was to see another endangered species, the following day, when a motorboat carried us out to Changuu Island. No longer used to confine slaves, but home to another unique creature. Huge grey domed geometrically patterned shells looked like massive boulders from a distance. A closer inspection revealed stumpy leathery legs with claws, short tails and a head merged into a long neck. When tempted with citrus fruit, these giant land tortoises would poke out their thick pink tongues before taking the food.

In the evening, I tried to phone Arusha Police Station, in the hope our belongings might have been handed in, but I couldn't get through. I'd a sneaking feeling that if our video camera was recovered, the police sergeant would be swapping it for a new car.

It rained heavily during our ferry trip back to Dar, making the crossing terribly rough. I sucked on some sugared almonds to keep my nausea under control. However, after three hours of being thrown around, I was pretty shaky when I got off.

We caught a train from Dar, on the TAZARA (Tanzania-Zambia Railway), via Kapiri Mposhi to Lusaka in Zambia. On arrival at the border station, the guards wanted to take our tickets and passports. We refused because we were extremely dubious about giving them anything as I'd heard they would ask for bribes to give them back.

We had to sleep in separate carriages because men and women were not allowed to share. It was a pleasant journey, although a long one.

On arrival in Lusaka, we got ready to disembark. The guards were getting passengers into queues with exceedingly long whips which seemed incredibly effective but rather intimidating. We hung back on the train to avoid the lashings. I hoped their accuracy was good, and they wouldn't hit us as I ducked my head, and we ran past.

We got our passports checked and then caught the bus into town, which took about three hours. There was little option on places to stay, so we caught a taxi to the YMCA. Once there, we discovered they had no running water, the toilets were disgustingly dirty and you had to tip a bucket of water into them to flush them. It was also a long way out of town, so we caught a taxi back to town and splashed out spending twice the price to stay at the Fairview Hotel.

'I cannot believe there is a clean bath and hot running water in the bathroom,' I exclaimed gleefully.

'I haven't seen you smile so brightly for months,' replied Russ.

'I'm going to soak in it all night,' I responded.

Unfortunately, first we had to go and find some food for dinner and then would have to leave on the bus to Victoria Falls, before daylight, the next morning. Stripping off my grimy clothing, I made the most of the bath that night by topping it up with hot water, so I could stay warm and comfortable.

I remembered what the young man in Uganda had said, 'If you can't have what you like, like what you have.' Africa made me appreciate the smallest things, like a hot bath, clean toilet and scrumptious food. I'd never take anything for granted again.

CHAPTER NINE – THREATENED SPECIES
Zimbabwe & South Africa

In Zimbabwe, white water rafting had been one of the highlights of our trip, even if I ended up covered in bruises. Moshe had been a great guide, and I was happy to have survived the river. Not wanting to outstay our welcome with Vincent, we boarded the once magnificent, but now jaded, old colonial train to Bulawayo. We had a compartment to ourselves bearing the insignia RR which graced the interior walls. This was an acronym for Rhodesian Railways, which it was called prior to independence. We had two bunks which turned into a bench seat during the daytime, a small table and a drop down sink where we could wash our hands. Soap was provided along with crisp white linen, blankets and pillows for our bunks.

In Bulawayo, we walked along the streets lined with jacaranda trees where their purple petals concealed the pavement. We visited some old haunts, such as Centenary and Central Park. They hadn't changed much, just looked a little more unkempt. Without transport, we booked on a coach trip to Matopos. The wind was freezing cold, so our first stop, to see cave paintings, was brief. We made the steep climb to Rhodes grave and Worlds View where the exposure made the wind feel bitter. Then it started raining heavily, so we proceeded to the game park. There, we saw a total of five white rhino which were difficult to spot because they were hidden in the tall dried out grass interspersed with bare trees.

We also saw the small sure-footed klipspringer walking on the tip of its hooves, the shaggy coated bushbuck with striking white spots above its nose and rotund zebra. The sable was majestic with a glossy black coat contrasting with its white facial markings and underbelly. It had the most superb long horns that curved backwards towards the tip.

Bulawayo hadn't changed much from our last visit, except most of our friends had moved overseas. It was time to move on and reconnoitre in South Africa.

When the bus careered out of control, my mind raced whilst I tried to figure out what to do in event of a crash. The bus was sliding sideways along the road and the driver struggling to keep control. Should I grip the seat in front of me, bury my head on my lap, or wake Russ, who was asleep beside me? My life didn't flash before me like they say it does, but I did think of the people I love.

It was difficult staying awake to catch the one o'clock bus that morning to Johannesburg. The old bus windows were drafty, but another passenger kindly lent us a quilt to keep warm. A tyre blew about seventy kilometres from Beitbridge, and the vehicle became uncontrollable. The driver skilfully saved it from running off the road, much to my relief. One of the wheel nuts had been welded, and the wheel brace didn't fit, so it took three hours for him to change the tyre. The border crossing went smoothly, and we transferred to a more comfortable bus for the rest of the journey.

I'd decided we could stay in Hillbrow, at a hotel listed in our guide book, and we'd organized to meet my parents in the local park the following day. The manager of a backpacker's hostel approached us at the bus station.

'It isn't safe to stay in Hillbrow and certainly not to hang around in the park,' he stated.

'We'll be fine because we're used to staying in the seedier areas of downtown,' I replied, trying to brush him off as I believed he just wanted our business.

'Seriously, you really don't want to stay there. It's notorious for crime, and your chances of being mugged, shot or raped, are very high,' he persisted.

Continuing to ignore him, I picked up my backpack from the luggage compartment and turned away.

He continued, 'You certainly wouldn't want to risk taking your elderly parents there. How would you feel if they were assaulted?'

Eventually I gave in, and he drove us to his hostel in Sandon which was ironically called "The Ritz". It turned out to be a good move as he took us to the airport to collect my parents and organized a hire car we could use for the next month.

'If you drive through any townships, don't stop at the traffic lights, even if they're red,' he advised us. 'Many people are carjacked in South Africa, so if you get held at gunpoint, just get out of the car, so you don't get shot.'

'Is it really that bad?' I asked concerned more for my parent's safety than my own.

'Yes, many tourists are violently robbed for their money, and it's usually a case of being in the wrong place at the wrong time,' he replied.

Many years later, I worked with a South African lady who'd done charity work in Hillbrow. She told me, when she went there, she always carried a pistol under the front seat of her car for protection.

At the Ritz, there was only one double room available, so we gave it to my parents. Russ and I slept in a large cupboard in the main building that night. We left early the next morning for Pilannesburg National Park. Stopping to stock up on food, on the way there, I noticed a guard holding an AK47 posted outside the supermarket. Luckily we could afford to pay for our groceries. I needed to cash some travellers' cheques, so we went in search of a bank. First, I was buzzed inside one set of doors but held there until I stated my name and nationality along with my purpose for entering the bank. After that, they let me through the second set of doors.

Mid-afternoon, we discovered we were staying in a rustic cottage where Russ and I slept in the loft on mattresses on the floor. It was a luxury to have our own cooking facilities and an alluring swimming pool. I was delighted to hear hornbills honk inharmoniously in the trees, in the back garden, whilst the warthogs scavenged below them on the lawn.

I wanted to share some of the amazing wildlife we'd seen in Kenya, Tanzania, Zambia and Zimbabwe, with my parents. I was lucky to have seen four of the Big Five with only the leopard proving elusive. I was thrilled to have seen a black rhino knowing they are close to extinction and rare to find. I loved the huge elephant which were easier to spot because they were so large, and I adored any type of cats including the lion. The Cape Buffalo were good to see, but there were other animals I preferred.

Russ drove us on a late afternoon game drive around Pilannesburg, which was nestled in the crater of a long extinct volcano. I scanned the spectacular landscape, from open grasslands to wooded thickets, for any sign of animals. I sat quietly and watched the white rhino on the bank. The waterbuck with its conspicuous white ring on its bottom and the wildebeest drank from the waterhole whilst a tribe of baboons communicated noisily. The rhino would be the first of my parents Big Five.

On an early morning game drive, we saw many elephant and waterbuck along with giraffe whose elegant necks were bent forward, so they could eat the leaves from the bushes. We spotted zebra, a stunning sable with its amazing long, slender horns and more klipspringer. The warthogs that had prominent lumps on the side of their heads knelt on their knees to snuffle with their flat snout on the ground. The mongooses were hyperactive, running around and quickly disappearing from sight whilst the baboons sat watching their young as they foraged for food. The black faced grey vervet monkeys looked at me appealingly, although I knew better than to fall for their charms. My parents had now seen the second of their Big Five, the elephant.

I hoped Kruger National Park would live up to its name. On the way there, we drove through the scenic Long Tom Pass as well as visiting Horse Shoe Falls, Mac Mac Ponds and Gods Window. I was excited when we entered the Paul Kruger Gate and travelled through Skukuza, Tshowane and Satara. During the journey, we sighted much wildlife including the most commonly seen animal in the park, the impala. It had a rich glossy chestnut brown back, which was separated from its white underside and legs with a black stripe. We also saw giraffe and Burchell's zebra which also had a white belly but a unique pattern of black stripes on the rest of its body. There was a kudu standing motionless on side of the road, so I was able to get a fantastic photo before it fled.

The elephant were fairly easy to spot, being the largest of the land mammals, even if they did camouflage well. Although covered in dust, it was still possible to make out their rough skin underneath. They used their muscular trunks to strip the trees of leaves. I was a little uncomfortable when they decided to cross the road in front of our car. Their tusks skirted the thirsty terrain and the matriarch stood guard less than a metre from our front bumper, waving her trunk in the air.

It was hard to believe the hippos were the most dangerous land mammal in Africa because they looked such gentle creatures. That is until they yawned, showing their teeth in their huge jaws. The spotted hyena was the most common hyena we saw. Its dark brown spots contrasted against its yellow-brown coat. We saw more waterbuck and the unsightly ground hornbills with their large bills and red throats which inflated when they called to each other. The starlings appeared black but glistened blue when the sun's rays bounced off their feathers.

I still wanted to show my Mum and Dad some lion and buffalo, although to make it perfect, we all wanted to see a leopard but knew our chances were slim.

The following morning we left a little later, arriving at Kruger around nine, and only seven kilometres into the park, spotted a leopard sitting near the roadside.

'Look,' I squeaked excitedly, pointing into the bush.

Many cars had stopped and the passengers were staring intently. It was difficult to see because its golden coat and black spots camouflaged well in the thick shrubs around it. Russ manoeuvred the car, so we could follow in its wake before it disappeared completely.

I'd finally seen each of the Big Five and was privileged to have been able to do so. I pondered how long they would all live on this earth.

Elephant delicately crossed the road, the soft pads of their feet leaving little impact. The black backed jackals had silver highlights shimmering in their fur. The heavily built water buffalo meandered in their herds like harmless cattle when really they were one of the most dangerous animals in Africa. Now my parents only had one more of the Big Five to see, the lion.

We saw more giraffe, zebra, waterbuck and the dainty bushbuck treading warily through the shadows whilst the kudu nearby listened alertly for any danger signals. The rusty coloured female nyala looked delightful with its white striped body. Impala, klipspringer and wildebeest gathered near the waterhole, awaiting their turn whilst the giraffe had spread their legs to lower their body, so their long slender necks could reach the surface of the water to drink.

The warthogs ran with their thin tails in the air like aerials with the tuft of bristles at the tip standing out. Wallowing lazily in the water, hippos grunted. Unfortunately we didn't see any lion before having to leave the park.

From Kruger, we travelled the garden route to Durban where we visited the Indian Markets via the old Fort and a diverse collection of Orchids at the Botanical Gardens.

Nearing East London, Russ asked my mum, 'What would you like for dinner tonight?'

She joked, 'Fish and chips,' which was her favourite takeaway at home.

Amazingly, Russ came across a small fish and chip shop selling hake and snoek along the back streets.

'Madam, as requested, here is your fish and chip shop,' said Russ in a plumy accent as he pulled over and parked the car.

We drove to Port Elizabeth and visited Happy Valley with its gentle lawns, lily ponds and colourful gardens before travelling on to Knysna where we spent several days staying in a lovely chalet on the east side of a protected lagoon. We had ducks on our doorstep as well as visits from a cat and a dog.

In the evening, we went to the cinema and saw Lion King starring "Simba" the lion, "Rafiki" the baboon who chanted "Asanta sana squashed banana" and "Mr Pig" who said "Hakuna Matata".

I hadn't heard Swahili spoken since we left Tanzania. I found it funny the baboon was called Rafiki, which means friend but also is a brand of toilet paper.

At Oudtshoorn we visited the Croc Ranch and Cheetahland. During the tour of the crocodile farm and endangered breeding facility, we saw cheetah, cougar, jaguar and lion. I decided it was worth paying extra to stroke the hand reared cheetah. I was surprised they had quite coarse fur and even coarser tongues which felt like sandpaper. Unfortunately we were only allowed a short time with them, and it was over too quickly.

Afterwards, we visited Highgate Ostrich Farm where we went on a tour during which the guide stood on an ostrich egg to prove it would not break. We were shown feathers, baby ostrich and incubators. I found it amusing when Russ rode an Ostrich. He was helped up onto its back and tucked his knees beneath its front wings, holding on firmly, so he didn't fall off. The ostrich was in a pen, so it couldn't run too fast. I was still worried it might bury its head in the ground, even though they don't actually do that. Perhaps it would catapult him off or reach round with its long neck and peck at him. He did a great job by managing to cling on the whole time.

Whilst in Cape Town, each evening we would return to the rented apartment and after dinner play scrabble over a few drinks. The plan was to return to Johannesburg via Pretoria, but when my Mum and I perused a beautiful book about South African game parks, one particular large glossy picture of a Cheetah with her cubs drew our attention. After discussing it with my dad and Russ, it was decided we would go to the Kalahari Gemsbok National Park instead. After all, my parents still hadn't seen any lion in the wild.

At Cape of Good Hope Nature Reserve, we saw vibrant protea in flower and unique wildlife including the almost extinct bontebok. They were a velvety chocolate brown colour with white markings on their legs, from their foreheads to their noses and around their tails.

As we drove around the park, we stopped behind a queue of cars watching the baboons. A teenage girl, from a nearby vehicle, walked up to a small baboon to feed it. There were signs everywhere advising not to feed the wildlife. However, this small baboon must have looked cute, so she approached it anyway. Unfortunately this attracted a large menacing male chacma baboon. She held the food high because he was taller than a metre, although not much shorter than she was. He must have weighed a good forty kilos so had immense strength. I held my breath when he grabbed the food in his right hand and attacked her with his left. Frozen in my seat, I was unsure how to help her. When she turned to run back to the safety of her car, he chased her and I thought was going to harm her, but he abruptly stopped more interested in the food he was holding. I could understand why people felt threatened by them, but they are the only baboon species that are protected, due to habitat loss, in the Southern Cape.

#

I gasped and tightly closed my eyes when the car skidded sideways in the dirt. We were travelling at one hundred kilometres an hour, and when the car started to glide, it did so quickly making my heart palpitate. Russ was driving at the time, some of the 322 kilometres of dirt road to the Kalahari Gemsbok National Park which bordered Namibia and Botswana. Luckily he was able to steer into the skid and saved the car from rolling. We shared the thirteen hours of driving, arriving after dark. Four wonderful days passed at the largest protected wilderness area in Africa where we drove alongside the dry riverbeds and through mile after mile of rolling rust-red sand dunes. Although semi-desert, it was richer than it appeared with solitary trees and scattered grasses dotting the landscape. It was eerily silent with only the sound of the car engine running. Social weaver birds had made massive nests on tree branches which would ultimately collapse from the excess weight.

I was lucky to see many antelope, especially the gemsbok which was extremely striking with long straight symmetrical horns and a muscular body. The black and white markings on their faces, body and legs were distinctive. I held my breath as I watched the young males rutting with heads down and horns interlocked. A sigh of relief escaped my lips when they parted unharmed.

In contrast, the red hartebeest (another large antelope) was a solid reddish colour with black markings on its face, a sloping back and heavily ringed horns. Once alerted to our presence, the antelope milled about and snorted nervously before bouncing into flight. The eland was unmistakable being the largest antelope with spiralled horns, whereas the klipspringer was tiny in contrast.

The ostrich covered an amazing distance in a short space of time and although one would think they were harmless, could be quite destructive. They were impressive, sprinting on tiptoe with their knees bent backwards to reach speeds far in excess of our Olympic runners. It was great to see so many black backed jackals, as well as lion sheltered beneath the shady bushes from the midday sun, in this land of drought. They looked stately with their black manes and black tuft at the tip of their tails. I was so pleased to have shared the Big Five with my parents.

Finally, we spotted the elusive cheetah we'd travelled all that way to see. It was only for a brief moment, just when dusk was descending, and she quickly disappeared into the undergrowth after her cubs. Had we arrived a minute later, we would never have known she was there at all.

Back at Twee Riverina, the ground squirrels clambered all over us to be fed peanuts. We also saw secretary birds with their long legs and crest of long feathers on top of their heads. One of a pair had a snake stretched between its beak and its toes, which it was battering to death on the ground. On the way to Mata Mata, we saw more jackals including a couple eating on the road as well as a lion and lioness sleeping.

Near Nossob, we watched, in awe, two lionesses with the cutest cubs tumbling around them. They played harmoniously, a perfect picture of family life beneath a cloudless sky as the golden rays frolicked across their hides. However, on closer inspection, we realized it was a sinister scene with four dead antelope casting dark shadows around them. Scavengers hungrily attacked one corpse. The vultures gorged themselves until they were too heavy to fly. Their unattractive bald head was an intelligent design since it allowed them to thrust it into carcasses and come out clean. The jackals were jostling each other to reap the more desirable parts. Three of the kills were hardly touched, and I wondered whether the lionesses had killed in hunger or for sport. Perhaps they had been teaching their cubs.

On the way out of the park, we were overjoyed to come across a brown hyena beside the waterhole. Different to the spotted hyena in many ways, not just because it had a long shaggy coat and pointy ears, but since it eats fruit as well as meat. Wavering precariously on the periphery of existence, they are endangered. My churning gut gnawed at my heart whilst my mind worked intensely, trying to come up with a solution to heal the world. So many species were in decline when they have as much right as any of us to flourish. The delicate balance of nature was too easy to unhinge, slipping into an abyss, as once one component was removed they could all fall off.

Back at "The Ritz", it was just as heart breaking saying goodbye to my parents because I never knew when I'd see them again. It had been great travelling together and being able to share our experiences.

Keeping busy, Russ and I went on a day tour of Soweto, which was about twenty kilometres south west of Johannesburg. Soweto, an acronym for South Western Townships, is a melting pot of South African Cultures and is segregated into townships creating separate areas for Blacks, Coloureds, Asians and Indians. There are also different areas depending on affluence.

The guide advised us, 'This is a dangerous area, and you need to be careful. Don't have anything valuable on show. Put your camera away in your bag with your purse or wallet concealed, and hold on to it rather than hanging it over your shoulder. Remove all jewellery, and dress inconspicuously. Stay close to me.'

I was a little nervous about the trip as when we returned our hire car, the day before, the lady that gave us a lift back to the hostel told us she lived in Soweto and hated it.

'I am scared for my daughters as there is a high chance of them being raped. It's not worth reporting as the police don't do anything about it. I'd like to move out, but nobody wants to buy our house,' she explained.

'How awful to have to live that way,' I sympathised, thinking it must be dreadful to exist in constant fear.

'It's got worse since Nelson Mandela became president as crime is rising dramatically,' she advised.

The only jewellery I wore was my cheap plastic watch. I concealed my purse and camera in my bum bag, which was tied around my waist and out of sight underneath my jumper.

A family of five welcomed us into their shack made of corrugated iron sheets. It wasn't much bigger than a shed. It housed a double bed, in which the parents slept, and another mattress that would be laid on the floor for the children to sleep on. There was a small two ring stove to cook on and outside, against the building, was a small table with a bowl of water on it. Nearby was a brick building with an iron roof which had one flush toilet and one tap of running water for seventy people to share.

It made me think, once again, about the words of wisdom a Ugandan had told me, "If you can't have what you like, like what you have". I'd find it extremely difficult to adapt because I took electricity and running water for granted at home. I could only imagine the stench from the toilet and the queues. Showing the greatest respect towards them, I wept inside wanting to hug them all for enduring such conditions which were all they'd known.

When we saw Nelson Mandela's home, which was given to him after he was released from prison, but at the time belonged to Winnie Mandela, we saw two of his daughters' arriving home in their school uniforms. Areas where barefoot youngsters played amongst the piles of garbage and ran along the pit holed roads, starkly contrasted with the clean, tree lined streets with well-kept homes and gardens where the children enjoyed the playgrounds.

I could have continued travelling indefinitely, but our money was running out, and Russ was ready to return home. The simplicity in which many African's lived was attractive. Life in Australia was too complicated and too materialistic. I never tired of watching the unique wildlife, experiencing their harmony and being close to nature. I respected the people but couldn't understand the violence between tribes or the cruelty some cultures had towards each other. Africa had stolen a piece of my heart, and I hoped to return again one day.

CHAPTER TEN – LEARNING THE ROPES
Australia

I was always looking for something different to do and fun to learn, so whilst still saving for our next trip, we decided to celebrate our tenth wedding anniversary by taking sailing lessons. I'd spent much of my childhood competition swimming but only had a brief encounter with boats when I joined the Sea Rangers. They had a small yacht, rowing boat and canoe stored on the Thames at Sunbury. Most of the time I spent canoeing, but I'd sailed a couple of times. Maybe this could be a new way of travelling the world.

The course we enlisted on was generally a four session course, but we combined the first two lessons, which we took on the day of our anniversary. As suggested by our instructor, Adrian, we stopped on the way there to purchase some gloves to protect our hands from rope burns whilst working the sails. Once on board a thirty-two foot Cavalier yacht, we were given a briefing and tried to take in all the different terminology used whilst navigating Pittwater.

Adrian explained some terms to us. What I'd consider "a rope attached to a sail" could have different descriptions.

'A rope is generally called a sheet if it controls any of the sails. However, a Halyard is what the sail is attached to at the top. The left side of the boat or surroundings is called Port, and the right side Starboard. The sail at the front of the boat is called a Headsail or Jib, and the bigger sail in the centre is called a mainsail,' he advised. My head was spinning as he continued, 'To control the boat, we wrap the sheets around a winch to determine the direction of the sails.'

I thought I'd got it, but there were many more new words to come to terms with.

The beams of sunlight, bursting through the downy virgin clouds crowding the celeste sky, were reflecting off the cerulean water matching my beaming smile. The bottle green rainforest melded onto the edge of the sandy beaches, secreting homes on the hillside. Whilst approaching Lion Island, a protected national park in the middle of Broken Bay, our lesson continued.

'The direction of the sails needs to be set according to the direction of the wind,' Adrian advised as he continued to explain how to tack and jibe the boat, which enabled us to turn it in a different direction each time we got close to the shoreline. 'You need to keep a look out for other boats and those who have right of way.'

When I was on the helm, which is what they call steering, he would help me keep watch because it was quite difficult to keep ducking down to look underneath the sails whilst at the same time concentrating on the wind direction and keeping the yacht headed on course. However, when it was Russ' turn, he told him it was the responsibility of the person on the helm and although he was also watching, made Russ look for himself.

The sound of a squeaky purr rose above the noise of the lapping ocean, drawing my attention away from the helm. It was hard to believe so much noise was coming from such a small creature. Swallowed by the sea, it disappeared for less than a minute before the pearls of liquid ran off its waterproof wings as it resurfaced nearby. It was an unexpected bonus as I hadn't realized fairy penguins nested as far north as Broken Bay. Just like the ones we saw in the rain on Phillip Island, this middy sized bird captivated me.

A dark shadow tracked towards me blocking out the light. I wondered whether it was a thundercloud but only until I saw a pelican flying overhead. I shivered. Although it was supposed to be lucky if bird droppings land on you, the thought of being whitewashed wasn't a pleasant one.

It wasn't long before we spent a day out on a friends' sixty-five foot steel ketch. Graham, a shipwright by trade, had built the ketch himself, although it took many years of hard work. When the huge boat, tied to the jetty at the bottom of his garden, came into view, I knew it would take several crew to handle it. It had a deep draft, so we left early as we had to time the journey to coincide with high tide because the creek was shallow in areas, and there were sandbanks in parts.

I turned towards the screeching call in the cloudless sky. Gazing steadfastly at the majestic raptor buoyantly gliding in circles, I couldn't drag myself away as the whistling kite caught the thermals soaring higher in the air.

The time whizzed by as I helped the crew adjust the sails and take my turn on the helm. Laying on the deck, the soft breeze loosened my hair from under my cap and whipped a few strands in front of my eyes, obscuring my view. Tucking it behind my ear, I felt at peace as my body moved in unison with the rocking motion which along with the warm touch of the suns' rays, lulled me into a mellow slumber.

I woke when we stopped for lunch at Coasters Retreat, a sheltered bay cut into the national park and edged by an elongated sandy beach. Jumping overboard, to swim ashore, I considered myself safe from sharks with others surrounding me. The heat of the day made my skin tingle as the moisture was sucked from it and left only the sea salt as seasoning. The cool water soothed my tired feet whilst I paddled along the shoreline.

In the afternoon, we sailed out of the heads into what is called blue water or unsheltered sea. The wind was stronger and the waves frothy. It took all my strength to hold the yacht on course. The sails were full, bulging like a melon fermenting inside. The fabric stretched taught like the skin of a drum. I called to the others to let out the mainsail, spilling some of the air and standing the boat upright.

My cheeks ached from smiling when I disembarked, jumping lithely from the deck to the shore. I was weary but content.

The following weekend, we shared our next introductory sailing lesson with another couple. It wasn't quite as inspiring as our first lesson, mainly because the other couple on board weren't happy if the boat wasn't upright. I grinned from behind the helm as I wrestled with the wheel when the boat leaned, or as they call it, heeled over. I felt alive as the tell-tales danced in the wind which cooled my face and moved the vessel along.

I didn't want the day to end so booked on a Competent Crew Course which I looked forward to as an escape after my mundane week.

Luckily it was just Russ and me along with Adrian that weekend on a forty foot Duncanson ketch. The vessel was a little too big to solo sail, so we worked together. Without a furling headsail, we attempted to hoist the jib ourselves by hand. The wind was like a demon, taunting me as it whipped the sail from my hands time and time again whilst I tried to feed the luff into the groove of the forestay. As soon as I got the top into the channel, the wind snatched it back out again. I summoned all my patience and strength, willing it to glide along the track. After several attempts I finally got there, and Russ pulled on the halyard to hoist it further.

'Stop,' I yelled.

'What?' he called back.

'Stop. Let the tension off as my finger's caught in the shackle.' My teeth were clamped tightly together.

'I nearly hoisted you up the track with the sail.' He covered his mouth, trying to suppress his laughter.

With my bruised and swollen finger stuffed in my jacket pocket, we sailed along Pittwater towards Lion Island and this time stopped for lunch at Great Mackerel Bay. Russ was on the helm steering into the wind, so I tackled my job. I pulled out plenty of anchor chain until it had gathered in a pyramid on the deck. Then I dropped the dead weight overboard. The water was shallow and clear, so I could see the equipment had transferred perfectly to the seabed.

'Okay, can you reverse?' I called out to Russ.

I heard the change in engine tone and the shift in momentum but wondered how to tell if the anchor had dug in as the sand had been stirred up and visibility was poor. I realized I needed to get this right otherwise the boat would drift away. My stomach was doing somersaults, and my appetite had disappeared. I nibbled at an apple, fully alert, watching the coastline to see if we were moving. When the wind swung around, so did the boat, and I couldn't be sure whether we'd dragged or not. I willed Russ and Adrian to eat their lunch quickly so we could be on our way.

I let out a sigh as we prepared to depart. Once again, Russ was on the helm. He motored the boat forward into the wind, hovering over the anchor to slacken the chain, so it was easier for me to lift. I wound the chain around the winch as instructed and with the handle attached, tried to lever it back on deck. Both my hands gripped tightly and pushed in unison. The chain rattled around the winch, clattering into the well before it stopped. I didn't have enough strength to do it singlehandedly. Adrian came up the deck to help.

'I want to do it myself,' I explained.

'Try turning the winch the other way,' he instructed. 'There are two speeds and you are trying the hardest.'

I pulled off my jacket as I was sweating, the beads running down my forehead stinging my eyes. Disappointed with myself, I moved aside, and he wound it easily like a clock.

'Here try now,' he said, it's come free.

I finished the job but think I'd be better on the helm in future, and Russ could winch the anchor.

Out at Lion Island, the breeze had dropped and darkness enveloped everything. I listened to the penguins unable to see them in the water. I tried on a harness which attached me to the deck lines. It was cumbersome, making it difficult to negotiate my footing, even in calm waters, but I was only likely to wear it offshore at night time or in bad weather.

It was time to take the sails down and motor into Refuge Bay for the night. I thought it must be far easier than getting them up. As I pulled down the jib and gathered the metres of cloth in my arms, I stepped back, to stop it from dangling over the side into the water, and tripped on a deck fitting, landing heavily on my bottom just millimetres from the open hatchway. I grimaced as another bruise was added to the ones appearing all over my body.

After a delicious curry for dinner, which we ate in the salon (lounge/dining area) where a sign said only dragons and mermaids were allowed, we had a peaceful night because the yacht was hardly moving. I soon learned there's much more to sailing than just getting from one place to another when the following morning, the toilet wouldn't empty. Luckily for me, Adrian and Russ figured out coral build up had blocked the pipes, and they cleared it.

Now keen to spend as much time as I could afloat, we chartered a thirty-five foot Jarkan yacht for a weekend. Russ' friend, Stewie, joined us. He'd sailed before and knew the local waterways better than I did.

I confidently hoisted the sails on my own, without incidence. The wind wasn't strong, so we sedately sailed along Pittwater, eating lunch on the run and again spending the night in Refuge Bay, which was set into the national park off Cowen Creek. Ashore, a freshwater waterfall cascaded from above, and a steep trail from the small golden beach led to the river at the top.

Before we could tackle the trail, I first had to try out another new skill and row us all ashore in a small dinghy. Normally, I don't think I'd have any difficulty because I'd rowed small boats before but generally bigger ones than the one we had at our disposal. Both Stewie and Russ thought it'd be great fun to rock the boat from side to side, so the oars were either deep in the water or high in the air.

'You're splashing us,' Stewie shouted. He laughed ruffling his short mop of dark hair.

'What do you expect when you can't sit still?' I replied.

'But I'm wet,' he yelled noisily.

'Shsh, people are staring at us,' I said, trying to quieten him down. 'You'll dry soon enough in this heat.'

Eventually we made it ashore and climbed up the hill to discover a fantastic view of the bay. The Jarkan floated grandly amongst an array of vessels in the calm anchorage as the sun danced across the glassy surface of the sea.

Back on board, we started to get organized for dinner.

'The gas bottle's empty,' Stewie stated as he turned the knob.

'How are we going to cook dinner?' I replied.

'There's nowhere nearby to get it topped up,' Russ pointed out as he went to investigate. Luckily Stewie had been mistaken, and there was plenty of gas, so we didn't have to survive on salad alone.

After a calm and peaceful sleep in the still bay, we decided to explore more of the area. The gentle breeze wasn't enough to transport us, so Russ motored to Hallets Beach instead. I rowed us ashore easily, without the antics of the previous day and watched the kookaburras swoop and dive. They were so graceful that I followed their every move.

We motored on to Little Jerusalem Bay, and I practised my anchor technique, so we could have lunch there. This time I managed to retrieve the anchor all on my own.

Back out in Cowan Creek, we discovered the wind had picked up, and we could sail. The Jarkan was rigged for solo sailing, and I wanted to try to sail the boat on my own. Whilst heeling over, steering through a fair swell, Stewie decided he was going to jump overboard to retrieve my camera case which he'd dropped.

I attempted to recall the man overboard technique. Steering the boat around to pick him up, I accidentally jibed the sail, and it crashed over to the other side with a loud crack. I started the motor for more control and slowed the speed when I neared him in the water, so Russ could drag him back on board.

'If you do that again, I'll leave you there next time,' I told him and laughed.

Keen to do as much sailing as possible, another friend, borrowed his grandfather's Northshore 38, and we sailed around Pittwater for the weekend. Another time, we were invited on Future Shock, a corporate yacht, but unfortunately it poured with rain.

I loved sailing, so we decided to look for a yacht of our own. I couldn't believe how expensive they were. After looking at many unloved and deteriorating vessels, we finally found Wimaway. Before committing to buy her, we thought it a good idea to charter a yacht for a few days just to make sure we really did love sailing as much as we thought.

I stood on the quayside mesmerised by the turquoise waters, glistening against the silhouettes of the islands of the Whitsundays. The warmth of the sun broke through the breeze to warm my skin. The trade winds usually blew at between ten to fifteen knots at this time of year. It was a perfect day for sailing. We'd chartered a thirty-four foot Columbia yacht for five nights. A huge boat, it sat high in the water with more than ample headroom and a wide beam. I felt guilty there would only be two of us on board such a spacious craft. Below the decks, was an inviting interior with carefully laid out dining and living areas, a small practical galley (kitchen), a navigation area, the head (which is what the toilet is called) and cosy berths to sleep in.

I stored our ample provisions on board and then listened to the briefing. I was concerned about our lack of sailing experience, but the boat manager put my mind at rest, saying we were more qualified than many others. The bilge pump wasn't working, so an electrician fixed it, but even he couldn't help us locate the dip stick to check the oil in the motor.

The Manager asked, 'Do you know what tack and jibe mean?' When we gave suitable explanations, he was more than happy to hand over the vessel. He motored us out of Abel Point Marina, then departed in his dingy leaving Russ and me to hoist the sails and set course for Nara Inlet where we needed to be anchored before four o'clock.

With the sails full, wind ruffling my hair and cool mist from the light sea spray cleansing my mind, I was in tune with the environment. There weren't any other boats in close proximity, and all I could hear was the splash of waves as the bow cut through the water. We passed Pioneer Rock on our starboard side and were just coming level with North Molle Island. From the chart, I could see Nara was the first inlet on our port side, and we'd a good south to south easterly wind carrying us there. I knew there was a large reef covering most of the entrance so needed to keep to the starboard side of the port marker. My polarised sunglasses enabled me to see through the shimmering surface and hopefully spot any isolated bommies and reefs. I was also wearing a wide-brimmed hat, to shade me from the sun, and applied a second coat of sunscreen as protection from the harsh rays.

Relief flooded through me when I spotted the port marker. Taking no chances, Russ started the engine. Heading into the wind, I furled the headsail and the mainsail slid rapidly down the track, expertly collecting inside the lazy jacks. Russ steered the yacht on a wide course to keep well clear of the reef.

According to the chart, the depth of the water was seven metres. Luckily there were hardly any other boats in the anchorage, which gave us room to lay plenty of scope when we anchored. I was fairly confident the tackle would grip on the soft mud bottom because we were in an all-weather-anchorage, only exposed by a strong south-south-easterly wind. Once happy the anchor had taken, I radioed in to confirm our position for the night, just making the deadline.

We motored ashore in the dinghy and climbed up the hill to see the aboriginal rock paintings. A goanna observed us whilst we took in the picturesque view of the bay. Back on the beach, I waded into the water, which soothed my warm skin, and watched the fish shoal around my feet. I slowly breathed the briny air, squinting at the golden sun setting behind the hills whilst listening to the gentle lap of the waves on the hull. In the dusk, I smiled to myself, elated at surviving so far.

The next day, we hoisted the anchor and once passed the reef at the entrance, hoisted the sails. We glided along the bottom of Hook Island on a beam reach with the wind on the side of our sails. Tacking up the west side of Hook Island put the wind behind us, and we moved slowly because there was little breeze. Russ pointed out a humpback whale near the island.

She was magnificent. The white patches on her dark body glistened in the light, and the grooves in her throat were like a pinstripe shirt beneath a tuxedo. The bumps on the rim of her pectoral fins looked like bulging muscles. I filmed and photographed the mother with her calf from a distance because I knew not to get too close. After a while, she got curious and surfaced about twenty metres from a collision course with our bow. Russ immediately steered forty-five degrees to port, to try to avoid a head-on crash, but when he turned the wheel, she appeared right alongside the yacht with all fifty feet of barnacled head and smooth back emerging above the water. I trembled, unable to pan out enough to fit her in my viewfinder. She was quickly claimed by the vast ocean, and we started the motor to deter another visit.

'What an amazing creature,' I said to Russ.

'She came a little too close,' he replied, all the colour having drained from his face.

When we got level with Bird and Langford Islands, we dropped the sails and motored the passage between Black and Hook Islands as the mild zephyr had disappeared completely. Hayman Island was in sight, and I beamed at the turtle surfacing in the water above a reef whilst we motored round to Butterfly Bay. I couldn't tell which species of turtle it was but was honoured to see one because all seven species are on the vulnerable or endangered list. Against all odds, I hoped they would never become extinct.

Having picked up a mooring in Luncheon Bay, we snorkelled from the yacht. Peering into another world, I spotted many vibrant fish, some of which were quite big. The coral was pretty, although not very colourful. I swam to the beach, basked in the sun for a while and then snorkelled some more. We couldn't stay there so motored round to Maureen's Cove where we picked up another mooring for the night.

It wasn't a well-protected bay, and the swell moved the boat creating a rocking motion. It was a dark night, without a moon to light up the sky. It felt eerie on deck in the blackness, and although it wasn't cold, I shivered. Looking at the surface of the sea, it was so murky I couldn't see beneath it and wondered what lurked there. I sweated as my mind conjured up images of large sharks with sharp pointy teeth. It was the first mooring we'd used, opting not to anchor, and I hoped it had been kept in good condition hence would hold well. Laying on my bunk, in the end, I drifted into a fitful sleep, dreaming the boat had broken free, and we were floating out to sea to be sunk on the coral. I wasn't sure what woke me, but I checked the depth gauge as an indication we hadn't moved. I knew the tides were larger in Queensland than New South Wales, but the depth gauge had dropped dramatically. This only contributed to my mounting fear. I was being unreasonable, but wrapped in the gloom with no other boats around, I felt vulnerable.

My muscles relaxed, and my dimples appeared as dawn washed in, and the sunrise brightened the day. I let out a deep breath when I noticed we were still on our mooring, in the same spot.

'Russ, last night I checked the depth gauge, and it must be faulty as it indicated we were in shallow water,' I explained.

'It works by sending a signal that bounces back. So there could've been something big, like a shark, underneath the gauge as it appears to be reading okay now,' he replied with a straight face.

'Mmm, I wish you hadn't told me that,' I said.

Motoring out toward Border Island, the calming cool wind stroked my brow. We picked up a buoy in Caterman Bay, so we could snorkel some more. Later, we motored around the top of Border Island before hoisting the sails, which I pulled in hard because we needed to sail close to the wind between Esk Island and Tongue Point. The wind and tide were against us, and we were blown toward Dumbell Island so decided to motor instead.

In the calm waters lapping Whitehaven Beach, on Whitsunday Island, we dropped anchor. I was uncomfortable though as we were a bit too close to another yacht, so we retrieved it and moved further out. I waited to check in with Airlie Comstat, then Russ took me to the beach in the dingy. Together, we pulled it up onto the soft white sand which stretched for miles and went for a walk in search of the palm tree in our guidebook. Whilst wandering back, I noticed the tide was coming in.

'Quick, the dinghy is floating out to sea,' I shouted as I ran towards it.

'That was a close call,' Russ replied, waist-deep in water, as he grabbed it.

'I didn't relish the idea of swimming after it,' I confessed.

'Not when there might be sharks,' he teased me.

Sitting on the yacht, I listened to instrumental music accompanied by sounds of orcas, by Pacific Blue, on the CD player.

I'd just put it on when Russ spotted a whale leaping out of the water near Haslewood Island. Her water spouts appeared gradually closer along the coast line, so I turned the music off, not wanting to attract her.

The next day, we motored through Solway passage because we'd heard how rough it can get there. Once through, I tried to hoist the sails, but the halyard caught around the anchor light that didn't work.

'I'm going to have to go up the mast,' said Russ.

'You don't have a harness,' I replied candidly.

'I'll have to go up without even a bosons chair.'

'Please don't. What happens if you fall? I'll have to sail solo to get you to a hospital.'

'I'll be fine.'

Just at that moment, the line freed itself and Russ quickly hoisted the sails.

We sailed along the south end of Whitsunday Island and headed out between Pentecost and Perseverance Islands. Whilst cruising across the south end of Hamilton Island, on a port tack, we spotted whales on our port side. They reappeared later on our starboard side, close to the shore line, so we started the motor as a deterrent, not wanting another close encounter.

Later, we attached to a mooring in Happy Bay where we took the dinghy across to the resort jetty and were able to swim in the pool, walk along the gritty, coral, shell beach and have a hot shower. It was time to head back to the yacht, but the fuel line on the outboard for the dinghy had broken off. I didn't fancy swimming so waited patiently as Russ fixed it. That evening, we returned to the restaurant for dinner. I guided the dinghy by torch light, and when I shone it on the surface of the water, fish jumped out. I guessed there were predators in there, and they didn't want to be in the spotlight. I laughed when one slapped Russ in the face with its tail, on the way passed before landing in the tender.

After a delicious meal, I felt at home, snug in the womb of the hull. The moon was out, and the wind whispered to me as I fell asleep with the salty aroma cleansing my nostrils.

We had a few more beautiful days and peaceful nights before we returned to Abel Point Marina. We got some good winds and sped along, but a couple of short showers of rain chased us to shelter below decks.

After such an amazing trip, we decided to purchase Wimaway. I thought back fourteen years, to when I stood looking at the harbour in Monaco and had never thought we would have our own boat. Admittedly, it wasn't a brand new sparkling motor cruiser worth millions, but a yacht was cheaper to fuel and much more exciting to pit against the elements.

Leaving Wimaway's mooring at Castlecrag, early in the morning, I quickly discovered the engine needed a fair bit of throttle to start from cold. We motored out to spit bridge and circled until it lifted. Continuing out towards the heads, we crossed the Sydney Regatta area which became "no go" from half past eleven.

We were out past the heads, where the two and a half metre swells were tossing Wimaway from side to side like a rag doll. I took the helm whilst Russ and Stewie hoisted the sails. It was funny watching them, at the front of the boat, whilst it rolled around. The halyard which was caught around the mast steps, needed to be untangled. Russ unclipped it whilst clinging with both arms around the boom. He passed the halyard to Stewie, who freed it, and because the boat swayed violently, he dived for the boom and hugged it cheek to cheek with Russ.

Laughing heartily, I called out, 'You look hilarious.'

Once the main and headsail were up, the wind died and became fluky. The pointer on the gauge turned 360 degrees, whipping the boat from side to side. We wallowed, for a while, until we all felt queasy, then pulled in the headsail and started the engine. A short distance later, I felt a gust from the North East, so we hoisted the sails once more. As we passed Manly Beach and Reef point, which we gave a wide berth, we managed five knots, in ten knot winds, straight up the coastline.

We entered the heads at Broken Bay mid-afternoon and sailed up the bay towards Lion Island on a starboard tack. Nearing the island, there were around fifty yachts racing across the bay. They were about three deep and overlapping bow to stern, so I handed the helm to Russ to get through them.

When we got close, Russ called out, 'Pull in the main sail.'

Just at that moment, Stewie woke up. He came wandering up the deck with the beanbag in his hand and dumped it on top of the sheets I was pulling in. We tacked around and found a gap in between the yachts. By the time we got through them, they'd moved in a swarm across the bay. Along Pittwater, we came across a race between skiffs, but Russ sailed us through perfectly. When we got to Scotland Island, we were on top of another race but heading towards McCarrs Creek where we took the sails down and motored to find our mooring.

We phoned the boat yard at Castlecrag to let them know we'd arrived safely, even though we'd towed the dinghy behind us, unaware it wasn't wise to do so.

Sitting in the cockpit, I sipped on my drink, listening to the kookaburras sing as the sun disappeared behind the hills. I felt calm like the flat glassy water surrounding me. Quietly, I left the guys chatting to retreat below decks which smelt a little musty with a hint of diesel. I soon changed that when I lit the gas ring on top of the stove to heat soup for dinner. The kitchen was compact and opposite the navigation desk, which had a fridge secreted below it. I searched in the locker for the bread, which was stored with other provisions. By now the aroma of pumpkins had permeated the cabin and was wafting outside.

The plates, bowls and cups were snuggly stored in a slot behind the cooker, so they couldn't move about. I slid out three large mugs and three plates after retrieving spoons from the cutlery draw. In the cosy inlet, the boat was stable, so it was easy to pour the soup before handing it to the guys. By now they were sitting on the comfortable cushioned bench seats, which concealed the water tanks in the middle section of the boat. They set up the collapsible table. It had a bead of wood around the edges, so nothing could roll off onto the wooden floor which was varnished to a high sheen, making it slippery.

After dinner, I boiled the kettle for a hot drink and to do the washing up. The foot pump dispensed fresh water from the one hundred litre tanks into the small, but deep sink, extinguishing the steam from the boiling water. I stacked the wet crockery on the draining board. After drying it, I put each piece on the navigation desk which was yet to be used for spreading out the charts. Behind it on the wall, were switches to turn on the speed and wind gauges, both the eutectic and electric fridge elements, as well as the mast and navigation lights. The controls for the bilge pump and engine were on the other side near the kitchen.

Later that evening, after darkness had enveloped our cosy home, I curled snugly in my warm sleeping bag, encased in the v-berth, at the front of the vessel. I stared at the stars through the overhead hatch. Slightly ajar, it invited a freshening breeze to caress my face whilst the moon smiled back at me.

Dawn appeared, having risen silently with the heat of the day yet to follow. Our new home had all the essentials we could need. In a tiny compartment, a manual pump toilet, sink, showerhead and cupboard completed the ablution block. Beyond the v-berth, a cupboard door in the wall hid the anchor chain. Beneath it, housed the spare sails, heavy ropes and other sailing essentials.

The unforgiving rays from the sun, like a blow torch, had baked the varnish on the woodwork until it bubbled and peeled. The teak decks, now grey, were relinquished of any trace of nourishing oils or colour. Our new abode was in need of a little nurturing.

The bay was scenic though. Its stillness calmed my spirit. I watched the two kites, circling high above us, reflected in water which was filled with floating jellyfish. After breakfast, I helped Russ fit the bimini and cockpit covers. We now had some shade. He then installed the twenty-seven megahertz radio whilst I rowed around Wimaway taking photos. She was a splendid boat, standing tall and proud.

Once the chores were completed, we were off. It wasn't long before we passed the moorings dotted along McCarrs Creek, hoisted the sails and I took control of the helm. I sailed us out to Lion Island whilst Stewie counted the number of yachts we overtook. She wasn't a fast boat, but with the wind on our beam and the right trim, she got up and boogied with the best of them. At Coasters Retreat, I insisted Stewie jump in the water first, giving me more than a fifty-fifty chance from any shark attacks. We swam the distance to shore whilst Russ slowly rowed across. After a leisurely walk along the beach, we all got in the dinghy to go back. I dared not move, frozen to the spot because it was sitting low in the water with three of us in it.

Over the next few months, we sailed almost every weekend. There was always somewhere new to explore and something else to learn.

One day, we sailed out past Lion Island in winds gusting up to twenty-five knots, which heeled the boat over at a strange angle and caused the sea water to wash over the decks. Russ turned to look behind us and noticed our towed dinghy was half submerged. It was difficult to pull in because we were travelling quite fast, but eventually he managed to tip the majority of water out without sinking it. When we anchored at Great Mackerel Beach, he rowed me ashore. I got out of the dinghy carefully but lost my balance and fell in the water with a loud splash and much laughter.

'It's strange, there are hardly any yachts around this morning,' I pointed out to Russ.

'I guess the sailors feel safer at home as the wind is a six on the beaufort scale,' he replied.

Wimaway was heeling over, and Russ was on the helm when an extra strong gust caught us, knocking the boat almost flat. Russ suggested we reef to reduce the surface of both sails. When we were passing Coasters Retreat, we spotted Graham's ketch moored there and decided to go and say hello. I picked up a mooring reasonably easily in the strong winds, although we needed more power than usual. Russ and Stewie went over to the ketch in the dinghy first, and then Russ came back for me. The sea spray was soaking him, and when I got in the dinghy, it spun around side on to the waves. A breaker came and nearly tipped us in, and although saved from turning over, we got drenched because the dinghy was half full of water. I'd made a bailer out of an empty drink bottle that morning, and I rowed across whilst Russ frantically bailed. We got near Graham's boat, and Russ accidently let go of the bailer, throwing it overboard. Luckily Graham threw us a rope and hauled us in.

We'd hoped to sail to Lake Macquarie for Christmas, but the current and winds were against us, so we changed plans and headed towards Sydney Harbour. The fifteen to twenty knots of stiff breeze whipped up seas of one to two metres with an additional swell of one metre, which made the sea like a rollercoaster. I put my wrist bands on before I left, which dug uncomfortably between the tendons, but I was still nauseous. Stewie slept on the bean bag and stayed there the whole trip whilst Russ and I shared the sailing before safely anchoring at Stores Beach near Manly, prior to darkness descending. The great thing about both Sydney Harbour and Broken Bay is there isn't a tricky bar to cross.

Stewie left the next morning, to spend Christmas Day with his family whilst we went shopping for some seafood and then relaxed on the beach. Although we were the only boat in the bay when we arrived, by Christmas morning the bay was full. I was disgusted, watching a group of young guys on a powerboat throw their empty beer bottles onto the rocks on the beach. There was broken glass everywhere for some unsuspecting person or animal to tread on. Another boatie yelled at them, and they seemed suitably ashamed as they went ashore to collect the deadly shards.

'Sailing could be a whole new way of travelling around the world,' I suggested to Russ.

'It might be cheaper than flying to places but would take much longer,' he admitted.

'It would be like having a holiday in a caravan that could travel overseas.'

'How would you feel about competing in the Sydney to Hobart race before sailing around the world?'

'I don't know much about it, but it could be fun.'

I wanted to challenge myself to steer us all the way back to Broken Bay. So when the water was glassy smooth that morning, I helped hoist the anchor and took the helm whilst we motored out of the heads making good time. The swell and waves were quite calm when Russ hoisted the main sail without any problems, but then we noticed a yacht, about fifty metres behind us, had set off a flare to attract our attention.

We turned into the wind, dropping the sail, then motored towards the boat in distress, arriving at the same time as a motor cruiser who was in a much better position to give them a tow. Experiencing problems with their motor not starting, they were drifting onto the rocks. We stood by whilst the cruiser threw them a rope to hold them securely until the water police arrived and dragged them to safety.

Russ hoisted the sails again, and we were back on course. Wimaway sliced through the sea at four knots for most of the journey, but rounding into Broken Bay, we sped up to six knots because the wind increased. Consequently, the waves picked up and with the boat pounding against the swell, I got pretty wet. I sailed down Cowan Creek with the wind behind us and picked up a mooring in Refuge Bay. Although proud to have hand steered the whole journey, my feet were aching from standing in the cockpit for five hours.

Unfortunately I couldn't get the coast guard on the radio or mobile phone to let them know we'd arrived safely, so we decided to head back to our own mooring and contact them from there.

Once out into Cowan Creek, the winds were howling, and we pounded against three metre high waves. I couldn't believe how quickly the weather conditions had changed. The water got through the rear seal on the front hatch and soaked our bedding. Along Pittwater it was calmer, although still windy, and it was getting dark when we reached our mooring, only to find another boat on it. I was exhausted because it had been a long and tiring day, but we had to wait for the owner of the other boat to fix his broken water pump before he could relinquish our mooring.

That night we heard on the news, a severe storm had struck the annual Sydney to Hobart race. Seventy knot winds were still battering the fleet and more than half retired early from the race. Rescue aircraft along with navy vessels saved over fifty sailors. Tragically, six people perished as boats sunk. I was shocked at how destructive the weather could be and dismayed about the loss of lives. Nature shouldn't be underestimated, and I decided that I no longer wanted to compete across Bass Strait.

The calm sheltered waters at Broken Bay still appealed. We often took a couple of friends sailing with us, but on this occasion it was our neighbours. It was the second time they had been out with us, and we decided to sail around to America's Bay to have a swim. Securely moored, the others all jumped off Wimaway whilst I climbed down the rear ladder and gently lowered myself into the water. It was cool and refreshing, so we swam around for a while before deciding to get back on board.

I'd left the ladder down, but the bottom rung didn't quite reach the surface of the sea. It was like doing gymnastics when I tried to curl my knees under my chin and lift my feet high enough to reach the first step, without my head submerging under water. I could manage to get my feet touching but didn't have the strength in my arms to then hoist myself up. Everyone was laughing at me by this stage, including myself, so any strength I had left exited my body when I collapsed in hysterics.

'I can't get up the ladder,' I said, giggling.

'Get out of the way and let me have a go,' replied my neighbour. She laughed but couldn't get out either.

'You try,' she said to her husband.

Each one of us had a go, but we all failed. People, on other yachts nearby, must have enjoyed watching our antics.

Russ finally got on board and reached down. 'Give me your hand,' he ordered and hoisted them on board one at a time. However, I couldn't be hoisted, so he got back in the water and tried to push me up onto the ladder. I was still laughing too much and lost my grip, falling back down onto his head and submerging him underwater. Newspaper headlines flashed into my mind, "Man Drowned by his Wife's Bottom". When I got back on board, we made the wise decision to fit an extension to the ladder.

Our next coastal trip was to Lake Macquarie. It was our first blue water trip to the north. As usual, Stewie was with us. It was an enjoyable trip, and we sailed far offshore, so we didn't have to avoid any of the reefs along the coastline. We made good time and arrived early at the entrance to the Swansea Channel. I knew the bar could be difficult to cross, especially in bad weather, and we needed to do so on the fifth hour of a rising tide because Wimaway had a deep draft of one point eight metres. We were a bit early, but the seas were calm, so we decided to go ahead anyway. After dropping the sails and starting the motor, we headed towards the bar. The waves were behind us, pushing us along. They were so strong, it made steering the boat on course quite difficult. We crossed without incident and followed the channel markers towards the bridge where we motored around in circles waiting for it to be lifted.

Our chart was reasonably new, but unfortunately not entirely accurate. I counted each port and starboard marker as we passed them on the correct side and was looking for the next set ahead. I turned to look to my right and saw a set of green and red markers there.

'What are those markers for?' I questioned the guys. 'They must guide you into a shallow bay.'

Before they could reply, we spotted a police launch up ahead madly waving at us. Unable to hear what they were saying, we slowed the engine to listen.

'Turn around, turn around,' they shouted.
I wondered why they were yelling at us. Was it because Stewie was wearing a Borat mankini? His daft sense of humour might have actually got him into trouble.

Russ steered the boat around, and we abruptly came to a stop on the sandy bottom below. The tug chugged over and threw us a rope to tie to the front winch and gently pulled us off the sandbank. Now I understood. We should have zig zagged between those markers on our right, but the chart had showed them as being in a straight line. Lucky the launch had been there to save us.

We still had to tackle the drop off into Lake Macquarie before we were safely into deeper waters. They do dredge the channel from time to time, but it had been a while so was shallower again. We were ready for this and motored slowly, keeping an eye on the depth. It wasn't long before we were safely on the lake, tied up to the jetty outside Wangi Wangi Workers Club.

I take pleasure in sailing and although the fury of nature can be scary and unpredictable, it has my great respect. I hoped sailing would be a great way to travel and see more of the world.

CHAPTER ELEVEN – INTO THE ABYSS
Borneo, New Zealand

I felt like a rabbit caught in a spotlight. My body was frozen and my feet wouldn't move. The aggressive screaming and barking was certainly working. The hairs on the back of my neck stood upright whilst I transfixed my gaze to the closest macaque. I knew they could jump great distances, and I didn't want to be attacked by one of the large intimidating alpha males.

We were trapped, surrounded on both sides of the trail as the long tailed monkeys returned from the water. When I first spotted them, I thought they were cute, but my opinion quickly changed when they challenged me. I knew they were just protecting their group because the lookouts kept the all clear whilst the rest crossed the trail in front and behind us.

Tiny black hands tightly gripped the branches. Light grey whiskers adjourned their little pink faces as they eyed us inquisitively. Their rusty brown fur looked soft against long, ash coloured tails. Once the crab eating macaques had all passed, the forest became quiet once again. The rotting vegetation filled the air with decay whilst we continued along the sandy trail covered in dropped leaves and crisscrossed with gnarly tree roots.

Pulau Sapu was one of the islands making up the Tunku Abdul Rahman Marine Park which we'd reached in an open flimsy speedboat. Alternately, we flew through the air and crashed back down causing plumes of salty water to saturate us. It didn't take long to dry off in the humid heat.

As we entered deeper into the rainforest, the mosquitoes appeared in swarms, so we walked faster, hoping not to be too badly bitten. The higher we climbed, the more bugs buzzed in our ears, so we were pleased to finally reach the coastline.

At the main beach, we entered the warm shimmering clear sea and watched the black and yellow stripped fish, intermingled with emerald green ones, swarm around us in shoals. I tried to touch one, but they were too fast and darted away as soon as I moved my hand. The brown fish that appeared must have mistaken the air bubbles on my skin for food when they started nibbling on my arms. Unfortunately they were not so gentle with Russ, giving him quite painful bites on his shins. We always joked his legs were like chicken legs, and the fish must have mistaken them for Kentucky Fried Chicken.

Borneo was intriguing and the wildlife incredible. When we arrived in Kota Kinabalu, I wasn't yet ready to face the onslaught of touts so was happily surprised not to find any. The locals were friendly and helpful without wanting to sell me anything in return. It was a laid back atmosphere, surrounded by some stunning scenery.

We were on our way back to England. Not for good, but to be there with my sister when she got married. I couldn't miss the opportunity to stop somewhere on the way and was fascinated by both the flora and fauna in Sabah.

When we arrived at Mount Kinabalu, the bus dropped us at crossroads in the pouring rain. I wasn't prepared for the cold mountain air, dressed in a cagoule to ward off the rain, shorts, t-shirt and thongs.

The mountain itself was spectacular, although its summit was hidden by fleecy white clouds. Towering above me, rising from the flourishing green jungle, its natural craggy exterior warned of the dangers that could be lurking on its trails to the summit.

In the afternoon, although we didn't climb the mountain, we followed many meandering tracks. Silau Silau led us to the Liwagu River, which wasn't crossable due to the torrent of water gushing along its path and forced us to turn back. We walked for many hours up steep hills and explored the Bukit Buran Trail and flower gardens. The landscape varied from lush green ferns, palms and colourful orchids to mosses and lichens.

In our chalet, we spread out our clothes, in front of the heater, to dry. I moved my bed closer to the electric fire, so I could get warmer too. When I turned out the ceiling light, I felt something small and soft drop onto my face. I froze, unsure what it was until it moved, and its tiny legs tickled whilst it gently walked across my cheek. It was joined by another, and then another, until I had goose pimples all over my body. The many little moths, no longer attracted by the light, fell where I lay, snuggled in my bed below. I wasn't prepared to share my sleeping arrangements with them so decided it was better to move further from the heat, so they dropped to the floor instead.

It was time to move on to Sandakan, and I was looking forward to the rest of the trip. I loved nature, especially the creatures concealed within the vegetation, which I hoped to see.

Rays of sunlight shone through the canopy of trees as I strolled along the narrow decked pathway. I was reminded of Clyde from Clint Eastwood's movie "Every Which Way by Loose". A huge Man of the Forest was determinedly walking towards me. His long powerful arms were stretched apart with one hand either side of the rails, and his shorter legs spread wide. He was impressive with an air of grandeur. His shaggy auburn hair hung limply on his muscular body as he determinedly advanced forward.

There wasn't any way to pass him, but I wondered about the protocol. Should I stand my ground? Should I back away, or should I just run? I was sweating, not from fear, but from the humidity. A juvenile orangutan swung down from a nearby tree and sat on the handrail. That put paid to Clyde because he had to let go and passed by as if I was invisible.

Sepilok is a wonderful place where orphaned and injured orangutans are rehabilitated back to the forest. They're fed twice a day, which gave us the amazing experience of getting close to these shy endearing creatures. One held my hand astonishingly gently. I wanted to hug him but held back with awkward restraint because I wasn't supposed to touch. I watched them swing on ropes, munch on bananas, groom each other and gaze at me with their enigmatic dark eyes. Their coats were the colour of rusted metal, returned to its natural unrefined state from the moisture in the forest, just like they had been rescued and rehabilitated.

At the nursery, the young ones hung upside down from a rope strung horizontally, gripping it with their petite fingers. Their tiny faces were adorable. There's something about babies that's always cute. I watched one whose hair stood on end as if he had been electrocuted. It framed his facial features perfectly. His tiny ears protruded on each side, and his innocent eyes, lined by long eyelashes, were above little nostrils perched over his wide flexible mouth.

I found it difficult to leave, wanting to linger amongst the apes. They had touched my heart, and I wished I had more time before exploring further.

My skin itched, both from mosquito bites and the writhing mass of cockroaches and beetles crawling on the floor as my feet sank in the foul smelling guano. I hoped the poisonous millipedes would stay on the wall of the limestone caves and not join the other bugs mountaineering up my shoes. The smell was pungent from the bat and bird excrement that had built up over many years. It was compacted by the yielders of the treasured bird's nests and aerated by the many creepy crawlies living inside it. The noise of thousands of swiftlets was amplified by the caves acoustics when they fluttered above my head.

The large opening of Gomatong Caves was partly camouflaged by the greenery growing around it. My torchlight bounced off the glistening ceiling and walls. A swiftlets droppings landed on my head. I believe it's supposed to be a good omen, but I was happier just staying upright as my feet slipped around. I couldn't understand why people would want to eat soup made from bird saliva as it didn't sound appetising to me.

It was a further half an hour along a bumpy dirt road to reach the river. A boat was waiting to take us to the environmentally friendly Sukau Rainforest Lodge, to indulge in luxury we weren't accustomed to.

The wooden canoe, powered by a quiet electric motor, left tiny ripples in its wake as we explored the tranquil Kinabatangan River. I could hear the call of the playful proboscis monkeys from high in the treetops along the riverbank whilst they swung from tree to tree. These fat bellied, orange chested monkeys with a pink bulbous nose, came crashing through the branches that couldn't hold their weight. Their red faces and pendulous nose gave them a comical look like a matured alcoholic whilst they foraged for food with their webbed feet.

Below their white bottoms, on the lower limbs, pigtail macaques came down to the water to socialise. As the evening cooled, the youngsters tip toed along the boughs stretching out across the river whilst playfully swiping each other but not losing balance or falling in.

Awoken the next morning by the whooping calls of the gibbons, we trekked into the forest to look for them and spotted them agilely moving under the canopy of foliage. Something bit my ankle and was excruciatingly painful as if a needle was embedded, but whatever had done it was long gone, leaving only a painful memory behind.

On a boat ride to Oxbow Lakes, the oriental darter, a large slender bird, was easily spooked and flew up high onto a tree branch. The kingfisher was tiny in comparison but vibrant with bright multihued feathers. Three storks flew overhead whilst more proboscis monkeys charged through the foliage, and a sole juvenile orangutan was draped artistically from a branch.

Chatting to our guide, I asked about the rainforest being logged.

'Somewhere in the region of 80 percent of the forest has already been logged,' Andrew advised.

'How can that be sustainable?' I queried.

'It isn't. It takes too long to regrow.'

'This beautiful wildlife is losing its habitat too fast. How is it going to survive?'

'Things are changing, and forests have been set aside for conservation at last.'

'Hopefully, it isn't too little too late,' I murmured as moisture formed in my eyes.

In the afternoon, one of the cleaners spotted a snake in our chalet under the bed. Our guide caught it and gave it to Russ to hold. Not much fatter than a shoe lace, it had colourful yellow, black and red stripes from head to tail like a kukri snake. I stroked it gently across its shiny scales before we set it free. It slithered straight to a skink and fastened its jaws tightly around it.

I was sad to leave this picturesque area, especially the native Bornean orangutan and endemic proboscis monkeys. I hoped it could be maintained for future generations to enjoy.

Days later, I watched transfixed when having emerged from the water, she slowly made her way up the beach and excavated a pit as a nesting place. Standing behind her, we watched whilst she popped out each soft egg, containing the beginnings of a tiny green turtle. The ranger reached down to remove them, one by one, to take to the hatchery.

A short walk away at the nursery, I watched the older hatchlings materialize from the ground and collected about six hundred of them, in buckets, to return to the sea. With our torches extinguished, in the black of the night, we freed the little critters from the pail, and they scattered instinctively towards the water. I picked one up, to find its tiny flippers amazingly strong. It automatically moved them, as if swimming through the air. On the ground, it raced for the sea, heading out towards the ocean in the dark ominous water as each wave brought it back towards the shore.

The ranger advised, 'The turtles are endangered for many reasons, but humans are their biggest predator because they harvest their eggs to eat, and kill them for their meat and shells. The turtles often get caught up in fishing nets or eat plastic rubbish. Their habitat is also being built out by development.'

I vowed to myself, never to buy anything made of turtle shell and certainly not eat their eggs or flesh.

As soon as the sun rose, I walked along the beach and found a stray hatchling which must have been confused by the lights of the chalet and headed in the wrong direction. As I set it free in the sea, I wondered if it would live to return and lay its own eggs on this very beach. Mortality rates were high with only one in a thousand hatchlings reaching adulthood, so the odds were against it.

Back in Kota Kinabalu, we checked into a moderately priced hotel, for a few nights of decent sleep, before continuing on our journey. I was roused by a rustling in our waste bin where I'd discarded the remainder of the dried fish that we'd sampled in the evening. I thought the fish was dead, so what was moving? An extremely large rodent scampered across the floor. When I say large, I mean it, not like a big rat but more the size of a small joey.

'Russ, wake up. Did you see that?' I was wide awake. 'It was huge. How did it get in here?' I ranted without letting him get a word in. 'Imagine if it had run across our bed or bit our faces whilst we were sleeping.'

'Calm down, it got in through the false ceiling and is not going to hurt you. It's only looking for food.'

'I'm sure it could administer a nasty bite. I don't want to sleep here again tonight.'

'Okay, we'll talk to them at reception.'

At reception, I explained the situation and she replied, 'There wouldn't be rats in our hotel. It's clean.'

'There definitely was one in our room,' I replied, frowning because she didn't believe me.

'It came down through the ceiling,' Russ joined in.

'No, not in our hotel,' she said bluntly.

'I'd like a different room. I'm not sleeping there with it again tonight,' I whined.

'Okay. I'll move you to a different room. Here's the key to one further down the corridor.'

'Thank you so much.' I was relieved to have somewhere safe to go.

That night, I had trouble getting to sleep because I kept opening my eyes, for just one more look, to make sure the rat wasn't there. Eventually I fell into a deep sleep, only to be woken by a loud crash. Sitting bolt upright, I checked to make sure Russ was awake too. There was the rat. It must have come along through the ceiling and was visiting all the rooms on the floor.

'That's it. We're not staying one more night in this hotel,' I said firmly.

'No we're not, as we are catching our flights tomorrow to the Philippines,' he replied.

'Oh yes,' I said meekly.

I still couldn't sleep because I was unable to take my eyes off the rat, just in case it headed in my direction. In the end, when it discovered there wasn't any food, it disappeared, and I got a few more hours of sleep.

It was time to move on from this extraordinary island full of unique and special wildlife. We were at the airport before the doors were even open, but when they did, our flight number wasn't listed at the check-in desk, so we found a seat to wait patiently.

As time got closer to departure, and it still hadn't been displayed, unsure what to do, I enquired at the desk. 'Can we check-in here as our flight number isn't listed?'

'Yes, this is the place, but your flight has been overbooked, and there are fourteen passengers including you, who cannot fly,' advised the clerk.

'How can that happen? Surely on such a small plane there shouldn't be extra people booked as you have to pay whether you fly or not,' I replied as my eyebrows nearly merged into my hairline.

'The airline always overbooks.'

'This flight connects us to another flight to the UK, and I cannot miss that flight as I'm to be Matron of Honour at my sister's wedding.'

'I can't help that. You should have checked in earlier.'

I was frustrated as we'd been sitting there for ages. There was no point in getting angry. If it was already full, it was too late. I couldn't believe how stupid I'd been to just wait.

As the departure time came and went, we waited to find out which day the next available flight would be leaving. Half an hour after the flight should have departed, they rushed us across the tarmac with our backpacks, stowed them in the oversize luggage compartment and seated us in business class. We got upgraded to the only two remaining seats. I was sorry for the other dozen people unable to join the flight but smiling as we wouldn't miss our connection.

Visibility was poor when we landed in Manila. The onslaught of rain drove people inside and flooded the roads causing traffic to crawl. A taxi driver promised to take us to our hotel but then wanted us to get out early because he was worried the water had risen higher than the floor and would come into the cab. I refused to do so having no idea where the hotel was or what was lurking under the water. By the time we checked in, the deluge had stopped, and we watched children swimming in the flooded streets.

That night, we ventured out for something to eat, but when we stopped at a bar, my face turned white because we were frisked for weapons before being allowed entry. Initially, I thought it was the establishment that perhaps attracted some undesirables and decided to try somewhere else, but it was the same at the next club and the following one. Although the bouncer might stop an armament from entering the club, I didn't want a knuckle sandwich for dinner, so we decided to head back to the hotel, instead.

It felt good to be headed to England, and I was looking forward to visiting my family and friends as well as attending my sister's wedding.

Safe in England, we had a late night drive back from Stafford to Canterbury. Russ' Mum was with us, and she agreed with me when I told Russ that we would both stay alert to talk to him, during the night journey, to help keep him awake. It wasn't long before Dee dropped off to sleep in the back seat of the car, but I was pretty nauseous so managed to stay awake for a while longer. With a pounding headache, in the end, I too succumbed with my chin resting on my chest, which left Russ to battle on alone.

The next day, I was feeling even worse. Dee insisted that I see her handsome doctor, who she adored. As I'd recently been travelling through Borneo and the Philippines, he suggested I should get a stool test done and prescribed Lomotil to take in the interim. I gradually deteriorated until I had no energy because I was constantly vomiting.

When Julia arrived to join us, she suggested having a takeaway for dinner. I'd been looking forward to a plate of good old English fish and chips. The cod in Australia is just not the same. So, tears ran down my cheeks in frustration because I knew I wouldn't be able to keep it down, and it was probably not a good choice of food with an upset stomach. However, unable to resist, I carefully ate the fish inside the batter, avoiding the fatty oil, but to no avail as minutes later it had all gone down the toilet.

My dad came and collected me because I still had to purchase a dress to wear to the wedding, and I needed to recover and prepare for the special day. Unfortunately I didn't seem to be getting any better. I was losing weight and fatigued so certainly in no condition to go shopping. The doctor had told me that he would have the test results in a week's time, which was a frustratingly long wait and just days before the wedding. I visited my sister for dinner and christened her toilet like all the others.

When the week had passed, I rang the doctor in Canterbury, whose receptionist insisted I had to attend the surgery for the results. I explained that I wouldn't be travelling back to the area, so she put me through to the GP, who informed me I'd picked up giardia lamblia.

Although a nasty parasite, it was curable with medication I'd been carrying all along. If only the results had come through quicker, I could have taken the pills earlier. The trick now was to keep the tablets down. I took all three and went to bed. The next morning, I was so much better. I finally could eat without vomiting and go shopping for a special dress for the wedding.

Our time in England was over all too quickly, but I wouldn't have to wait long before meeting up with my family again.

#

I shivered as I tried to see my hand held out in front of me. The darkness was impenetrable, having swallowed everything in it. It smelt damp, and I was cold. My body stiffened whilst I listened. The eerie silence gave me a growing sense of isolation. Tentatively, I took a step forward and then another.

Abseiling had never been one of my favourite pastimes, and my feet didn't touch the sides during the 110 foot drop into an abyss. Each time I let off the brake, I'd descend with a jolt, a little further into what seemed a bottomless cavern, and the warm enticing sunshine would fade some more. I'd always been scared of heights, so why did I chose to push myself to do things I didn't really enjoy?

I was relieved when my toes touched the ground, and I could unhook myself from the line. I must be in a cave of some sort, but I couldn't tell because it was jet black. The guide had said just to walk forward, and I'd come to the flying fox. I inched ahead until I could feel the handle, which I hung on to tightly. I whizzed along the zip line, with the air whooshing past my face, until I arrived in a grotto lit up by torchlight.

When Russ joined me, we jumped off the ledge together into the ice-cold underground river. I shut my eyes and held my breath whilst water filled my ears and nostrils.

'It's freezing,' I exclaimed gasping.

'I'm glad we're wearing wetsuits,' he replied.

After wading and partly swimming upstream, we leisurely floated back down in inner tubes like a chain with each person's feet under the person in front's armpits. It was a serene experience, gliding along in the dark and looking up at the sparkling glow worms on the crystal mosaics of limestone formations whilst our talented New Zealand guide sung a melodious tune which echoed around the underground passageways.

We stopped to touch a whale tail fossil whilst we scrambled and splashed along. My chest tightened, and I wanted to scream as I crawled through some tiny tunnels and crevices. I was beginning to regret having eaten a large sandwich for lunch because I felt like Garfield squeezing through the cat flap, but flooded with water. Forward was the only option with people both in front and behind me.

I could hear the subterranean waterfall long before we reached it. The twin cascades poured down on me with a force threatening to dislodge my grip on the wet slippery rocks whilst I climbed up through a narrow vertical opening and emerged out of a small hole on the river edge. I couldn't have been happier to gaze upon the rolling grasslands above Waitomo Caves with the sun caressing my face. Now I remembered why I challenged myself as the satisfaction warmed my stiff, cold body.

I chose to visit New Zealand because my parents were travelling with us, and I thought it was a safe country to explore. I'd hired a car and pre-booked cabins in various caravan parks across the North and South Islands. The roads were easy to navigate, and there was little traffic outside the major cities. There was so much to see in this diverse country with a warm climate in the north and glaciers in the south.

As the sun rose, partly hidden by cloud, it revealed a chilly day. A fine drizzle of rain splattered down. I thought it was going to be damp if the weather didn't improve, and I wanted to stay dry. At Taupo, we all boarded a Huka Jet, on Waikato River, which carried ten passengers.

'You sit on the end where you will have a better view,' Russ insisted with a naughty grin. Pointing to a seat he explained, 'Park yourself in that row behind the driver, and I'll sit in the middle.'

The boat rode within inches of the banks of native bush, trees and cliff face. At speeds of up to eighty kilometres per hour, my vision was blurred and objects merged into one. My knuckles were chalky from tightly grasping the handrail in front of me. The 360° rapid spins were disorientating, but the view of the white water cascading down the Huka Falls was quite spectacular. However, Russ wasn't happy because I was still reasonably dry.

He complained to the driver, 'I'm not wet enough yet as I'm sitting in the middle.'

'Hold on,' he replied, making many sharp turns which made the water stand up in plumes and splash down inside the jet, drenching everyone except Russ, who was laughing gleefully. Now I understood why he chose to sit in the centre.

After being chilled on the Huka Jet, it was soothing to soak in the forty-two degree mineral pools, at De Bretts Thermal Resort, which warmed me. My muscles slowly relaxed, and the tension from the ride ebbed away. It had been an adrenalin charged day, and I relished the experience but was content just to spend time with my family.

It took me a while to understand that to get from the North Island to the South Island, we'd have to travel in a northerly direction. I couldn't see the logic until I looked at the map. The ferry departed from Wellington, which is geographically located further south than Picton, which is where we landed on the South Island. The crossing was fairly smooth, and we passed the time quickly by watching a movie in the theatre. It was only a couple more hours by road to Kaikoura.

After our trip had been cancelled the day before, I was relieved the weather had improved enough for us to head out to sea. We boarded a large motorboat and set out in search of our quarry. The skipper tuned in the radio, and I could hear there had been a sighting of a pod of five hundred dusky dolphins. I couldn't stand still as I was excited, but it quickly turned to apprehension when I heard there was an orca amongst them. I knew killer whales ate dolphins but wasn't sure if humans were on their menu too.

The diesel smell and bumpy motion of the boat made many more than myself queasy. The anxiety wasn't helping either. I tried to fix my eyes on the horizon, but it kept disappearing. The drone of the engine was dulled by the slapping of waves against the hull. Salt water stung my eyes, coating my hair and face whilst I peered out to sea.

Finally the captain shutdown the engine, and the boat monotonously rolled from side to side.

'The orca has departed,' he advised. 'Please don't touch the dolphins, but to attract them and keep their attention, it's a good idea to hum a tune, such as "Yellow Submarine". Anyone feeling seasick should get in the water first.'

I didn't need any encouragement and jumped straight into the freezing water. I fitted my snorkel mask, buried my face into the surface of the sea and looked around at a completely new world whilst humming the Beatles melody as instructed.

Almost immediately I spotted them, bluish black in colour with white bellies and flippers as well as two white stripes from their dorsal fin to their tail. One dolphin and her calf swam straight towards me, so close, I could've reached out and touched her. They were so graceful and seemed just as curious about me as I was about them. The pup came to investigate, swimming beneath me and briefly alongside. I was fascinated, and when given the opportunity to stay in the water for a second session, was overjoyed.

I barely noticed the icy water trickling down my back when the Velcro on the neck of my wetsuit came undone. My intimate encounter with the dolphins captured my undivided attention. They all swam too fast for me to keep up when they leapt out of the water, tumbling in the air. They seemed excited too and when they came close, appeared to look at me inquisitively.

Eventually I had to get back on board and after a quick hot shower was soon feeling seasick again. I sipped on a cup of hot chocolate and watched the dolphins bow ride alongside the boat, listening to their squeaks and clicks. I wondered what they were communicating to each other.

We had to move on if we were to keep up with the accommodation bookings along the way. I was sad to leave the natural wonders of this unique place and wished I could have spent longer there.

#

I trembled at the top of the mountain. My ankles were securely tied together, so I couldn't run, and only jump tiny steps. My rapid breathing seemed to hinder my hearing whilst I awaited instructions. Could I turn back and escape the situation? I told myself I must be strong and keep moving forward. I can do this, I repeated over and over in my mind.

We caught the cable car to the top of the mountain where Russ and I had our weight written on the back of our hands. I insisted on going first, in case I changed my mind and didn't have to queue for too long. The view of the sapphire blue lake, Lake Wakatipu, surrounded by mountains was stunning from four hundred metres above Queenstown.

What did I have to prove? Only days earlier, I'd abseiled 110 feet. Now I was going to jump forty-seven metres off a platform called The Ledge. I waddled to the edge of the deck like a penguin but didn't dare look down. It was so difficult to stand right on the edge with nothing to stop me falling off. Although I had turbulence in my stomach, I kept telling myself it would be fine as long as I didn't look down. Then mechanically my arms moved above my head, and without thought, I dived into the air, no longer worried about slipping or tripping.

What an amazing feeling of weightlessness. I was falling through the sky. Being head first, the tension built up blocking my nose and pressurizing my eyes. My heart was beating rapidly, and my brain wasn't quite sure what to think. I reached the bottom of the bungy cord and bounced back up. I decided that I preferred going up. Although I immediately thought, what goes up has to come down again. A few bounces later and it was all over. I let out the breath I'd been holding and gasped for oxygen. I was lowered to the floor, dangling upside down.

'I feel like a trussed up turkey,' I confessed whilst I was untied. The muscles in my legs reminded me how steep the climb was back to the top where Russ was waiting.

He questioned me, 'Did you enjoy it, because you didn't even scream?'

'I was too terrified to scream. I certainly won't be doing multiple jumps like you.'

The next morning, when I looked in the mirror, I wondered how I'd got black eyeliner under my eyebrows. I wiped them with my finger and then scrubbed at them with a wet cloth. Was I seeing things?

'Russ, I can't get these marks off above my eyes. Can you help me?' I asked.

'It's bruising where your blood vessels have burst from the pressure of the jump,' he replied.

I now have a certificate to show that I came to terms with the realities of extreme gravity. Although I'm not sure I agree when they say there is only one way down.

I smeared the salty tears across my cheek with the back of my hand, hugging my parents tightly as I said goodbye and hoped it wouldn't be long before we met up once more. New Zealand was a great country to visit. It was so versatile with much on offer, but it was warmer in Australia and time to explore more of Africa.

CHAPTER TWELVE – CLASSICAL ELEMENTS
Mauritius, Namibia, Botswana, Zimbabwe,
Zambia, South Africa, Madagascar

I'd been looking forward to returning to Africa for a long time. It was as if an invisible thread was pulling me towards it. I couldn't wait to see the lemurs in Madagascar, a tropical paradise with white sandy beaches in Mauritius, the Okanvango Delta in Botswana and the wildlife in Namibia. They were all places we hadn't been able to see on our last trip.

By the time the plane landed in Mauritius, it was dark, so we stayed near the airport, catching the bus to Port Louis the following day, passed fields of erect sugar cane undulating in the breeze. To get to Perebeyere, we had to change buses in Port Louis, which was fairly straight forward but meant a walk to the other side of the capital city which was crowded, dirty and had a thick smog hovering over it.

The bus, although belching diesel fumes, was comfortable, and it was good to get away from the bustle of the city. Sitting upstairs, I watched as marvellous beaches edging dazzling azure seas came into view. The sun lifted my spirits, and I relaxed in the laid back atmosphere.

Whilst staying in a rented two bedroom villa with a lovely view out to sea, we rescued a bird tangled upside down in the bougainvillea on our balcony. It had cotton entwined tightly around both feet. I wasn't sure whether it had caught itself or someone had done it on purpose. Russ gently held the bird whilst I unravelled and cut the cotton away. It was patient and held still and quiet, flying off as soon as it was free.

Wanting to wash some clothes, I tried to fill the laundry sink. I called out to Russ, 'I think the water's turned off. Can you check the bathroom sink?'

'It's not working either,' he replied, twiddling the taps.

'Let's go for breakfast instead,' I suggested, getting ready to leave.

Locking the front door of our second storey apartment behind us, we headed to a café where we lingered over a leisurely breakfast. On returning an hour or so later, we discovered a waterfall cascading over our balcony.

'Oops, we must have left one of the taps in the on position,' I said to Russ sheepishly.

With the water restored, it had flooded the floor of the unit. Luckily it was all tiled, so there was no damage, but it took us some time to mop up all the water.

A flight took us from Mauritius to Johannesburg and another on to Windhoek. During one flight, Russ sat next to the emergency exit and was shown how to operate it if necessary. He carefully listened to the attendant who also left him an instruction card to read.

Later, when he was snoozing, the air hostess woke him saying 'My assistant, you are not allowed to sleep because you might have to open the emergency exit.' I sincerely hoped he wouldn't need to.

From Windhoek, we drove about five hundred kilometres to Sachsenheim, only stopping to pick up some biltong on the way. The dried meat was made from many different animals, but it was unusual to see elephant and giraffe biltong on sale. It must have been for the tourists.

At the game ranch, we walked a long track to a deserted waterhole where we climbed up into a rickety old hide and sat waiting patiently. At first, there were only cattle and then slowly, as the heat of the day died down, more animals started to arrive. Guinea fowl and other birds came to drink, followed by two female kudu and a couple of dik dik with dark tufts of hair on their foreheads. The kudu were extremely wary and must have picked up on our presence because they quickly vanished. Later, when seven of them came back to drink, a smile spread across my face, and I struggled to keep silent. A warthog appeared with her baby. I don't think it matters what type of baby it is because they're all cute, but this pint sized piglet certainly fitted the bill.

The sun was just disappearing, and we packed up to leave when two Eland appeared. They were big antelope with horns that spiralled at the base. We stayed briefly to watch them drink but then had to leave because we needed to walk back to camp before the sun set. It took longer than we anticipated, and my torch broke, so we had to find our way along the last bit in the dark. All my senses were alert for the slightest sound of trouble.

The mosquitoes in our room were annoying, buzzing close to my ear. I didn't have any insect spray so decided to light a mosquito coil and stood it on a saucer on the table beside the bed. Russ was trying to shower under the tepid trickle of water emerging from the head, so I read my book whilst I waited.

He appeared from the bathroom yelling, 'Put the fire out.'

'Where?' I asked, looking around to see a blaze growing along the coil. It wasn't smouldering like it should but had a large flame which had ignited the lace doily on the table. I hastily smothered it and accessed the damage. I was apologetic when telling our hostess about it as we checked out, but she seemed unconcerned.

Etosha, meaning "Place of dry water", was quite different to most of the national parks we'd visited. It was arid, so surprising to see that many antelope, zebra and giraffe on rocky barren land. I loved the braying noise the zebra made similar to a donkey. They sounded excited and happy romping around.

A huge herd of around thirty-nine elephant chased away about fifty zebra drinking at the waterhole. It reminded me of the queuing system in Southern Europe when I patiently waited in line and other people would storm straight up to the front of the column and push in. There were many calves, and I was enthralled watching them play in the water. A little one slipped in the mud which came up to its tummy. Filling its miniature trunk with water, it sprayed the liquid over its back. Out of the water hole, it quietly trumpeted whilst it dashed around between the legs of older elephant and underneath their bellies.

The smell of faeces trampled into the mud, from hundreds of creatures going to drink, was quite pungent, but this particular day the smell in the car became overwhelming.

'What is that smell?' I asked Russ.

'What smell?' he replied with a look of innocence.

'I wish I could open the car window to get rid of the disgusting odour,' I replied, putting my hand on the handle.

'No, it wouldn't be safe to do that. Aren't you enjoying the scent from my fart?' His laugh sounded wicked.

It was unusual to see the generally elusive leopard walking through the bush, and I was excited because I'd only seen one amongst the scrub in South Africa once before. They're such majestic creatures with beautifully marked fur. The black dots and rosettes on their tawny and white coat look exquisite as well as helping them to camouflage. Cautiously, it made its way forward, fully alert and listening for danger. Spellbound, I was disappointed when it disappeared from sight.

Russ carefully drove past the two giant bull elephant that were close to the road as they can be unpredictable. We saw many large herds at different water holes. Like watching an enthralling theatre show, I was hooked, unable to take my eyes off them, observing their antics and never wanting to leave. The oldest female, the matriarch, was in charge, and the whole herd protected the young ones.

It was rewarding to see the black-faced impala which is bordering on extinction and now only found in Namibia and Angola. It pulls at my heart every time I see a creature threatened with elimination.

I found it amusing watching a springbok chase a jackal around the thicket. It had started out with the jackal chasing the springbok, but whilst they were running in a circle, the springbok ran so fast it ended up behind the jackal and thus chasing it.

We pulled into the lodge where we were to spend the night and watched birds pecking their reflection in the hubcaps on a mini. Guinea fowl were running around being chased by a dachshund puppy. Although an impressive resort, it reminded me of an English farmyard.

Back in Windhoek, I was sitting on the cool tiled floor by the toilet. I had a terrible migraine, and every time I was sick, sweat beaded on my brow as I struggled to breathe. I'd been vomiting for hours, and each time I tried to go back to bed, it would trigger the nausea and pounding pain in my head again. It didn't help that I was worried about not being in any condition to board a flight to Maun, in Botswana, the following morning.

The guesthouse owner kindly drove me to the hospital in his van. I sat in the front with a bucket, and Russ perched in the back on top of the tools. It wasn't far away, and the clinic was surprisingly modern. A kind nurse gave me an injection to stop the vomiting and relieve the pain. Tucked up in bed at our lodgings, I was asleep almost immediately and recovered enough to travel the next day.

#

I held my breath whilst I watched the solitary elephant just metres in front of me. He was magnificent, standing out clearly on a patch of parched grass scorched to straw. I knew lone rogue bulls are the most dangerous because they're outcasts and unpredictable. I was down wind and hoped the direction wouldn't change to reveal my presence. I stood perfectly still so as not to make any noise and dared not speak. He flapped his ears to cool his body, waived his trunk in the air to smell and then put it on the ground. My broad grin enticed my dimples to appear as notches in my cheeks.

Cowboy drove us to the Mokoro station from where Brendan poled us in a dugout canoe to Palm Island, through the reeds and passed delicate white water lilies with yellow centres. The Okanvango Delta was quiet with only the sounds of a few birds. Ducks swam on the glassy smooth water whilst egrets took flight when we approached them.

Brendan explained, 'The water is less than two metres deep but covers thousands of square kilometres.'

I thought that I didn't want to fall in anyway because I wouldn't be able to stand up. Although on the other hand, it was a tempting thought, having been sitting on the hard carved out bottom of the wooden vessel for too long.

When Brendan led us around the island, herds of springbok, zebra, tsessebe and wildebeest scattered when we approached too noisily. They were easy to spot in the low scrubland and fascinating to watch running but difficult to get close to. The elephant was much less skittish.

Back at the lodge, we chatted to a couple from Zimbabwe. They were looking at relocating to Botswana as they had squatters on their farm. I thought how awful it was for them to lose everything they had worked for. They told me about her cousin who runs elephant safaris at Victoria Falls. I'd always fancied travelling on an elephant through the bush, but the price to do so was beyond our budget. She gave me her relative's phone number, after explaining they were suffering from the reduction in tourism, and it was possible to ride for just a few hours. We hadn't intended going to Zimbabwe, but it was an option to consider as the border wasn't far from Kasane.

The three hundred kilometre bus journey from Maun to Nata was quite comfortable. I was looking forward to staying at a lodge in a luxury tent, and it didn't disappoint me. It was luxurious with an ensuite bathroom, fan, tea and coffee making facilities, and charming furniture. There was no power, as although the generator came on briefly during the night, it wasn't working the next morning. It didn't bother me, because we left early on a trip to Makigadikgadi Pans at seven.

The pans, which used to be salt pans, were overgrown with grass and looked like a savannah, but where it had flooded made a sixty kilometre lake. I watched springbok and jackal but only through binoculars because they were a long way off. The flamingos were just young ones that hadn't migrated so weren't pink yet. When we walked close to them, they flew around in a big circle settling back where they started. Herons, pelicans, kestrels, geese and ducks also gathered in the water.

We stood around the boot of the vehicle whilst eating sweet rusks and sipping tea. I thought it an unusual combination as I believed rusks were for babies when they were teething. We chatted to the two lads who were our driver and guide, and because they wanted to get away from their work at the hotel, they suggested we ask for them to take us to town that afternoon.

Back at the lodge, there was still no electricity, so we decided to walk the ten kilometres into town as there was nothing else to do. It was a hot and dusty two hour walk with the sun beating down on us. The anti-malaria tablets I was taking made my skin sensitive to the sun, so I'd applied plenty of block out. However, I couldn't have coated my toes well enough, and exposed in open sandals, I got large blisters on the tops of all my toes around the nails.

The children in the village called out 'Hello,' and a few held our hands whilst we walked passed the fence of branches and wire that enclosed a compound where chickens and goats roamed freely beside the round thatched rondavels. They walked a little way with us before turning back. A refreshing drink in town went down well before starting the long return journey.

I wasn't looking forward to the walk back and was pleased when part way there we were offered a lift. To finish the day on a high, the electricity had been fixed in our room, and a hot shower was perfect.

The next morning, at reception, I asked, 'Can the lads that drove us to the pans yesterday, drive us to the bus station?'

When they appeared, they were quite indignant saying, 'You walked to town yesterday, instead of asking for us, so you can walk again this morning.'

I was amazed at their response. This was the first time I'd encountered this type of behaviour in all the time we'd spent in Africa.

Unperturbed, we hitched a free ride from other travellers and then squashed into a minibus where we were unable to move for the three and a half hour journey to Kasane.

At Chobe, I was ecstatic to have a clean bathroom with hot running water and a bathtub. Our room was spacious with a large soft comfortable bed, television and native works of art. The Lodge was the height of luxury. Sliding doors opened onto a patio which led to a lush green lawn where a warthog buried his snout and vervets clambered on the building.

'We must remember to keep the door closed so the monkeys cannot get inside,' I said to Russ, remembering the ones that tried to pinch my lunch in the Masai Mara.

As we walked around the gardens, we noticed a minivan in the carpark had left their windows down and cheeky monkeys had climbed inside and helped themselves. One sat munching on the crisps it was eating from a ripped open packet, another was licking sugar emptied onto the ground and a third rifled through their belongings stacked in a trailer. There was no point in chasing them away as the damage was done, and we couldn't make the vehicle secure. However, I was sure the owners wouldn't be impressed when they returned.

Later that afternoon, perched on a bench seat in an open truck, I was exposed without walls or solid roof to protect me, but it did make game viewing much easier. A kudu with large curling horns stood just inside the entrance. White stripes lined his body below a shaggy mane. His ears were erect, listening warily, ready to flee at the slightest indication of jeopardy.

Near the Chobe River, a male lion was dragging its kill, a baby buffalo, towards the road. Two lionesses followed, keeping a watchful eye on six gorgeous little cubs which were only a few months old. Several safari trucks blocked the road, so they couldn't cross.

Our driver moved our vehicle forward slightly saying, 'I know this lion, and it's not good he is angry so best to get out of his way.'

'Good idea,' I replied thankfully, because I was vulnerable in the open truck.

I then watched, in awe, from our new position as the male charged directly at us. There was nothing between him and me except air. I prayed he wouldn't choose to attack. He dropped the buffalo and ran forward, stopping less than a metre short of the truck.

My breath quickened and heart pounded when he retreated and charged again. Headlines flashed into my mind, "Australian couple mauled by lion". My muscles relaxed when he collected the kill and found a gap to run through. I smiled, pleased the pride had escaped into the bush, because it wasn't fair to corner such a splendid family.

I was privileged to see the rare Puku, a lovable sandy brown antelope, but after spotting another six lion relaxing under a tree, wondered how they would survive.

I'd not seen red lechwe before, so it was great to spot them. These golden brown antelope had white bellies and the males were adorned with long spiral horns. The solitary male sable was also spectacular with elongated straight horns curving backwards.

As usual, the elephant were easy to spot because there were so many large herds. I sat watching them eat from the trees, tearing the leaves and branches down. A juvenile bull swiftly charged our truck. He trumpeted loudly whilst he ran towards us, ears forward and trunk high. I was spellbound but started laughing when he retreated and mock charged again and again.

'Don't worry he is practicing,' advised our driver.

I was soon distracted by a couple of duelling elephant. I hoped they wouldn't injure each other. Hippos and crocodiles lazed in the water whilst the pachyderms drank from the bank, and the sun set a deep tangerine as it disappeared into the water.

The following day, we decided to go on a fishing trip. I'd no idea how to fish but thought it might be fun from a small boat along the river towards the rapids. I think Vincent felt sorry for us when we only caught a few tiny bream, which had to be thrown back, because he took us into the game park.

'Oh my Lord,' gasped Vincent as he opened the throttle to full thrust, and the vessel slowly picked up speed. The hippopotamus was charging straight at us, and all I could think was that they're said to have caused more human deaths in Africa than any other large animal. Of course, their tiny counterparts, mosquitoes, kill many more people worldwide. We'd seen the hippo and her calf half out of the water on a mound in the river, but then Vincent shut down the throttle whilst we watched the animals around us. There were a couple of big crocodiles (one on a nest), monitor lizards, red lechwe and herds of buffalo. We slowly drifted backwards towards the cow, and before we knew it were way to close for a mum protecting her young. Good job Russ tapped Vincent on the shoulder, so he looked behind him and saw her closing in on us quickly, or we could have been another statistic.

I wished we could have spent longer at Chobe, but we'd much to see, so it was time to move on. Victoria Falls was just a short bus ride away, and although we had to go through passport control and buy a visa, the whole journey only took an hour and a half.

It didn't take me long to convince Russ that an elephant safari was an opportunity we couldn't pass up, and he was keen to go white-water rafting again.

Zimbabwe was suffering, no longer like we remembered it as the bread-basket of Africa. Its currency had devalued with inflation at 65 percent, so we got a good exchange rate for our US dollars. I still struggled to comprehend the violent invasion of white commercial farms and was glad we'd not been able to settle in Zimbabwe years earlier. Fuel shortages and power cuts were a daily problem, and we hoped we would be able to get out of country when the time came.

On the way to meet our elephant, we were driven through the bush to the camp and saw many kudu with their corkscrew horns and elegant giraffe. Russ and I were to travel on a bull called Sabu (pronounced Sah-boo). Our Induna (driver) was called Wellington. I opted to sit on the saddle between Russ and Wellington, which turned out to be the most comfortable option. My feet were vulnerable being at Sabu's most rotund point. For an hour and a quarter, I made sure he didn't trap them against the trees or drag them through camel thorn bushes, because he only allowed for his own girth. He moved through the bush, swinging his trunk, flapping his ears and swishing his tail and even pulled off branches to eat along the way. I spotted giraffe and guinea fowl roaming the surrounding scrubland.

When Russ dismounted, I asked him, 'What's the matter?'

'Sabu keeps whipping me with his tail, and I was uncomfortable enough sitting on his backbone anyway.'

'Okay, as long as you are happy to walk,' I replied from my safe vantage point.

I was Sabu's only passenger when he entered the lake. Up to his tummy in water, he sprayed a trunk full of liquid behind his ears, but I was far enough back it didn't wet me.

Back at the camp, I was able to stroke his rough hairy trunk, and he dribbled on me whilst taking food out of my hands. It was a memorable day, and once again I was wishing I could have spent more time there.

The next day, I went kayaking whilst Russ tackled the real rapids. I'd a sense of deja-vu when crossing over into Zambia and hoped this river trip would be much tamer than white-water rafting years ago. There was only one other couple and since the kayaks were tandem, our guide, Tiki, took the other older lady whilst I shared a raft with her husband. We paddled for fifteen kilometres downstream, close to the Zimbabwe side along the Zambezi National Park, looking out for wildlife. I spotted ground hornbills with their distinctive red skin on their faces and throats, noisy baboons, mighty elephant, impala and people who were fishing on the Zambian side.

Our guide advised, 'Give the hippos a wide berth, and if one overturns your kayak, swim away from it because it will see the biggest object.'

I immediately thought of the size of my bottom and realized the raft was much larger, so I should be okay.

'However, do not let go of your paddle,' he continued.

'Don't tell me, as I'll need it to smack the crocodile I've attracted on the head,' I interrupted.

'No, because it will cost you $50 if you lose it,' he said straight faced.

I laughed since I'd no intention of getting anywhere near a hippo as I was wary of them, especially after being charged by one in Botswana. Anyway, the flimsy inflatable kayak would be ineffective against a hippo's huge jaw.

Either I, or my companion for the day, didn't know the difference between right and left. When I called out instructions, we went round in circles, got stuck on the rocks, but most scarily got way too close to the hippos for our guides liking.

Consequently, I found our kayak tied to the back of Tikis, so we merely had to paddle and not steer. Unfortunately this made it rather uncomfortable when we crossed many small rapids. Although they were only about a grade one, they seemed choppy. Whilst each raft bounced over the turbulent water, they would collide together, and at one stage we almost capsized.

The pleasant afternoon passed quickly, and once back on dry land, I was taken on a game drive through the Livingstone Mosi-O-Tunya Park, in Zambia. It was delightful to see more waterbuck, impala, zebra, baboons, vervet monkeys, giraffe, water buffalo, elephant, wildebeest and warthogs. I just couldn't get enough of all the wildlife. However, it was the four white rhino that made my day. The park was home to five of them, so I was overjoyed to see the majority. It is distressing that they have been poached almost to extinction. I thought we should nurture and cherish the creatures on this planet and not greedily hunt them for profit. I waited a long time to be picked up to return to Zimbabwe because our driver had trouble getting fuel and ultimately had to buy it in Zambia.

Unfortunately the trains from Bulawayo to Gaberone were no longer running, so I tried to find out if we could catch a bus instead. Both the bus companies I knew about had ceased operation, so we were hoping to succeed elsewhere. In the end, we caught the famous, but run-down RR (Rhodesian Railways) train from Victoria Falls to Bulawayo where we hoped not to get stuck.

There were quite a few vehicles leaving Bulawayo, and we managed to find a minibus headed for Gaborone in Botswana. As usual, we were squashed in to more than the maximum capacity. It reminded me of the time when it was a fad to see how many people would fit in a mini. To make it into the Guinness Book of Records, they simply had to stay that way for five seconds and didn't have to travel for hours over pot holed and bumpy roads.

Although difficult to get to, I really wanted to see the wildlife at Mokoldi Nature Reserve because they had ten of only twenty-six white rhino in the whole of Botswana.

On arrival, a park ranger introduced me to their two male hand-reared cheetah. The next forty-five minutes flew by as I stroked them, listened to them purring and had my hand licked by their sandpaper tongues. Their coats were stunning, and they were more portly than the ones I'd seen in the wild so well fed.

They seemed to be loving the attention. When Russ stopped stroking one, the cheetah reached out to pull his hand back. Because these big cats cannot retract their claws, it accidently tore open his skin. I felt a special connection, was completely at ease and loved every minute with these gentle felines.

Throughout the rest of the park, I spotted duiker, kudu, impala, ostrich and four young elephant, one bull and three cows. Finally, I spotted two white rhino which were a mother and her eighteen month old calf. I wondered how many more generations would have the opportunity to see this species, since the fight against poachers isn't very successful, although I admire the park rangers willing to sacrifice their lives in the battle.

Back at the guesthouse, we booked a taxi to take us to the station the following day. It never arrived, maybe because it was a public holiday or as it was only four in the morning. We couldn't afford to miss the bus so started walking until we found a vehicle going in the right direction.

I was worried because we had a flight to catch, and if we missed the transport to Johannesburg, we would miss the plane to Mauritius.

Russ asked a driver sitting in a minibus, 'Where can we get a lift to the main bus station?'

'I will drive you if you pay me a taxi fare,' he replied, his eyes shining.

'Thank you. That would be great,' I intervened.

From there, we were able to squash three people onto two seats in another minibus travelling to Johannesburg. At the border, although departing Botswana was easy enough, we had to queue for over two hours to get into South Africa. It was a good opportunity though to stretch my legs and get some blood circulating again in my bottom which was numb.

Eventually the driver of the minibus chucked us out on a street in Hillbrow, late in the afternoon. I'd no idea of our location so at a phone stall nearby rang the backpacker's hostel because they had offered to collect us.

'We have arrived. Please can you come and pick us up?' I asked the receptionist.

'Sure, I will send someone to the Rotunda coach station now,' she replied.

'We're not actually at that station.'

'Well, where are you then?'

'I'm not exactly sure.'

The lady in the booth took the phone from me and explained where we were.

'You have to come and pick them up. You cannot leave them here,' she reprimanded the receptionist, who was reluctant to send anyone.

Whilst Russ produced his wallet to get the money to pay for the phone call, a guy ran up behind him and tried to snatch it out of his hand. Luckily Russ had a good hold, so the thief was unsuccessful, but he ran off after him down the street.

It must have looked quite funny when I ran after them to stop Russ. I caught up with him just as he was entering a building.

'Please stop. We have no idea where we are. It obviously isn't a good neighbourhood, and you might end up lynched by a gang in there,' I explained, gently guiding him away.

'I hadn't thought of that. I only wanted to catch the guy,' he replied, his eyebrows drawn closer together.

'What for? He didn't get your wallet, so come back to the phone stall with me.'

We waited an hour and a half for the driver to come for us and were kindly allowed to sit inside a hairdressing salon, in the meantime, to keep out of trouble.

The driver explained, 'I don't like visiting this area. When I come here, I leave all my money at home because it's extremely dangerous. I haven't brought the car here either, so we will need to walk to it as I didn't want it damaged.'

During the journey to the backpackers, he kept laughing and saying, 'You survived, you survived, that was close, you survived.'

A little later that afternoon, we went for a walk, and a dear little Jack Russell dog decided to follow us. I thought that eventually he will turn back and go home, but there was no deterring him, and he followed us for ages. As we neared the hostel once more, we ran inside and shut our room door because we didn't have the heart to shoo him away.

The hostel receptionist was surprised, querying, 'Where did that dog come from?' and then chased him out.

When we left the hostel for dinner that night, there he was, still waiting for us and followed us all the way to the restaurant.

As we went inside, the waiter told us, 'Sorry, no dogs allowed.'

'That's alright because he's not our dog,' I replied.

However, once again he waited for us on the mat outside. I felt so sorry for him that we kept some of our dinner, which we fed to him when we left, so he wouldn't follow us anymore.

#

I hadn't expected as much poverty as I saw in Antananarivo or Tana as the capital of Madagascar is called for short. Small children running around on dirty roads wearing torn clothes contrasted drastically with the upmarket French patisseries selling fancy cakes and pastries. One street vendor had just one mouldy orange for sale whilst others had stale donuts or a few vegetables. I hoped our visit would help get money to those who needed it most.

We didn't plan to stay in Tana long and headed out to Perinet where we stayed in a chalet at Andasibe which was a couple of kilometres from the park entrance. A guide took us along the Indri Circuit. After spotting a couple of varieties of chameleon, he showed us a cute family of woolly lemurs snuggled up together in a branch of a tree. Their brown grey fur looked thick whilst their amber eyes were tiny lights that stood out from their dark faces. They sported long thin tails and five tiny digits on each hand and foot.

A congress of common brown lemurs leapt through the trees using their adapted first toes to grasp the branches. They looked so cuddly with soft fur, long slender limbs and endearing faces. I was in my element.

The next morning, I could hear the loud melodious howls of the critically endangered Indri from our chalet and set out early to find them on the Circuit Grande. Although the largest of the lemurs and noisy, they were difficult to spot, sitting up high in the treetops. Their prominent black ears' were tufted like a teddy bear, and their black faces, body and hands contrasted against their white arms and legs revealing their position in the canopy of green leaves. I was reluctant to leave them but hoped to see more lemurs on the rest of our trip.

It was a long and challenging journey to Mahajanga, a crumbling dry and dusty old colonial town which would once have been magnificent. Without the murmur of a breeze, the sun roasted everything it touched, and although we were beside the water, it was hot, so we decided to catch the ferry across to a small fishing village called Katsepty. I'd read about Madame Chabaud's incredible French cooking and her seafood in particular. It had been a long time since I'd used the French that I'd learnt many years before.

The ferry was popular, crammed full with passengers, vehicles and produce. We were lucky to find a seat sheltered from the wind when the crowds descended and the noise rose to a crescendo. It was an enjoyable hours crossing in the sunshine. We alighted the ferry, onto a sandy beach which surrounded palm trees secreting thatched buildings. Walking through the village we discovered the famous restaurant.

Russ enquired at the bar, 'What is included in the set menu for lunch?'

The attendant replied in French, 'Sanglier.'

Russ explained to me, 'It's lobster for lunch, sanglier.'

'That'll be delicious,' I replied because I'd been looking forward to some seafood. 'I thought lobster was langoustine in French, but I am not entirely sure,' I pointed out, puzzled by the description.

'Never mind, it'll be delicious anyway, as Madam Chabaud is such a great cook.'

I enjoyed the light tangy crab salad we ate for entrée but would only partake in the vegetables when the wild boar was served on a huge platter with its fatty hairy skin still attached. I don't eat red meat, but Russ enjoyed it though, even if he had also been looking forward to some "fruits de mer".

#

It was mid-morning when we landed on Nosy Be, a tropical island off the Malagasy coast. Taxi drivers shouted, competing against each other to take us to Andoany, better known as Hell-ville. We had a pleasant journey to our cabin whilst listening to a running commentary. Our driver stopped to pick me some strong smelling ylang ylang flowers and point out pepper plants and coffee trees on plantations.

This small town, once a fishing village, was quite pleasant and although the mosquitoes were a nuisance, it was a good base from which to visit other islands.

A catamaran sailed us to the smaller island of Nosy Komba where we landed at the fishing village of Ampangorina and walked to visit the resident Black lemurs. I'd bought bananas with me, hoping to entice them down from the trees, but they were semi-tame and jumped onto us before we could even get the fruit from our daypack. When Russ finally held out a banana, four or five lemurs mobbed him for it, and one got so excited it peed on him.

They had such soft fur and soft fingers without claws. The males were raven black like a panther whilst the females were rusty brown with long white ear tufts similar to whiskers. Both had long fluffy tails.

They were jumping around eagerly, grunting like pigs. A female sat on my shoulder which, although lovely, gave me goose bumps. I then spotted a tiny baby clutching tightly to its mothers back and blending in so well that it was difficult to see.

An enterprising young boy, dressed only in tatty shorts, held out a large chameleon on a stick. Its vibrant turquoise tail was curled like a Catherine Wheel, and its bulbous globe eye roamed continuously as it tightly gripped the twig. I took a photo and paid the lad the tip he demanded.

Later, we motored across to Nosy Tanikely, a little isle west of Nosy Komba, where we went snorkelling in the protected marine reserve. I saw many shimmering fish in and around the coral which came close to me. There was a glittering silver one, similar to a hairtail, swimming just below the surface as well as a cuttlefish and colourful parrotfish amongst many others.

We returned to our cabin, later that afternoon, kissed by the sun and invigorated by the fresh sea-air and salty water.

The next morning, our guide, Jake, was extremely frustrating. After wading through the mangroves to our pirogue, I paddled for some time before arriving at Lokobe where the sun beat down on me during the long walk along the beach. I was glad to have taken a bottle of water with me as we set off into the forest at an extremely fast pace, and I struggled to keep up.

Jake told us in hushed tones, 'Keep quiet so you don't scare the lemurs away.'

The first one we saw was a sportive lemur. I managed to get a photo, but as soon as Russ turned on the video camera, Jake shook the tree, so it jumped away. He continued to find us lemurs and then frighten them away, all morning, which was extremely annoying.

Eventually I asked him, 'Why do you keep scaring the lemurs?'

'I want to give you an action shot,' he replied.

'Thanks for trying to be helpful, but please don't make an action shot as my photos will all be out of focus,' I explained.

We saw a conspiracy of black lemurs, a boa constrictor and two other snakes, one black speckled with yellow dots and another taupe in colour as well as a few chameleons.

'Ouch,' I exclaimed loudly when I found myself sitting on the dry leaves coating the steep slope.

'Are you okay?' asked Russ, unable to stop laughing.

'I slipped and have landed heavily on a sharp stump protruding out of the ground.'

He helped me to my feet, but we were both hot, sweaty and exhausted by the time we got back to the village, and by then I had a lovely bruise on my bottom as a souvenir.

It was early morning when we departed from our tropical paradise and caught the fast boat to mainland. I was uncomfortable when the craft slammed against the waves because my bruise got a pounding. Then I was squashed into the back of a truck with another twenty people, for the next hour, on a hard wooden bench seat. Travelling along rutted roads, which were only passable in the dry season, was almost as bad as the boat. I wasn't sure if I could endure the rest of the seven hour journey to Diego Suarez until we reached Amjanya and transferred to a minibus. The rest of the journey was more comfortable.

Parc National de Montagne D'Ambre was about thirty-five kilometres south of Diego in the mountains, so we booked on a tour. A guide was compulsory in the park and traipsed us up and down steep hills through the forests. The Grande Cascade was a vision to observe plummeting down to the chasm below. On the way back, I watched Sanford Brown lemurs. They had beautiful chestnut brown fur on their bodies which was complemented by creamy buff coloured thick whiskers lining the sides of its face. Its dazzling amber eyes shone each side of its dark chocolate brown nose as it gazed back at me.

I was tired after trekking to Antakarana Waterfall, Petite Cascade and Lac de la Coupe Verte where I was mesmerised by a small kingfisher perched on a branch protruding from the lake. Its tangerine coloured chest contrasted well with its azure wings and head. During the steep climb out of the forest, I saw another large family of Sanford Brown Lemurs and the welcoming sight of the taxi waiting to take us back to our room.

Two flights were leaving within half an hour of each other, and there was no queuing system, just bedlam. Everyone crowded the check-in desk, pushing and shoving but getting nowhere. I'd read about the airline over booking and flights being full so worried we wouldn't get on, especially after our experience in Borneo. A flight to Tana left before ours, so when Russ finally got to the counter, they wouldn't issue our boarding passes until all the people on the earlier flight had been processed.

In the end, we stood to the side, squashed against the wall by the melee and later passed our tickets from one person to another until they reached the front. We did the same with our backpacks, and it was amusing to watch as they travelled over a sea of dark heads to the counter. I wondered whether I'd ever see my belongings again, or even if my pack would be loaded on the right plane.

I'd hoped to visit the Ampijoroa Reserve because I'd have liked to see Coquerel's sifaka, but there were bushfires raging through it.

On making enquiries about a day trip, the hotel manager, who only knew a little English, advised, 'The forest is on fire, and the animals are grilled. Nothing left to see.'

I was distressed, not just for missing out but because of all the wildlife perishing. Nature could be harsh at times, and the animals had enough to compete with as their habitat dwindles.

I much prefer to see wildlife in its natural environment, but having failed to see aye ayes and fossa, we spent our last day, in Tana, at the zoo. The nocturnal aye ayes were asleep, so I couldn't see them, but the fossa was in view in its cage. An extraordinary creature, similar to a dog, but apparently related to the mongoose. Because it appeared cute and cuddly, I couldn't imagine it being one of the lemur's only predators. Its nose looked more like a canines and its reddish brown fur like a cat's coat. I was surprised to learn it spent as much time in the trees as on the ground where it would need to use its long tail for balance.

Other lemurs we saw at the zoo were the crowned lemur, red bellied lemur and a dwarf lemur with purely its bottom on show. However, it was the troop of ring-tailed lemurs that captivated me with their antics. It bought back memories of Johnny Morris' television show called Animal Magic, which I watched as a child, where his companion was Dotty a ringtail lemur.

A tiny pup clung to its mothers back, winding its long fluffy black and white ringed tail around its body. Their tiny fingers appeared to have nails on them, and although they had a thumb, it was only pseudo-opposable, which meant their hands were not perfect at grasping objects.

I was concerned for the endemic creatures in Madagascar with 80 percent of the forests already logged due to poverty and overpopulation. Various species of lemurs are said to be the animals closest to extinction. I hoped they would survive, as their spirit will stay with me forever.

Africa is somewhere I'll always want to return to. I'm drawn towards its natural wonders, which continue to surprise and amaze me. Now I am honoured to have travelled to a quarter of the countries in this unique continent. Its diverse landscapes and cultures are fascinating, but it's the wildlife that has captured my heart. I'd fulfilled my dream to explore one of the five continents I studied as a child and hoped one day to investigate the other four.

CHAPTER THIRTEEN – GIFT OF THE GAB
Estonia, Latvia, Lithuania, Southern Ireland
England, Australia

I thought I was going to get pushed back down the escalator and take everyone with me when the person in front of me stepped backwards onto my feet. I was three-quarters of the way up with a queue both in front and behind me. I could see the landing at the top, and it was full. Nobody could get off quick enough and were bumping into the crowd in front of them. I couldn't move backwards because two people were on the step below me. The person standing on my feet pushed me just as the guard hit the emergency stop button, and we came to a standstill.

I was at Heathrow, London's major airport, where I met my parents, and together we caught a small plane to Helsinki. Russ wasn't travelling with me this time. This trip to Europe was different from my travels in the eighties as I'd pre-booked our accommodation over the internet, although I still used a guidebook to work out how to get around. Internet cafes made it easy to keep in touch with friends, and my camera was now lightweight with a built-in zoom lens.

Although I'd enough annual leave to cover the six week trip, unfortunately my employer would not approve the time off. This was the first time I'd been made to decide between travel and work. Undeterred, I resigned as I was keen not only to travel but see my family in England once again.

I checked us into a hostel, but the computer was down. They gave me the key to a room on the fifth floor, but after trudging up the stairs, I couldn't open the door. I went back to reception and was told to bump it with my hip. This worked, but there were only two single beds inside. So back I went to reception again and got a key to a room on the fourth floor which, this time, had three single beds. Now we could all sleep well.

The next day, at the ferry port, I handed my passport to the officer in a booth.

'You are travelling alone and have only spent one night in Helsinki. Why are you moving on so fast? Are you carrying drugs?' he questioned me in impeccable English.

'I'm travelling with my parents, but because they have European passports and mine is Australian, we had to queue at different kiosks,' I explained. I went on to mention, 'Our holiday destination is the Baltics, but our journey there necessitated an overnight stop in Helsinki, and we don't have enough time to spend here as well.' Fortunately he stamped my passport, and I was able to join my parents on the ferry to Estonia.

At Parnu, my mum and I decided to go for a mud bath. It seemed more like an old hospital rather than a health resort. The walls were covered in brick style navy blue tiles. We paid our money to the receptionist and as instructed, followed a lady along the corridor. She looked matronly with blond plaited hair curled around her ears. She issued short sharp instructions to us. When we entered a small room, where another lady sat with a towel around her, we started to change into our swimsuits.

The lady just looked at us and said, 'No clothes.' I looked at my mum with surprise, and she wrapped her towel tightly around herself.

There were two tiled benches on each side of the room and a shower head at the back.

The matron ordered us, 'sit,' and then, 'lay,' indicating towards the tiled benches each supporting a tarpaulin full of hot mud.

I exclaimed, 'ooh,' when a bucket of piping hot mud was poured over my naked body.

She replied, 'Good, very good.'

The wax covered canvas was wrapped around me along with a blanket to keep in the heat. I could move my fingers and wriggle my toes but found I was getting extremely hot. I felt like the centre of a "pig's blanket", the sausage wrapped in bacon. We could've been in a "Carry On" movie. Both Mum and I had the giggles because we found the whole experience hilarious, especially as the tarpaulin was neatly folded back at one corner to leave my right breast exposed.

After fifteen minutes we were released, and told, 'Stand,' and then, 'Shower.' The lady washed the mud off my back and then gave me the shower head to finish cleaning myself. Mud was everywhere, under my nails and behind my ears. I hoped after all the effort the treatment was beneficial.

The next morning, I was beginning to wonder whether we were at the right bus stop and if in fact the bus to Riga stopped there. Each minute seemed such a long time whilst I peered into the distance, down the road, in the hope of seeing our transport. I couldn't even ask anyone, because I couldn't find someone that spoke English. We waited for over an hour, almost ready to give up hope when the bus arrived.

We had a comfortable trip to Latvia, watching the movie "Legally Blonde". I started to giggle when Reese Witherspoon along with the other characters spoke in Russian. Not because of the language, but as the dubbing wasn't in synch with their voices. It had English subtitles which seemed unusual as surely it should have been the other way around.

Riga was a bigger city than I'd expected. Each day, we would venture outside into the drizzling rain. It was challenging trying to find somewhere to change currency and difficult booking tickets for the bus to Vilnius.

It didn't matter how long we spent exploring, it was always still light when we returned. Although exhausted from walking all day, it was difficult to sleep since it didn't get dark until after midnight, and the sun was up again by four o'clock.

In Lithuania, it was still raining and quite chilly, so I put on my thermal vest, long pants and joggers. We all donned our raincoats and headed into town. By the time we got across the bridge, it was bucketing down, so we took shelter in a cafe. When it eased off a little, we headed towards Old Town and had the same problems as in Latvia trying to change money and book on the bus back to Estonia.

It was a long walk up Gediminas Hill to Gedimino Tower, and the cobblestone track underfoot was slippery from the downpour. The climb was invigorating, and from the top of the tower, I let the charming vista over the Old Town take me back in time. I could see the crosses in the distance, perched on top of Three Crosses Hill. My legs were wobbly, and my stomach fluttered when I looked down from the fourteenth century defence which was twenty metres tall but much further to the square below. I struggled dizzily to get back down the seventy-eight steep spiral steps, but my heart rate returned to normal whilst heading back down the hill and through the park.

Undeterred by my acrophobia, I started climbing the 227 acutely steep steps to the three crosses Triju, Kryzui and Kalnus. I tried not to peer downwards, only looking across at the Tower on the adjacent hill. It was a good way to curb the reactions my body produced.

Walking back to the hostel, I stopped to listen to the people singing. Dressed in folk costumes, with garlands of flowers in their hair, it was a celebration of Midsummer's Eve. Some people were bungy-jumping off a crane in the park. Having already jumped off The Ledge in New Zealand, I didn't feel a need to do it again.

A day trip to Trakai enabled me to sail on Lake Galve, around the spectacular Island Castle, on a twenty-five foot yacht of Swedish design with a one and a half metre draft. The skipper had sailed a different yacht in the 1998 Dubai Olympic Sailing Championships and was an experienced sailor. He started to release the ropes and push off, so I automatically helped by untying the rear ones.

He kindly let me take the rudder, so I could steer for most of the trip. I was even allowed to tack once when we needed to move the direction of sails. Due to the angle of the wind, which was quite strong at times, it caused the boat to heel over a fair way. I loved the wind on my face but worried about my dad when I looked into the dark unfathomable waters. He couldn't swim, and the lake was forty-five metres deep in some parts. I didn't fancy trying to find him if he fell overboard.

I had to sail through the reeds, close to land in one area, as the main channel was only one metre deep near the castle. I'd a fantastic time though and thought it a great way to view the fortress.

Returning from a long day out, we decided to duck into McDonalds, near the train station, just so we could use their clean toilet. Unfortunately they were locked and a token needed to gain entry.

On enquiring at the cash register, the attendant advised, 'You must purchase something before I may give you a token.' Not sure I could wait until we got back to the hostel, I purchased a small portion of chips to share. However, I didn't end up using the token, because when we went to use it, the person exiting held the door open for us to enter.

#

Back in England, we left early to catch the ferry across the Irish Sea. We were making good time until we got to junction eleven on the M4 motorway. An accident ahead caused the traffic to come to a standstill, and six police cars, five fire engines and an ambulance attended. A lorry had shed its load, but two hours later they cleared one lane, and we continued on our way. The ferry was late departing, which was handy because of our tardiness. The crossing was rough, and whilst I laid in the top bunk, I'd fly off it, just touching the ceiling before bumping back down. Strangely, perhaps because it was so stormy, I wasn't seasick, although I had great difficulty getting any sleep.

It was raining when we arrived at Blarney Castle. My dad stayed at the bottom whilst Mum and I climbed the 107 steps to the top. I coped quite well climbing the stairs but started to get wobbly legs walking along the battlements because I could see down.

I was here to get the "gift of the gab" as it was called. Millions of pilgrims had gone before me, but I was still terrified. I'd watched the Sherlock Holmes mystery where a man fell to his death trying to do just that. I had collywobbles when I leant backwards whilst vainly clinging to an iron railing, so I could kiss the Blarney Stone which was set on the outside of the castle under the parapet. I was impressed with my own courage, but my legs were like jelly all the way back down the steps to terra firma.

Around Southern Ireland, we often stopped to look at ancient stones, some dating back as far as 1100BC. I found it amazing they were still standing today. I read about the Kilnaurane Pillar Stone in a guidebook, and we decided to trek out across the farmer's field to have a close look at it. The monolith had some rare ninth-century depictions carved into the stone. I climbed into the fenced-off area and was engrossed studying the pictures and talking to my dad for some time. When we turned to leave, I discovered we were the centre of attention and completely surrounded by cows.

'We are under scrutiny,' I said to Dad. My eyes were wide.

'Maybe they think we have food,' he replied, shuffling his feet.

'I hope they don't bite as they're blocking our exit. It's late in the afternoon, and we can't stay here forever,' I said, stating the obvious.

'Quick follow me,' I called as I plunged over the enclosure hoping there weren't any bulls in the field.

'It's a fast pace you have set,' puffed Dad as we half walked and half ran back to the car.

It was fabulous to spend time with my parents and sister, although I miss them more and more the longer we are apart. I certainly had found the opportunity to discover much of Europe, visiting almost half of the countries which were rich in history, diverse in culture and gastronomy. Lots of nationalities spoke English, which made travelling easier with such an abundance of difference dialects and languages. I'd been lucky to live there for many years and satisfied to have experienced another continent I learned about at school, but Australia was calling me back to the sunshine and my husband.

#

Something brushed against my ankle, then grabbed it pulling my leg under the water. My breathing quickened, and I held back a scream whilst trying to keep my head up.

When our guide described the different sharks we might encounter, I was worried because they're not my favourite fish. Although it was extremely unlikely a timid reef shark would attack a snorkeler, there was always a first time. I thought that I'd prefer not to see one.

I awkwardly twisted around for a better view, just as Russ surfaced from under the water, laughing when he let go of my leg.

It had seemed like a long journey out to Hastings Reef, off the coast of Cairns, although it had only taken two and a half hours. The swell and smell of diesel made my stomach churn. I'd put on my pressure wrist bands, but they didn't repel the nausea. There was a light drizzle of rain and far off sound of thunder whilst the boat rocked from side to side.

I was keen to get in the water, to dispel the horrible queasy feeling but then reluctant to do so on hearing about the sharks. All I could think about was the movie Jaws. We were only on the outer edge of the reef because the steep waves made it unsafe to swim over the top in case we were pounded against the coral. Once in the water, I initially kept checking behind me because one of those sharks might have me in its sights, but I soon relaxed and went with waves.

The water was murky, stirred up by the storm, so it was difficult to see too far. I loved having the schools of fish swirl around me as I floated motionless on top of the ocean. The parrot fish were vibrant, standing out against the reef, turquoise blue with milky tangerine markings. Ebony and ivory striped fish grouped together underneath the bottom of the boat.

The buffet lunch helped to settle my stomach, and I was feeling much more my usual self when I entered the water off Michaelmas Cay. The reef itself was colourful, and I enjoyed watching the pretty fish dart in and out of the coral and around the clams. Parrot fish were vivid. One was a bluey green with lilac and indigo markings.

As I pulled my head from the water, Russ called to me from the boat, 'Quickly get out the water. There is a fin coming towards you.'

I panicked and doing the worse thing possible started splashing around as I frantically kicked my legs, trying to propel myself towards the ladder. I was sure the shark could smell my fear and would zone in on it. I dragged myself up the ladder and looked around for the shark fin. I couldn't see one. I turned to Russ, who was laughing.

'See that person over there in the water?' he said, showing no emotion.

'Yes,' I replied dubiously.

'She's from Finland and was swimming towards you just now.'

'You think you are so funny.' I couldn't help but laugh.

I was enjoying the adventure sports in Cairns. At least that is what I called them, but maybe they are just games.

Ernest Hemmingway is quoted as saying, "There are only three sports, bullfighting, motor-racing and mountaineering: all the rest are merely games". I wondered what he would make of bull-running, drag-racing and the luge today.

I was lucky to have experienced many games during my travels, including whitewater rafting, sky-diving, bungy-jumping, para-gliding, skiing, sledding, horse and motorbike riding, mountain climbing, wind-surfing, kayaking and black water rafting. Some I was hopeless at, and some I enjoyed more than others. I thought it might be fun to go whitewater rafting again so booked on a tour.

I knew the Tully River wouldn't be quite as ferocious as the Zambezi but was surprised by the experience. It's said to be the best rafting across Australia and New Zealand, so I thought it would be wild, although the African river is said to be the best in the world with its fierce current.

On the Tully, the rapids were classed as grade three and four with many of them in quick succession, whereas many on the Zambezi were a grade five and classified as extremely difficult, long and violent.

I was apprehensive, remembering the bruised muscles I'd sustained from a raft flip years earlier, and the moments of near suffocation from being submerged for so long but realized this might be a tamer journey. The scenery was striking as it traversed through ancient rainforest, and although there were crocodiles in the river, I never saw any.

As before, we geared up with crash hats and life jackets, but this time were given our own paddles. I found this perplexing as I wondered how I could hang on and paddle at the same time. Ready for the journey through forty-four rapids, I climbed into the inflatable.

It turned out to be a pleasant leisurely trip, with very little white-water, so no raft flips or even a submersion. I enjoyed swimming in the river and being carried along in my life jacket, but it really was only a strong current, not an aerated washing machine. Whilst in the vessel, the wettest I got was from other passengers flicking water at me with their paddles or when the guide held the inflatable underneath a small waterfall, just to get us wet. To try to spice up the trip, we even went over rapids backwards in the hope we would fall out but to no avail. However, the day was enjoyable and bought home the ferocity of the Zambezi.

Early another morning, when the wind wasn't right at the first site, we drove on to the next. Russ helped roll out and inflate the balloon. It was cumbersome to climb into the basket which had three compartments. There were four of us in each with the pilot centred in the middle. He controlled the hot air which regulated the height of balloon, and the hotter it was, the higher we rose. Unfortunately by the time we took off, it was already daylight, so we missed the sunrise.

I had collywobbles when I peered over the side of the basket at the flat landscape below with rolling hills in the distance. A kangaroo hopped along as I clutched the edge of the basket whilst standing as far back as I could. I was never good at heights, especially in an unstable carrier hanging by rope. I tried to look at the view in the distance rather than directly down, because it was too late now to get off. It was hot and noisy when the burner heated the air to raise the balloon, but the wind was gentle when we reached two thousand feet. From above the clouds, we floated gently across the Atherton Tablelands and Mareeba Town at ten knots. I took deep breaths to slow my pulse and concentrated on the moment.

Our pilot informed us, 'I have the most balloon flying hours in the world, so you are quite safe with me.'

He was right because he landed easily at two knots and missed the power lines. We all helped roll up the balloon and pack it away. Another balloon wasn't so lucky when it landed on its side in the forest, making it difficult to get the gear out.

I enjoyed our adventures in Cairns and thought about how much Australia had to offer. Although the whitewater rafting might not be the most adventurous, it was safe along with the ballooning. The Great Barrier Reef is the largest in the world. Although it is a unique and special ecosystem, it is under extreme threat with a huge area of it already dead. At risk from rising water temperatures causing bleaching, more acidic water caused by too much carbon dioxide, oil spills, over fishing, shipping accidents and too much sediment, its survival is being challenged. Storms may cause damage, although they can also cool the higher water temperatures said to be caused by global warming. A solution was found to control the crown of thorns starfish, by destroying it with an injection, so I hope that solutions can be found to overcome the other threats, as without the coral, a ripple effect will follow for all the fish and organisms that live within it.

Rather than meet somewhere else around the globe, my parents decided to visit us in Australia this time. Having stayed with us before, I wanted to take them somewhere different. Knowing they weren't fans of the heat, I thought Tasmania would make a good destination in summer.

Whilst there, we visited the Tasmanian Devil Park, in Taranna, because I wanted to contribute to their efforts to save the largest remaining meat-eating marsupial. It was a cold day with the chill sinking through my clothes. There were a couple of devils running around a pen waiting to be fed, but the keeper headed for a newer enclosure housing another three. They seemed to instinctively know there was food around, or perhaps they could smell it in the air. He made them jump up for their first piece of meat, which they clasped in their powerful jaws, and then he threw the other two pieces into the enclosure. I was surprised at how high they could jump on their stumpy little legs and at how long they took to find the rest of the meat which they fought over.

It was distressing to learn many wild Tasmanian devils were suffering from fatal facial tumours, characterized by cancers around the mouth and head, causing the population in the wild to shrink dramatically. I was delighted to learn the Tasmanian Devil Park along with many other organizations was breeding healthy devils in captivity, so they could eventually be released into the wild and not become extinct like the Tasmanian tiger.

When we first arrived at the caravan park, Moggy, which is what we named the cute tabby feline, was waiting to be invited inside our cabin. The cabin was compact with just one bathroom, open plan fully equipped kitchen/living area and two sleeping areas. That night, we slept in a fridge because even two blankets on our bed didn't warm us. I tried not to think Moggy might be sleeping outside and took comfort believing she must have a home to return to. However, the next morning, she was back on the doorstep, so I gave her a saucer of milk for breakfast which she lapped enthusiastically.

Every day, when we returned from sightseeing, Moggy would be there on the doormat, waiting for us to return. If we had a long day, she would be quite indignant that we were back so late and meow loudly to complain about where we'd been. I fed her some leftover chicken, and then she settled on our bed for the night. I didn't have the heart to put her outside, so decided she could stay. She woke me at six, in the morning, to be fed. Once she had filled up on chicken and milk, she was happy to sit outside on the doorstep.

It dawned a glorious day with the sun's rays roasting the atmosphere to thirty-three degrees centigrade. It was chilly on the peak of Mount Wellington, from the strong wind, so I was happy to descend and head south.

I'd read there was a platypus platform in Geeveston but didn't have any expectations about spotting any, so I was excited when Mum pointed one out from the footbridge. I quickly spotted a second and watched enthralled whilst they swam backwards and forwards searching the water for food. It was easy to see their dark duck-like bill and deep brown fur as they moved, leaving a bow wave on the surface and then disappearing underwater for a while, trailing bubbles. I could understand why the European naturalists originally thought this duckbilled monotreme was a fake, as it looks like it is a combination of many creatures in one.

Moggy spent another night on our bed and, in the morning, finished off the last of the chicken and milk. It was hard to leave her because she had found a special place in my heart.

When checking out, I asked the receptionist, 'Who does she belong to?' It turned out that she was a stray. I was upset to think she might be back out in the cold that night but hoped the new guests would open their hearts and cabin to her as we had.

We travelled on to Morton Island, in Queensland, leaving Moggy behind. At Tangalooma, as dusk neared, lightening lit up the dark skies and thunder rolled ominously around us. The sparkling clear blue water of the Coral Sea now looked angry, black and uninviting.

Mum and Dad went to change into shorts we'd lent them because they didn't possess any of their own. They had tried them on the night before, so Mum was surprised the shorts she wore fell straight to the ground. She put a few safety pins in them to hold them up. However, my dad found his shorts much tighter than he remembered and struggled to get the button done up at his waist.

When they showed them to me, I couldn't help but laugh, explaining, 'Dad you are wearing my shorts, and Mum has Russ' on by mistake.'

We all watched the dolphins from the jetty whilst they slapped their tails as a sign of anger, did spy hops (poking their head out of the water), breached, surfed and swam upside down to see the fish they were catching. There was a shovelnose stringray in the shallows too. One of the dolphins had a baby, and before it got dark, I saw her playing when she circled under the pier.

The Marine Biologist instructed us to form a line on the sandy beach and wash our hands with a special solution, so we wouldn't pass on any germs. I took a fish from the bucket and followed him into the water. By now the sun had set, and it was completely black, except when the lightening set fire to the sky. Heavy droplets of water struck my face as I waded in up to my waist with the cold water swirling around me and tugging at my clothes. The white caps crashed into me, and it wasn't long before I was soaked up to my shoulders and shivering. Underwater, the dolphin gently took the fish from my hand before swimming away and coming back for more. I was fortunate to watch such a powerful creature so tender and agile.

As we rushed towards the last ferry, not wanting to miss it, we were told it had been evacuated due to the lightening. It was another half an hour before we were allowed to board. If I thought the trip there had been uncomfortable, the trip back was one of my worst nightmares. It was so dark that there was no sign of a horizon to fix on. Inside the catamaran, it was warm and muggy as the rain lashed at the vessel. At times, I found myself flying above my seat and banging back down the other side of the wave whilst water washed over the windows. It was like being on a rollercoaster ride but became more unpleasant when passengers vomited. I held scented wipes to my nose to try to ward off the unpleasant smell and nausea. It seemed much longer than the hour and a quarter it took to get to the wharf, and I was glad I hadn't eaten any dinner.

Australia has wonderful wildlife which needs balancing as much as the endangered animals in Africa and Asia. It has its own unique species that should be protected for generations to continue to enjoy. I missed my parents now they had returned to England but was looking forward to seeing more of this land down under.

The grid hung out over the water, and I could see between the squares that it was a long drop down. That old sensation returned when my legs became shaky and my heart started to pound. All I could hear was my thumping heart as the other sounds around me tuned out. Don't look down, I told myself and wrenched my eyes from the sea to look in front of me. The wind was strong, battering against my overalls and moulding them against my skin. I can do this, I know I can, I repeated over and over inside my head whilst I firmly gripped the handrail. I knew the harness wouldn't let me fall, but it was that same phobia I couldn't control.

It was our wedding anniversary, so we wanted to do something special to celebrate. We'd spent some time at the base being briefed and fitted out with overalls, harnesses and a helmet. I was disappointed at not being able to take my camera but understood how much damage it could do if I dropped it on traffic or pedestrians below.

As I stepped off the grid, back onto solid bridge, I could again hear the voice of our guide explaining the history of Sydney Harbour Bridge, and my heart slowed back to normal. I climbed vertical steps, holding each side and moving each foot, rung by rung, to get up above the traffic driving below and then continued up more stairs on a gradual slope. I relished the amazing sights around me, but didn't dare look down. At the summit, I was proud to have reached 134 metres above sea level. The Opera House looked small in the distance, and I was satisfied to be heading back to ground level.

Each year, I tried to find something different to do to celebrate our wedding anniversary, something to challenge us. We'd tried sailing and bridge climbing. I wasn't keen to try some of the newer extreme sports like high lining as I knew I wouldn't be able to keep balance on the tightrope with my wobbly legs. Base-jumping wasn't a consideration for me, either. Instead, we took a trip in a seaplane, over Forster, thinking perhaps this could be a different mode of transport for us.

The plane was parked at the end of a wooden jetty, so it was easy to climb on board. It wasn't long, and we were racing across the water before the nose lifted, and we were flying higher and higher into the sky. Fitted out with headsets, we could hear the pilot's commentary whilst we buzzed along. The view was quite spectacular, and I was reasonably comfortable because the windows were tiny, so I didn't feel as if I might fall out. I had an eagle's eye view over the lakes whilst we travelled further south and along the coastline where we could see dolphins riding the waves close to the beach.

Another time, we celebrated with a helicopter ride. My heart beat loudly, and I was pleased to be sitting because my legs had lost their strength. I shut my eyes as I didn't want to look down. There was a great view below, but I preferred to look out the window of the helicopter rather than through the glass floor at the front.

It was more like going up in an elevator, than a plane taking off, because the gravity pulled downwards, instead of pushing me back in my seat. It was good to have headphones as the noise from the rotor blades was loud when they spun round and round.

I was floating in the sky, although there was a slight turbulence buffeting the aircraft. It seemed to manoeuvre easily, but I squeezed Russ' hand tightly as the aircraft tilted when the pilot changed direction, and I was glad the doors were safely shut.

The view of Newcastle's coastline was quite dramatic. Deep blue seas washed in on a long stretch of sandy beach. The houses and roads seemed like a model village. The cars buzzed similar to flies zooming along the streets.

As we dropped from the sky, the pilot gently landed the helicopter on the pad.

I guess every fear can't be cured, but I could try to conquer my acrophobia time and time again. I was falling in love with Australia, its picturesque scenery, fabulous wildlife and never-ending "games" or adventure options as I prefer to call them. It was great to see some of our country, but I still wanted to see more of Asia and Oceania, and at some stage, I needed to visit that fifth continent I'd learned about in geography classes.

CHAPTER FOURTEEN – POINT OF NO RETURN
Sri Lanka, Vietnam, Cambodia, England

Russ and I were staying with friends in Queensland, on Boxing Day 2004, when we heard the terrible news. We were horrified at the devastation and loss of life when a huge tsunami hit southern Asia. A massive earthquake in the Indian Ocean generated huge waves, killing thousands of people without warning. Nature could be cruel.

We had flights booked to meet my parents in Sri Lanka, in a few weeks' time. There was no way I'd ever put them in any danger, so we discussed the matter and monitored the health situation because diseases like malaria, typhoid and cholera were likely to spread easily. I also didn't want to be a burden on Sri-Lanka whilst they were recovering. When the tourist minister called for visitors to return, I wanted to help build the economy so definitely didn't want to cancel our trip. The World Health Organization confirmed there weren't any outbreaks of disease, and my parents still wanted to go.

For a change, I'd booked on a tour through a Sri-Lankan company, for part of our trip, as far as Delhousie. I worked out the cost for the four of us to do everything backpacking on our own, and it was about the same price. I tend to avoid tours, but this one was just for the four of us, so I decided it was worth trying.

We started out from Negombo, thirty-seven kilometres north of the capital city Colombo, and toured the ancient cities, none of which had been affected by the tsunami. Our driver, Kasun, was extremely helpful and informative. There was so much to discover in Aukana, Anuradhapura and Minhintale, so we crammed in as much as we could see, which made long interesting days. At Minhintale, a couple of touts latched onto us and followed us, continually trying to give us advice to earn a tip, but we didn't need a guide, as we had Kasun.

Russ and I climbed Aradhana Gala (Meditation Rock), up a steep path and over sun-heated rock leading to a point where there were great views. I sat down whilst looking across to Mahaseya Dagoba on an adjacent hill and a statue of a white Buddha on another. It was serene and quiet with nobody else around, so I took a moment to just absorb the atmosphere.

When I stood up and looked back the way we'd climbed, the adrenalin kicked in causing my legs to wobble and my heart to race. I was terrified of tackling the steep ascent so took it step by step, hand over hand whilst I clung to the handrail petrified I'd fall. I was relieved to reach the bottom but disappointed I'd such a strong reaction. I needed to get my phobia under control.

There was certainly more chances to challenge myself. At Sigiriya, it was quite a climb to the summit 660 feet up.

Our guide suggested, 'Slowly, slowly catchy monkey.'

I laughed because I hadn't heard that expression for a long time, and it conjured up images of someone stalking a monkey.

We entered the complex through Kasyapa's beautiful water gardens, then started to climb up a pathway, clinging to the sheer side of the rock, to the Mirror Graffiti wall. Protected on the outside by a five metre high wall, I was reasonably comfortable until I came to a modem spiral stairway affixed to the cliff face. I dislike spiral steps as there is never enough room to place my whole foot on each step, and it also enables me to look down. It was a long drop, so I hurried on before my legs became jelly and held my head high. I climbed through the Lion's Paws, up the grooves cut into the rock face and then ascended the metal steps. There was plenty of room at the top of the rock, which meant I could keep far away from the edges and absorb the scenic panorama.

Another day, I visited Pinnawela Elephant Orphanage and watched the elephant bathe in the river. One of the calves was only one month old, and its mother stood between us as protection. On the endangered list, these impressive creatures were fighting extinction. Human over-population was diminishing their habitat. I struggled because I love all animals and want them to be safe and have a good life, but I could understand people needed to farm the land to survive as well.

These Asian elephant were quite different to the ones I'd seen in Africa. Smaller in height with slighter ears and a different shaped head, they had quite a unique look.

I was grateful the orphanage saved orphaned and abandoned wild elephant as well as setting up a breeding centre to ensure there were generations to come.

A keeper fed one of the babies a bottle of milk, but it wanted more and when it wasn't forthcoming, bit the keeper hard making him angry. It reminded me of the saying "Don't bite the hand that feeds you". I thought, someone needs to explain that to the calf, because elephant never forget.

The drive to Nuwara Eliya, known as Little England, was a windy mountain drive through hillsides of charming waterfalls and tea bushes where workers were picking. Roadside stalls overflowed with all manner of vegetables grown in abundance. The area was the favourite hill station of the British, who kitted it out like home. The old pink-brick post office, the stately home type Hill Club and Old English style phone and post boxes certainly made it seem like Britain. On the way back to the hotel, a crow caught me by surprise when it bombed my head the same way the magpies do at home.

The air was cool and fresh during the day but freezing at night, so we wore our warm clothes to bed.

'It's so cold that my feet are ice blocks,' I moaned to Russ as I shivered.

'I'm not warm either. I have goosebumps,' he consoled me before getting up and raiding the laundry cupboard for extra blankets.

'Thanks for the extra cover. If I can warm up, I might be able to get to sleep.'

The day after our tour ended, Russ and I set off on foot with a breakfast of cold toasted sandwiches in our daypack and followed the signs towards the 7,362 foot high mountain. My parents were not coming with us. They opted to explore the local town of Delhousie instead.

The morning was cool with an eerie mist suspended in the air. I'd been looking forward to this moment for some time. I wanted to challenge myself and prove I could do it.

Many stalls lined the villages, mainly selling lollies but also selling ornaments and souvenirs. It reminded me of a funfair with prizes on display. We wandered through a village, arriving at the entrance archway from where it was a seven kilometre climb to the summit. The gentle slope was easy on the other side of the archway but led to a junction where a flight of steep steps headed in one direction or a path to continue around the hill in the other.

I didn't know which way to go, so we started up the flight of steep steps, at the top of which I saw a temple, but there didn't appear to be any way around it. Assuming we were going the wrong way, we turned to head back, but a villager stopped us pointing out the right direction. We ascended the temple steps and discovered another pathway to the left, which we followed. However, further along was another fork in the road. Signposted, one went to the Japanese-Sri Lanka Friendship Dagoba and the other guided us up the mountainside.

The stony top of Adams Peak broke the surface of the thick lush emerald forest which concealed the trail. My sights were fixed on the tip.

About an hour and a half after we left, I was running out of energy. The steps where tall, and I was struggling just to put one foot in front of the other. My body was devoid of energy and muscles refusing to lift me upwards. After all the training I'd done, I was already thinking that I wouldn't to make it to the top.

I'd been training for ages, climbing up and down the dozen steps at the back of our house leading down to the garden. Pale and sweaty, I'd collapse in a heap twice a week after running up and down three hundred times.

Why couldn't I do this? I should be able to. Why was my body refusing to co-operate? How could I be exhausted already? I needed to make it to the top. I'd come all this way and now barely started. Disappointed, I thought what a failure I was.

Mount Kosciuszko, the highest mountain in Australia, stood at 7,309 feet, only fifty-three feet shorter than Adams Peak. Although it was a much gentler climb from Charlotte Pass until closer to the summit, it wasn't that many years ago that I'd reached the top fairly easily.

We stopped, sitting on the edge of the stairway, so I could catch my breath and eat the toasted sandwiches in the hope they would fuel my body. Continuing up the uneven steps, I took them one at a time. Slowly, but methodically, I moved forward and upwards until we reached one of the tea houses. Inside, I indulged in a bottle of sugary coca cola and sucked on a polo mint. Surprisingly, this refreshed me completely, my energy not only returned, but I buzzed, eager to get going again. Almost bounding up the stairs, we continued to climb the five thousand steps. Gradually, the tea houses thinned out, and the stairs got steeper and steeper. People were coming back down, having already watched the sunrise from the peak, but I couldn't see anyone else going up. It was pilgrimage season so supposedly the busiest time of year, but I found it extremely quiet, probably because of the tsunami.

We climbed on for a total of four hours, but on reaching the pinnacle, realization hit me. I needed to enter the temple so removed my shoes, but I hadn't brought a sarong to cover my legs. Dressed in shorts and t-shirt, I panicked because it wasn't like I could nip back down and get one. I was stupid to have not thought about bringing it along.

I so wanted to ring the bell and write my name in the book, at the summit, but now I doubted myself once more as I believed I'd be turned away.

A monk with a shaved head, wearing orange robes and slip on sandals, appeared and beckoned us inside where I saw the footprint of Adam, Lord Shiva or Gautama Buddha, whichever you believe it to be. I rang the bell that pilgrims are entitled to ring as many times as they have successfully ascended the mountain. Unfortunately there wasn't a book to write in, but I guess it would have to be huge if everyone that visited signed it. I wasn't disappointed though, since the view from the top was splendid. Standing higher than the cumulus clouds, I could see Colombo sixty-five kilometres away. The tranquillity was calming. I breathed slowly and deeply, savouring the atmosphere.

It was a long walk back down, and I only stopped briefly at one tea-house, to have a soft drink. Amazingly it only took two hours to descend at a constant pace. By the time I reached the bottom, my legs were faltering. Not from my fear of heights this time, but because they were worn out. I expected to be sore the next morning, however, the Siddhalepa Ayurveda Balm I'd rubbed into my calves, back at the hotel, had done its job, and I could've tackled the mountain again.

 A minibus took the four of us to Tissamaharama, the following day, so I'd plenty of rest during the journey and a good night's sleep at the hotel.

 It was dark when we arrived at the gates of Yala National Park where a compulsory tracker clambered on board our open top fifties jeep. The park was a mixture of open parkland and dense jungle.

 We drove along the ocean side of the park. I could see much damage to the vegetation where the tsunami had hit. The first animal I spotted was water buffalo, but it was the elusive leopard I wanted to see most. There were approximately thirteen in the area, but they're difficult to spot because they spend most of the day sleeping.

 Amongst the scrub, I started to see many spotted deer, wild boar, the occasional mongoose and land monitor, as well as a jungle fowl, which is Sri Lanka's national bird.

 Our tracker was good, and it wasn't long before he spotted paw-prints in the sand. I spent a long time scanning the bush and listening for the raspy cough the leopard makes.

 There were quite a few small herds of wild Asian elephant, and the most satisfying were a group in a waterhole. One of the older elephant was trying to teach the baby to bathe. She rolled over in the water, demonstrating how to lay down and squirted it with water. It was captivating to watch.

 In the afternoon, I spotted cute grey langur monkeys. Further along the road, beside the river, were a whole troop of macaques. They're not my favourite monkeys and when the head monkey aggressively charged at me, I wasn't impressed and quite happy to move on in search of leopard.

 I'd long since given up hope when our tracker spotted one sitting in the undergrowth. When he reversed back, it started to move away. I thought it was gone, but it had to cross the road behind the jeep, and I was waiting with my camera ready.

Unfortunately it was facing away from us and quickly disappeared into the undergrowth on the other side of the road. It was brilliant to see if only for a brief moment and left lasting paw-prints, not just on the ground, but across my heart.

Covered in a fine red dust, I had a spring in my step as I exited the jeep back at the hotel.

'How lucky were we to see a leopard?' I questioned, my face glowing with delight.

'I didn't think we would find one,' replied Russ, sharing in my happiness.

In contrast, the journey to Hikkaduwa was a shocking experience. The damage the tsunami had wreaked on the coastline was gigantic. Mile after mile of devastation. We passed numerous camps set up with tents to house people and tanks which were being constantly filled with fresh water. I was terribly concerned for the people that had lost their homes but even more so for the loss of lives. The journey took five hours, but finding somewhere to stay in town wasn't easy because there had been much damage caused. Hikkaduwa was one long street along the waterfront.

Chatting to a shop owner, he told us, 'The tsunami came in and smashed the front of this building. I lost several of my motorbikes that were out on hire and three computers which were downstairs.'

'It must have been upsetting for you,' I said, my lips drooping.

'I wasn't there when the tsunami hit, but my sister was and couldn't understand what was happening,' he replied with sadness in his eyes.

'What did you do in the aftermath?'

'The roads were blocked with rubble, but everyone just got out there and cleared the section of road in front of their premises, by hand.'

'It's great when everyone bands together to help each other. I'm so sorry for all the damage.'

We walked further along the road to see the display of aid work being carried out in the area. There were many projects operating, including housing, schooling, hygiene and boat building. The biggest project was yet to start. The red-cross were relocating a whole area that had been devastated and rebuilding homes for them inland. It was great to see charities working there from all different parts of the world, including Japan and Europe.

The following day, Russ organized a van to take us to Brief Garden, which was about ten kilometres inland from Bentota. The devastation along the coastline continued for miles. The derailed train was still there, lying on its side, the carriages ripped apart like the lives of the locals. Some rebuilding was taking place, and fishing boats were being repaired, but there wasn't the hive of activity I'd expected to see.

On the way, we stopped at a turtle hatchery which had been totally destroyed by the tsunami.

The owner had tears in his eyes as he told us, 'I have lost not only my home and business, but also all of my beloved hand-reared turtles.'

He had a Readers Digest article written about the great conservation work he had done over the last twenty-six years. Looking at the calm sea, it was difficult to comprehend that something many people depended on for their livelihoods had turned into a monster taking away lives in an instant.

'We are so sorry to hear what has happened and would like you to have this donation to buy some more turtle eggs to restart your business,' I said.

'I have received no assistance from the government, yet they have given new boats to people that never had boats before,' he informed us.

'It's not much money but hopefully enough to get you started once again. I know it will never replace what you had, but it's a step forward.' I hoped he would be able to make a new beginning in the admirable profession of conservation of turtles.

On the way back from the gardens, we found another turtle hatchery still open. I wondered how their turtles managed to survive, perhaps they were just in the right location. With only seven species of sea turtle in the world and all of them endangered by extinction, I was thrilled to hold a baby loggerhead turtle that was four days old. It was fantastic to see the tiny critters swimming strongly in the tank. The olive ridley turtles were born the previous day and hopefully would be a whole new generation. In captivity, they had a much better chance of living a long life. The eighteen month old hawksbill that I cradled in my arms was heavy, but quite charming, and I was glad the green turtle, loggerhead and an especially rare albino would be well looked after.

Having survived three years, the olive ridley turtle weighed twenty kilograms. I was pleased to see many older turtles and hoped the hatchlings would continue to flourish.

It was time to head back to Negombo. On another muggy day, Russ went in search of some transport. Mum requested he find a Mercedes with air-conditioning. Eventually Russ recruited a driver and asked him to tell her his beaten up old van was a Sri-Lankan Mercedes.

'Here is our transport,' said Russ, revealing our driver.

'What type of van do you have?' he asked the driver, who looked at him blankly. 'Remember what I told you to say?'

'No, I forget.'

'He has a Sri-Lankan Mercedes,' said Russ. 'Well, not really, but I told him to tell you it was. At least it has air-conditioning.'

It was cool, well, at the beginning of the trip until the system broke down. The journey was horrendous. I was sitting in the front and definitely regretting it because I'm sure the driver was kamikaze.

His breath stank of arrack, the local brew, and he kept saying, 'I am so tired.' I thought it was because the buzz from the alcohol had worn off. We had several near misses, and he tried to console me by saying, 'I good driver. I have sixteen years' of driving experience.' I thought to myself that he'd been lucky to survive that long.

I hoped Sri Lanka was able to repair the damaged communities and the optimistic people could rebuild their lives and overcome the grief of losing family and friends.

#

Another trip to the UK presented the opportunity to stop-over in Asia, and we decided to spend time in Vietnam and Cambodia to break the long journey.

After checking in at the guesthouse, we left our shoes on the rack and climbed the eighty steep stairs to our room. Our cosy chamber was air-conditioned with a fan, television and fridge. We also had at least one mosquito for company, so I plugged in the repeller to try to keep it at bay.

We explored the streets of the Pham Ngu Lao which is often called Saigon. It was a bustling hive of activity with much life taking place on the streets. A jumble of markets, shops, outdoor cafes and vendors selling their wares, competed for space between the parked vehicles.

The roads were congested, perforated with potholes and the alleyways often just dirt paths. They were packed with scooters, cars, trucks and locals pushing their stalls. Motorcycle riders often wore masks to protect themselves from the pollution and dust. Families of four squashed onto one tiny bike, and once I saw as many as five.

There was no limit to what could be carried on a bicycle, moped or motorbike or to how high it was stacked. Merchants carried their wares this way. There was everything plastic on one, from bowls and cups to buckets and brooms. Florists had flowers, plants and bonsai aboard. Stacks of delicate china seemed more than a little risky. On another, all things straw, including hats and baskets, wobbled dangerously as the rider weaved in and out of the traffic. Cages were strapped down and held chickens, rabbits or puppies, and there were even goldfish in plastic bags filled with water. I saw large items of furniture and rugs rolled up which were balanced precariously. The essentials for tourists, such as bottled water and freshly baked bread, were left uncovered, to collect a coating of exhaust fumes whilst being transported the same way. More food, including fruit and vegetables, even kegs or cases of beer, vibrated with the rhythm of the engine. Then there were the construction workers carrying building materials and tools like ladders, bamboo poles and long pipes. They would definitely be pulled over in Australia for such long loads.

I thought we were liberal at home, not just letting our dogs stick their heads out the car window, but also carrying them in the back of a utility truck. This was nothing compared to the canines enjoying themselves on bikes. Their fur was ruffled and faces distorted from the wind generated from forward momentum, as they sat in the foot well of a scooter or poised on a pillion seat. What a crazy country I was exploring.

Initially, it was extremely difficult to cross the road, but after a while, I got the hang of it. Motorcyclists would string in a long line across a junction, similar to on a race track, although I'm not sure how they decided who got pole position. Crossing the road reminded me of trying to manoeuver our boat through vessels racing across the bay. Generally the motorists would try to dodge pedestrians, unlike yacht competitors who would collide rather than give way. After walking a few blocks, we stopped for a drink at a local bar where we sat on the sidewalk and watched the melee unfold. Hawkers walked by selling books, piled high and tied together with string. Young children were selling Zippo lighters, sunglasses or chewing gum.

By now it was dark, but we decided to head off to Ben Thanh markets anyway. Because they drive on the right, I found it confusing, not knowing which way to look whilst crossing the road, especially when a few would travel the wrong way up the street and ignore the red traffic lights. There were many more roads to traverse, and I quickly jumped out of the way when a motorcycle rode along the pavement. I didn't feel safe anywhere, well, until we got to the roundabout outside the markets, and a tourist policeman came to help me across the road.

There were a couple of streets with food stalls on one side and clothing or general wares on the other. I was fascinated by the seafood, prawns, crayfish, pippies and crabs that were alive in tanks of water on display. Numerous fruit stalls sold exotic fruits such as rambutans, mangosteens, longans, pomelos, jackfruit, dragon fruit and custard apples, which I wanted to try. There were souvenirs for sale including clothes, shoes, bags, hair accessories, paintings and lacquerware.

Exploring the local area, the following morning, we walked to the Saigon Zoo and Botanical Gardens which had many interesting animals, either rare or threatened with extinction, on display. Once again, I was saddened by this knowledge but fortunate to have the opportunity to see them.

The marbled cat appeared about the size of a domestic cat with an extremely long and bushy tail, whereas the fishing cat was about twice the size. It was stocky with a relatively short tail compared to the length of its body. Reading the sign, I found it fascinating that it can focus on animals under water because its eyes are closer together than other cats.

The Binturong looked cute, and I was interested to find it was from the same species as the fossa that we'd seen in Madagascar. To me, its build was similar to the red panda, but it was covered in thick dark hair. I didn't want to get too close, because I'd heard if they were frightened, they could spray a foul smelling liquid similar to a skunk.

I'd never seen a yellow-throated marten before. It looked exquisite with its magnificent walnut coat, golden throat and dark bushy tail.

When Russ beckoned, the gibbon came down from its perch and automatically turned its back to the bars for a massage. It was déjà vu when he recalled another gibbon in Thailand returning the favour by searching through his hair for nits.

Nearby, at the Museum of Vietnamese History, we watched a water Puppet show, a performing art which I read has been around since the eleventh century in Vietnam. The puppeteers hid behind a curtain, standing waist-high in water and controlled the puppets on sticks. I found it quite comical, maybe because of the slight resemblance to the Punch and Judy shows from my childhood or perhaps my lack of understanding of what was happening. I could sense the building tension by the music and was just waiting for the puppets to beat each other with sticks, but it never happened. I imagined the puppeteer's skin being wrinkled and soft from the long emersion in water.

I hadn't heard of the Cao Dai temple but found the concept appealing. Caodaism is an attempt to create the ideal religion by mixing and matching all other religions. So you have pieces of Buddhism, Confucianism, Taoism, Hinduism, Christianity, Islam and the traditional Vietnamese Cult of Ancestor Worship all mingled together. I thought a religion that stresses love for one another can't be bad.

On arrival at the temple, there was some confusion as to which entry to use since there was one for males and one for females. Whether it was because I had my hair stuffed under my hat, or I was a tourist, it turned out that we both needed to go through the door for males after removing our shoes. Walking around the lower level of the temple before the ceremony started, we encountered a vibrant blend of different styles of architecture with paintings of Chinese unicorns, phoenix and turtle, together with Victor Hugo on whom the saints bestowed sainthood along with Winston Churchill. The temple was built on nine levels representing nine steps to heaven.

We watched the ceremony at noon, from the balcony, and listened to the worshippers, dressed in colourful robes, chant and bow, on the lower level, before a large sphere with an eye which is the symbol of the religion and represents truth. The worshippers clothed in yellow robes were Buddhists. The Confucians were in red whilst the Taoists wore blue and other religions or women donned white.

Later that day, as we were leaving the markets, the late afternoon deluge started. We took shelter in a t-shirt shop, but when the rain wasn't easing, dashed to a bar to have a drink. Russ befriended the puppy there which took great delight in trying to nip him. I know his legs are skinny, but the dog seemed to think they were a bone to chew on.

Later, I decided to try the unknown fruit we'd bought earlier at the markets and carefully peeled it with our penknife before passing a slice to Russ. He spat it out, so I tried a slice. It was revolting and took all the moisture out of my mouth. I can only assume it must have needed cooking before eating or just wasn't ripe. Luckily we'd also bought some jackfruit which tasted smooth and creamy.

We checked in at the airport fairly quickly, but the queue through immigration moved slowly. We nicknamed our processor "The Snail". Due to engineering problems, our flight was delayed for four and a half hours and the tuk tuk driver from the guesthouse had been waiting that long to pick us up in Cambodia. At the guesthouse, we checked into a spacious room, on the second floor, overlooking the river. By now it was dark and wet, but we walked to town along the riverside where there were many market stalls, shops and street vendors.

Back in our room, we had fun trying to turn the lights out because the switches were all linked to the power sockets. Eventually I discovered everything had to be turned off to get the lights out. Consequently, we could not leave the camera battery charging for the night nor the mosquito repeller plug working.

Our trusty Tuk Tuk driver took us and our guide to Angkor the following morning. When Angkor Wat came into view, I was stunned. As usual, I was lost for words and only managed to say, 'Wow,' over and over again. I could see why the area is considered the biggest temple complex of the world as it's a massive majestic structure. On foot, we crossed the sandstone causeway, spanning the wide moat, to closely inspect the famous decorations of unique heavenly nymphs (Apsara) on the walls and in the niches. It really did represent one of the greatest architectural achievements.

We walked around the outside of the temple. Some local kids were playing in the forest and had a bat trapped down a storm water drain. We could only hear the children talking in the drain, so Russ crept up and made loud bat noises which echoed eerily in the confined space, giving the children a fright and our guide hysterics.

After climbing the steps to the first level of Angkor Wat, our guide described the scenes in various bas-reliefs which contained sandstone carvings. The detail and execution were superb. Columns along the outer wall created a mix of bright light and shadows on the reliefs.

I climbed the extremely steep steps to the top of the inner sanctuary, gripping with my hands as well as treading with my feet, to find a spectacular view from the top. The steep stairways represent the difficulty of ascending to the kingdom of the gods. However, it was descending that was to challenge me. I was more than just frightened, I was terrified trying to get down. From looking at the views, my heart was already beating too fast, and my legs were unstable, as usual.

There was a handrail but little space to place my feet, which meant stepping sideways down the sheer staircase. I don't know how I managed, but I clung to the railing whilst I carefully took one step at a time, holding up everyone after me. As my legs shook, I found it difficult to place my foot and often it would tip, almost sliding off, causing my legs to wobble even more. When I finally reached the bottom, it was to a round of applause. I hadn't realized that many people, sitting on the wall at the base, had been watching me. I was so embarrassed but extremely pleased to have made it.

As with many ruins we'd visited in Africa and Asia, there were troops of monkeys clambering the structures and sitting under the shade of the rainforest trees. Although the macaques looked cute, some were quite aggressive, so I was happy to watch them from a distance.

Back outside the temple, we sat by the moat and ate our sandwiches, which we had bought with us from the guesthouse, whilst our driver and guide went to the restaurant to eat. We were soon joined by a group of young children who spoke good English and even knew the name of the new prime minister in England. Some of the children had been swimming in the moat, fully clothed, so were dripping wet. I gave them some brittle Jila mints, which they proceeded to try to crunch. I'd images of broken teeth, but they survived well. There was a rope running on one side of the market stalls, and they explained vendors were not supposed to cross this line. There was a policeman to enforce it, and apparently if a salesperson did cross with merchandise, they would be fined. I thought what a great way to keep the touts at bay.

We found our driver and guide before entering the city of Angkor Thom through the South Gate, a sandstone tower rising twenty-three meters to the sky and topped with four heads, one facing each cardinal direction.

From a distance the Bayon looked like piles of rubble, but once closer, I could see the towers of stone and hundreds of faces of Avalokiteshvara smiling at us.

Having seen the movie Tomb Raider, I was intrigued to visit Ta Prohm, which was used as the main location, but unprepared to be ambushed by touts.

They started offering goods. 'Hey Mister, please buy one for a dollar.'

'No thank you,' we replied in unison whilst walking away.

'I give you two for a dollar,' the children sang back.

'No thank you,' became our standard response whilst they gradually increased to three, then four, until finally they tendered ten for a dollar.

Once passed the entrance to Ta Prohm, the touts couldn't enter, and it was a peaceful walk to the temple, other than the coach loads of chattering tourists.

In awe, I surveyed Ta Prohm, which blanketed in dense jungle was left untouched and partly crumpled in neglect whilst nature penetrated it and branches of leaves formed a canopy to protect and shelter the monastery. I noticed the enormous silk-cotton tree roots and those of the strangler fig pushing apart walls and stone blocks, like Sid (our pet python) pushed our sofa away many years ago, making space to invade.

I got lost amongst the closed courtyards and narrow passageways because although cleared of vegetation, many were impassable blocked by piles of stone, dislodged long ago by now lifeless trees. Walking through this maze, there was only one way in and one way out. Outside the inner haven, the complex was still in the vice-like grip of the trees, slowly declining.

On the way out, we listened to some blind musicians playing traditional Cambodian music and purchased their CD before dashing for the tuk tuk to avoid the touts.

I found the historic temples in Siem Riep interesting, but after three days of exploring various sites, I had temple overload and was looking forward to seeing our relatives in the UK so quite happy to move on.

Whilst in England, I got double enjoyment as I got to see my family and indulge my passion of close encounters with animals. England might seem a strange place to see primates considering that most species are found in Africa, Asia and the Americas. These were not monkeys endemic to the United Kingdom but rescued ones in either sanctuaries, zoos or wildlife parks. I prefer to see animals in their own environment, but with monkeys either vanishing from the wild, as they border on extinction, or difficult to spot, this was a great way to learn about their conservation and see them close up.

We visited the Monkey Sanctuary in Cornwall which is home to a large colony of South American woolly monkeys as well as some rescued capuchin.

We watched them forage and play in surroundings built, as closely as possible, to replicate their natural habitat. The woolly monkeys had adorable silver grey coats. Because their heads were black, they looked like they were wearing cardigans. Their fur was short, and their eyes were pools of dark liquid ink. One hung from its prehensile tail whilst it picked at the chopped apples and pears with human like hands. Two more sat on the ground looking grumpy with their arms folded in front of them, or perhaps they were just enjoying the sunshine.

I could hear the dominant males testing the security of the enclosures by vigorously shaking the bars, which caused much screaming amongst the different groups.

After watching the woolly monkey's antics, we moved on to see the capuchins. These cute little monkeys had a crop of black fur on top of their heads, golden fur covering their upper arms and body, and black fur on their lower body and legs. One swung on the ropes provided and opened its mouth revealing long sharp canine teeth. I wondered how people could keep them as pets.

We were in for more monkeying around at Dudley Zoo in the rain. The foliage shook when they approached and little faces peered at us in the warm forest enclosure. Both the endangered Goeldi and Squirrel monkeys sat close to me whilst they inquisitively looked around. I thought they were sweet little critters. The White Faced Saki, a large monkey, crept forward along a branch to peer at us but being much less confident, it didn't get quite so near.

As we walked through the one-acre wood, curiosity got the better of the inhabitants. As soon as we were through the double gates, black and white ruffled lemurs tried to get in my backpack. Sitting on my shoulders, they searched for food, but I didn't have any.

Both the male and female looked the same with ebony and ivory markings as well as a ruff of long white fur around their ears and neck. The lemurs made a loud alarm call when Russ imitated the call of the black lemur. It reminded me of our time in Madagascar.

Several of the ruffled lemurs were attracted to Russ' sister's bag.

'Why do they keep trying to get inside?' she asked me, puzzled by their actions.

I'd a broad grin on my face as I explained, 'At the café, whilst you had gone to the toilet, Russ put hot chips inside your umbrella. He did this so that when you opened it, the chips would fall out onto you.'

'The lemurs must be able to smell them,' she replied, shaking with laughter.

The ring-tails, collared and black lemurs watched from a distance. They were all curious and came up pretty close, but only the black and white ruffled lemurs climbed on me.

I only saw the female black lemurs which are actually brown in colour, as only the males are black. They are usually shy nocturnal primates but were busy interacting and defending their territory from the other lemur species in the wood.

It was a great experience to get so intimate with the lemurs, watch them play and listen to them calling. It brought back fond memories of Madagascar where I'd love to return to one day.

The following day, we went to the Monkey Forest where it was drizzling with rain, although brief interludes were dry. One hundred and forty Barbary macaques were roaming freely in the sixty acres of forest. I remembered this highly endangered species from our trip to Gibraltar, in 1985, where they're the last remaining wild population in Europe. They still exist in the mountains of Morocco and Algeria but are under threat from logging.

A ten week old baby, carefully watched by its mother, got up to all sorts of antics, climbing trees and hanging upside down from branches. All babies are cute and this one was no exception, especially when it cuddled into the welcoming arms of its mum to suckle on her nipple. It leapt around, chasing its father, who protected the apple he was eating, and then rode on Mum's back. It was interesting watching them go about their daily lives.

The adults had luxurious dense fur coats. They looked to be wearing Russian sable hats with a reddish tinge on their heads. Grey fur on their backs and limbs contrasted with their white bellies. Only their pink faces and ears were uncovered. Some appeared to be wearing powder blue eye-shadow, which was fashionable in the seventies, whilst they foraged for food hidden in the long grass.

The monkey's tiny feet squeezed at my heart as it pumped faster. I was so lucky to have seen these American and African primates but sad that many were becoming endangered, meaning they might not be around in a few decades time for others to see. It was great these organizations had breeding programs to increase numbers, but I hoped they would fare well in the wild.

It had been a great trip and fantastic to see my family again, but I was looking forward to going back to Australia which had so much more to offer than just sunshine.

CHAPTER FIFTEEN – SHIPS IN THE NIGHT
Fiji, Tonga, Australia

I often wondered about living a more simple life. Some of Africa offered that, although at the same time could be extremely frustrating and didn't provide a stable platform to live in. I loved the wildlife and enjoyed being closer to it, but Australia had its own unique fauna too.

I thought Fiji might be a simple place to live. We could purchase property there, unlike Vanuatu and some other countries in Oceania. It could also be a great place to sail to, so I thought we should take a look.

A couple of thousand kilometres north east of Sydney, I watched as Viti Levu came into view through the plane window. A large sign saying "Bula" welcomed us to Nadi International airport. It was warm outside and dry but threatening to rain.

Our lovely airy room had a view of the two mile long Wailoaloa beach and out to sea where a ship wreck was decaying in the shallows nearby. Whilst paddling in the sea, we were joined by a couple of dogs. At the same time as the mongrels, we spotted a frog hopping towards the sea. We distracted them so the tiny amphibian could make its escape.

Sunday dawned another beautiful day. Uncluttered skies revealed a blinding sun as we headed for Sigatoka. I saw several mongooses run across the road that day. Although cute little critters, I knew they had been introduced to Fiji to get the snakes out of the sugar cane fields but ended up contributing to the extinction of numerous endemic species of birds and skinks. The balance of nature is so fragile and hard to control once it has gone wrong.

Once passed Sigatoka, we arrived in Korotogo where we stopped at Kula Eco Park which was nestled in a valley of coastal forest. In the main building, there were displays including a Fiji boa, Fiji tree frog, preserved insects as well as some of Fiji's larger sea shells, butterflies and moths.

Once outside, I was given a baby Fiji boa to hold. I loved the exotic markings on its shiny scales which reminded me of Muscles, the boa we had as a pet for a while. However, I was distracted when banded iguanas were placed on each of my shoulders and a striped iguana on my head.

'Fiji banded iguana are currently regarded as vulnerable but are now being reconsidered endangered,' explained the guide.

Presuming mongooses were contributing to its downfall, I replied, 'I'm privileged to have held one.' However, what I hadn't realized was the iguana was also prey for the lovable boa I was cradling.

'It's a protected species and being bred to increase their numbers,' she continued.

I smiled hoping they would survive in the wild.

A coconut weather station sign hung beside the wooden walkway between enclosures of native birds and reptiles. It had a coconut dangling on a string beside it and an explanation that tells the weather.

It stated if the coconut is: Wet – It's raining, Swaying – It's windy, Hot – It's sunny, Cool – It's Cloudy, Blue – Its Cold and Gone – It's a Cyclone. I decided today was sunny.

We saw many other birds endemic to Fiji such as the orange dove, sulphur-breasted musk parrot and collared lory which is called kula in Fijian. I never tired of seeing new species.

Fiji was an ideal place to relax with a slow pace, warm weather and splendid scenery, but I couldn't spend the whole time visiting offshore islands.

I browsed through a list of day trips, most of which were water based. The only land based activities were sky-diving and zip-line, both of which I'd tried before. Many of the water activities didn't ignite my enthusiasm. I'd previously tried fishing, windsurfing and parasailing and already enjoyed sailing or cruising to the islands where I snorkelled and kayaked for many hours, even sailing a small Hobie Cat. That just left a day out white-water rafting, and I thought it might be fun to try to recapture the excitement of the Zambezi.

The following day at Navua, we transferred to a motorised canoe which motored for at least an hour up stream. I was uncomfortable sitting on the low seats with a bulky life jacket on, so the time passed slowly. The scenery along the river was wonderful. The mountain sides were steep and covered in leafy green foliage including ferns and bamboo. Winding along the river, we passed several waterfalls and a few cows grazing near the water's edge.

At an upstream village, we transferred to an inflatable raft to travel back down the Navua River. Rafting was peaceful, although I was concentrating on paddling. We stopped for a swim at the base of a waterfall whilst our guide cooked a delicious lunch. The rapids were tame though, so much so, I didn't know there were any. They were certainly no competition to the ferocious Zambezi, not even to the Tully River. I was disappointed. If it hadn't been for the drizzling rain, I'd have barely got wet.

I loved Fiji and enjoyed slowing down, but although a great place to visit and unwind, it wasn't somewhere to settle permanently. I loved the people and the beaches, but Australia was calling me home.

#

The moon was completely extinguished by the black clouds, and a thick fog had descended, cloaking me in a dark haze. The muggy air blanketed the night, reducing visibility, so it was difficult to even see the bow of the boat. It was deathly quiet with just the sound of the waves against the hull. I could see the headland, faintly silhouetted against the sky, because there were lights on the mainland beyond it. I thought these lights must be from Palm Beach, stretching towards Sydney. However, once we passed the lights on shore, I realized there was another headland. It wasn't illuminated so completely impossible to tell where the land started and more importantly where it finished. I didn't know how far offshore we were, which was frightening, because our navigation equipment was no longer working, and I didn't know which way to steer to keep away from land. For the first time, I wondered if we would make it home safely.

"Man cannot discover new oceans until he has the courage to lose sight of shore" was printed on my bookmark and inspired me to keep travelling. Because I suffered seasickness and migraines, I needed to make sure I'd be able to cope with long blue water passages. So back home once more, I planned to sail to Port Stephens from Broken Bay as it was an ideal opportunity to test myself.

It was my first overnight blue water trip on our beloved Wimaway. Russ was the skipper, and I completed the crew along with two others John and Michael. Whilst I finished packing the perishable provisions into cool bags, John loaded the other bags onto the utility truck and munched on a couple of Kwells because, like me, he was prone to seasickness. It reminded me to wear my pressure bands on the trip. Russ drove, and they let me sit in the front as I was worried about suffering motion sickness on the way to the boat.

We hastily loaded the gear on board. I went below to start packing the provisions away and set up the navigation equipment. We were running interactive marine charts with a Holux GPS to track our position on my ipaq. The GPS connection was by blue tooth, which I mounted above the cupboard beside the navigation desk and plugged it into a twelve volt power supply. The ipaq and the backup Garmin GPS got power from the outlets in the port pocket, in the cockpit. I was relieved to see a strong connection was made to the GPS, and it wasn't long before it had secured our position from several satellites which showed on the chart as a red circle with a cross in it.

The sun was already setting when we departed around five in the evening. Although the forecast was for twenty to thirty knots of wind, with up to four and a half metre waves, it was eerily still. The water was flat with barely a ripple on it, and the only breeze was from the forward motion created by Wimaway under motor.

It wasn't long before daylight disappeared, leaving just a tiny arc of light radiating from the moon through the insubstantial cloud cover. The night air was warm and humid with an impending sense of a storm. We ate dinner whilst motoring towards the heads. Russ ducked below and radioed the coastguards to let them know of our trip. They suggested we log in again when we reached Swansea.

We took it in turns to steer to a compass course of about thirty degrees. It was now completely dark with the sky lighting momentarily by flashes of lightening in the distance. The faint rumble of thunder broke the quiet lapping of water. Apart from the noise from the engine, it was peaceful. There were many lights from massive container ships in the distance. The illumination on the bow and stern of a boat appeared to be two separate vessels, but when we got closer, I could make out the outline of the craft in between. Wimaway glided between the motionless hulks.

Russ went below to the v-berth to sleep, and I took the helm for the next couple of hours. At first, it was only a few fat droplets of rain, but slowly it turned into a deluge. I must have looked comical in my raincoat and shorts with bare feet and legs protruding. Once it stopped drizzling, I decided to try to sleep so went below too. I stretched out on the starboard bunk for about ten minutes before I couldn't stand the nausea any longer and had to go back on deck. In the meantime, Russ had got up, so the other guys took the opportunity to sleep.

On the helm, I tried to fend off my seasickness but was getting pretty tired as I'd been awake for seventeen hours, and the excitement of the trip was catching up with me. I'd previously been steering using the lights on the shore or boats on the port side as a fix, but now there was nothing ahead in the dark to steer to and without a horizon, my nausea increased. So I used the navigation system because as long as the course arrow was aligned with the plotted route everything should be fine.

At last, Port Stephens lighthouse appeared in the distance. It would flash four times and then stop for a phase. The swell was washing in behind us and turning the boat, so often the lighthouse would be sighted on the starboard side, instead of the port. After another few hours of steering, I was exhausted, so Russ programmed, "Raymond", our autopilot to steer. It did a much better job than I did of keeping Wimaway on course. I remained standing because having to continually shift weight to balance seemed to slightly relieve my sickness.

As daylight slowly illuminated the horizon, marking the start of a new day, the wind started to increase, and I longed to rid myself of this weary nausea. Bottlenose dolphins weaved and dived in the warm waters from the north, which the offshore current had carried here. Russ logged off with the coastal patrol at Port Stephens when we entered sheltered waters and tied up in the marina at Nelson Bay. Finally I slept, oblivious to the symphony of groaning ropes and clanging halyard.

Since it was raining, we spent the rest of the day in the pub watching people pass by. I slept well that night because I wanted to be refreshed for the return trip. Before I knew it, it was five in the morning, so I cooked bacon, eggs and toast for breakfast. After a quick shower, I washed up the dishes, and we quickly readied the boat to leave.

Everyone put on their wet weather gear as the ocean mirrored the dreary sky, masked by heavy grey clouds laden with moisture. John appeared in his fluorescent yellow waterproof jacket and pants. At least we'd spot him easily if he fell overboard. I wore Russ' old blue and white Burke jacket with some cheap yellow plastic leggings.

The winds were strong, around fifteen to twenty knots, and the seas and swell were several metres. We had to head away from the bay and sail close-haul to head in the right direction. It was going to be a long sail home, beating into the wind all the way, because the forecast change in wind direction never eventuated.

I sat on the cabin top to take some photos of the spray. Russ came and joined me, and we took turns standing at the bow getting soaked. The front of the boat would bounce high above the horizon and then pitch down the next wave spraying plumes of water into the air and all over me. Wimaway was heeled at a forty-five degree angle with strong gusts of up to twenty-five knots occasionally knocking her further over. The decks were flooded with water, and the spray would, every so often, make it into the cockpit and drench everyone there too.

When the winds increased to a constant twenty-five knots, wading through the ankle deep water on the low side of the deck, Russ reefed the mainsail.

I returned to the cockpit to steer. I was envious when Michael read a magazine in the cabin as I couldn't even cope with a quick trip to the toilet and back, without nausea enveloping me. On the helm, I got a regular dousing in sea water. Only once did I manage to duck, and the wave bounced off my back straight into Russ, who was sitting on the wooden seat behind me. My feet were wet along with the bottom of my track pants which were protruding from beneath my waterproof leggings. Later, Russ lent me his thick socks to wear because I was getting cold.

I hogged the helm for the next five hours until Michael got up and wanted to steer, so I reluctantly relinquished the helm on the provision I could have it back if I felt sick again.

He told us, 'I got "psst" on whilst sleeping in the starboard bunk. I was lying underneath it, yawning when it went off.'

I laughed as I knew Russ had put the air freshener in the bunk above and every few minutes it would squirt perfume into the air.

It was time to tack. I furiously pulled the sheet to bring the headsail over to the starboard winch whilst Russ let it out on the port side. The boat bounced over another big wave, and my feet lost contact with the deck. Still hanging on to the sheet, I pitched backwards and the back of my arm just saved me from falling down the companionway. I quickly got back up to winch in the rest of the sheet, accompanied by much laughter.

I explained, 'That was my newly invented quick tacking method.' I don't think anyone believed me though.

We headed into the wind, as close as we could, and almost managed to clear Stockton Bight. We could see the wreck of the Sigma as well as the four wheel drives speeding along the beach, so it was time for another tack. Off we went in the wrong direction again because we needed to get further offshore to be able to tack back down the coast.

About an hour before dusk, the winds started to drop. Once they were consistently under ten knots, we decided to furl in the headsail, so we could motor past Moon Island outside the entrance to Swansea channel. We still had a long way to go. John noticed the ipaq was no longer working. It must've got doused by a few of the bigger waves. Without it, we would need the GPS waypoints to steer to in the dark. I took the helm and headed towards some ship lights ahead of our course. I could see Norah Heads Lighthouse blinking intermittently on our starboard side.

After we'd eaten, Russ went below to get some sleep, and Michael set up his GPS, to show the waypoint to clear at The Entrance, before also going to sleep. By now it was black with only the lights on shore for illumination. I called to Michael to find out the name of the next waypoint to set. We seemed to motor on and on for hours. At one stage we passed a fishing boat, but there didn't appear to be anyone else around.

Finally we set the waypoint for Broken Bay and had lost sight of Norah Head Lighthouse behind us, yet we couldn't see Barren Joey Lighthouse ahead. John steered whilst I grabbed a chart from the table which accentuated my nausea and made it difficult to think clearly. It looked like we should have three unlit headlands, third point, second point and first point to pass before Broken Bay would appear. What I thought was the first of these headlands came into view.

Unable to see where we were through the darkness and worried about hitting land, I pondered which direction to take and if we would make it home safely. Michael awoke and came on deck. He motored the boat a bit further offshore and pointed to Barren Joey Lighthouse. I couldn't see it at all. His eyesight was much better than mine. He explained normally we would've seen it from much further away, but the fog was limiting its reach.

He said, 'I'm not well. It must have been the smoked salmon sandwiches and biltong I ate earlier.' Then he promptly spewed over the side. At least I'd managed not to vomit so far.

I woke Russ to come back on deck because we needed a good pair of eyes, and I still couldn't make out the lighthouse. Resiliently, Michael got back behind the wheel and continued to steer us towards Pittwater saying he now felt better.

Pittwater was well lit from the houses on the shore, and it was easy to make out the port and starboard markers. Relieved we were back in sheltered waters, I went below to pack up our gear whilst Russ logged off with the coastal patrol. I was tucked up in a warm bed, snug in a cocoon of blankets, by three o'clock in the morning.

I couldn't see myself sailing to Fiji, or even very far along the coastline, unless I could stop and sleep every night. Motion-sickness was something I had to live with, and I decided I was better at backpacking than sailing.

#

Having decided I didn't want to sail around the Pacific, I booked a trip to Tonga, the first Pacific Nation to welcome a new day. I thought it might be convenient to have everything organized for a change so booked an on-line airline's package trip which included flights and accommodation.

Once our flight landed, we got through customs and walked out into the night air on the island of Tongatapu. A taxi, which we shared with a couple from Campbelltown, took us to our hotel. They couldn't remember what hotel they were booked into for the night, only that it had a red roof. So when we arrived at our hotel, at eleven thirty in the evening, they got on the internet to check their email confirmation. Unfortunately I arrived to a blank look from the receptionist, who went and found her boss.

'We don't have your booking and are fully booked,' she informed me.

It had been a long day, and I was tired and frustrated having already paid for the holiday in full.

'Where can we stay? It's late at night and everywhere will be closed,' I asked stifling a yawn.

'I have just phoned, so you can stay at another lodging further along the road.'

'Who will be paying for it?' I frowned as we didn't bring money to pay for accommodation.

'It depends on who has made the mistake with the booking.'

I sighed, relieved to have a comfortable bed for the night but not looking forward to trying to fix the problem. This was supposed to be a relaxing trip, a retreat from the stresses of work and fast-paced life in Sydney.

The next morning, we walked to the "fully booked hotel" for breakfast. The owner arrived and beckoned us to a quiet table to talk. Tonga was two hours ahead of Sydney, which meant the company we'd booked through would not be open yet. So I envisaged the day slipping away whilst we tried to resolve our accommodation situation.

The owner said, 'Because you have a booking number, the fault must be mine, and I'd like to make amends.'

'Thank you,' I replied, raising my eyebrows.

'Are you happy with the new hotel?'

'Yes, it's comfortable, although it doesn't have an ocean view, which we paid extra for at your hotel.'

'I'll lend you a hire car for the week and organize tickets for you to go to a cultural show, free of charge, if you will stay on at the other hotel.'

I was amazed at her generosity as I'd anticipated a struggle to get a refund and then being left to sort things out ourselves.

'Please also come here for your breakfast, each morning, as that is part of your package,' she informed us.

'Thank you so much,' I replied, the tension releasing from my shoulders.

Russ needed to get a Tongan driver's licence. At the Ministry of Transport, we took a ticket and waited our turn. It was difficult to know when that was because they announced the numbers in Tongan. The lady serving us was wearing a ta'ovala (a mat wrapped around the waist and tied with rope). It looked most uncomfortable to be sitting in all day, and it made me think about the clothing women endured for fashion. I wore stiletto heels for many years but not any longer. It wasn't long before Russ had his three month visitor licence, and we were on our way.

The car was turning out to be invaluable because Russ was suffering from sciatica and experiencing a lot of pain when walking. The speed limit in villages and town was forty kilometres per hour and sixty-five in between. However, it was difficult for us to know when a village ended and a new one started. Some of the roads were badly pot holed and with pigs, chickens and cows roaming freely, forty was a good speed to keep to.

We drove to the west coast and stopped at a beach resort for lunch. I was thrilled to see humpback whales spouting out at sea and frolicking just beyond the reef. Whilst we were eating lunch, the couple from Campbelltown who we shared a taxi with, arrived. It was good to see them again, and they explained this was the resort with the red roof they had booked. We walked a short distance along the beach before driving on to the Blow Holes at Houma.

They were quite stunning and ran about five to six kilometres along the west coast. When the waves hit the terraced coastline, water ejected through the natural vents in the coral rock causing high jets and a vertical wall of water. Russ tried to get me to pose for a photo in front of them, but I was wise to his plan to get me soaked after he tricked me on the New Zealand Huka Jet.

On the way back to Nuku'alofa, we stopped to watch the flying foxes clinging to the casuarinas trees at Kolovai Village about eighteen kilometres from town. They were quite noisy, hanging upside down and flapping their wings. Further towards town, we drove past a large field of coconut palms with cows grazing.

'Look, it's a coconut milk paddock,' I said to Russ jokingly.

'I always wondered where it came from,' he replied with a straight face.

Another day, a small motorboat took us across to Pangaimotu Island where we strolled along the sandy beach with dogs running beside us. The sea transformed from smalt to cyan, lapping the golden sands covered in scattered shells, small pieces of broken coral and eel grass.

When I neared the first bend, the sand bordered flat rock with pools of captured water which had been warmed in the sunshine. The centre of the island was covered in a thick forest of coconut palms. The north side was edged with mangrove bushes whose roots wound their way into the salt water. They made a neat home for the hermit crabs which crept beneath them. Around further, we came across a deserted area where water must be able to flood in but at the time was dry. Some of the palm trees had been chopped down, and it was unnervingly desolate because the only trees were the few coconut palms edging the barren area.

We watched the birds fly close to the ground and pick up tiny crabs scuttling along the water's edge. Workers were collecting shellfish further along the bay, before we reached the platform area where we'd started from. I snorkelled around the boat wreck but only saw a couple of sandy coloured fish which blended well with the seabed.

At breakfast another morning, the hotel owner gave us free tickets for a day trip to Fafa Island Resort which is situated on its own private tropical island. There were strong winds on the journey there, so the captain rolled out the sail on the motor sailor to catch the breeze. The sea was corrugated with the wind making white caps on the tips of the waves.

Once on the island, we walked along the deserted beach, around the eighteen acre palm covered atoll, with the wind gusting strongly. The coral sand was crunchy under our feet whilst we watched the frigate birds search the rocks for food. I snorkelled off the rocks, but it was shallow close to the shore, and the jagged coral scrapped my hand and knee.

Russ laughed at me when I tried to put my snorkel mask on over my sunglasses.

Later I told him, 'You would've laughed louder when I put my head underwater and took my first breath as I got a mouthful of water, having forgotten to put the breathing tube in my mouth.'

I saw vibrant corals which swayed with the movement of the water and hid the tiny black and white fish amongst the fronds. An electric blue fish darted from another patch of coral and back again whilst larger sandy hued ones swam around less timidly.

The generosity of the hotel owner didn't stop there. She lent us her own private convertible car for the day, so we could drive around the island. She also booked us into a beachside resort for a night, to give us a more laid back atmosphere, and when we returned to the first hotel, we were upgraded to a suite.

To show our gratitude, we wanted to give her a gift that would last. We could only find plastic flower arrangements in the shops and bars of chocolate so decided a shrub for her garden would be a good idea. The question was, where to buy one. After many discussions, we were directed to the Forestry Commission. Unfortunately it was pouring with rain, and their plants were in the ground rather than in pots. I slipped and slid in my thongs as we looked at the seedlings growing in increasing soggy soil. On enquiring at the office, the lady suggested we drive her to her home where she had potted plants for sale. She gave us a running commentary on the way there which was lovely. We bought a plant from her that apparently flowers, but it weighed a ton in its large pot. It was still pouring with rain, and I squeezed in the back of the vehicle, again squashed between our backpacks, and found a plastic bag, so the lady sat in the front with the plant on the bag on her lap.

Not realizing the custom in Tonga was to reciprocate when a gift is given, we dropped off the plant, with a thank you card addressed to the owner, at the hotel we'd originally booked. Consequently, late on our final evening a package arrived of handmade Tongan place mats. She had made our holiday exceptionally delightful. Her warm generosity and kind hospitality was a refreshing change.

Having visited a third of the countries in Australasia, the world's smallest continent that I learned about at school, I was content to be fulfilling my dream. We were relaxed and ready to head home, to plan our next adventure.

CHAPTER SIXTEEN – EVER DECREASING PAW PRINTS
Thailand, Hong Kong, China, Laos

I wished it wasn't quite so windy when the cable car swayed back and forth. I still didn't really cope being that high off the ground, and although the view was spectacular, when I looked down, my stomach churned.

'Did you know, recently two pods collided, and passengers were stuck in the air for three hours before they were rescued?' asked a gentleman seated beside me. I thought that I didn't have three hours to wait because we had a flight to catch.

We just had a few hours in Hong Kong and were amazed at the generosity of local passengers who kindly paid one of our bus fares to Tung Chung Station. It was a dollar, and we only had enough change to pay for one fare because the driver insisted on the exact coins.

The queue for the Cable Car was long, and we wasted an hour getting our tickets. I was glad the five point seven kilometre ride took merely twenty-four minutes. Although we had a dazzling 360 degree view over Tung Chung Bay and the South China Seas, we were high up in the air and balanced on a cable like a tight rope walker. When the pod turned sixty degrees, the International Airport came into view, and we perused the undulating floral foam of the dense woodlands through the Lantau North Country Park. At last, the Tian Tan Buddha Statue came into view, which is what I'd come to see.

I was pleased to plant my feet on solid ground whilst we wandered through the Chinese style setting of Ngong Ping Village, passed quaint shops and restaurants along the roadside. It was challenging climbing the 268 steps to reach the lotus throne, on top of a three platform altar, on which the dignified Buddha sat serenely atop Ngong Ping Plateau. My guidebook stated his right hand was raised to represent the removal of affliction whilst his left hand rested on his lap in a gesture of giving. He symbolized something I believed in deeply, the harmonious relationship between man and nature, people and faith. I do have faith that people can keep the delicate balance with nature but sometimes am disappointed.

Although the sky was grey and misty, the view from the platform was glorious where he sat, amid the peaks and troughs of mushy pea treetops, facing north.

The weather deteriorated, making it a long journey back to the airport where we caught an evening flight to Chengdu. Seated in front of the exit meant our seats would not recline, but exhausted I fell asleep immediately.

I'd wanted to volunteer to work with Pandas in Wolong, but Russ wasn't keen. He didn't relish the idea of cleaning up panda poo on what was supposed to be an enjoyable holiday. I'd have loved to have seen pandas in the wild, but unfortunately, not long before we were due to leave for China, in 2008, they had a devastating earthquake.

It made me think back to December 1989 when I was working at my computer, on the third floor of an office in Australia, and my chair seemed to have a mind of its own when it started vibrating. Dizziness overwhelmed me momentarily, but I thought I'd imagined it. However, there'd been an earthquake 160 kilometres north in Newcastle, one of Australia's worst, measuring five point six on the Richter magnitude scale. Lucky to have only experienced the tremor, I knew how much devastation earthquakes can cause, having also seen the aftermath in Sri Lanka. I was worried about the pandas' safety.

We checked in at the youth hostel in Chengdu and after getting up, the next morning, went in search of breakfast which turned out to be quite a difficult task. We walked many side streets and saw several restaurants but nobody spoke English. In a tiny café full of locals, we sat and made signs with our hands. They served us steamed dumplings which we think were filled with spicy meat dunked in chilli, and we drank a bowl of hot water. We were supposed to put wontons in the hot water but didn't know how to ask for a drink to accompany the other food.

We had to cross several major intersections. When the lights were green, it was for both the pedestrians and bicycles, so I still had to ensure I didn't get run over. Then, although some of the cars would stop, others, along with the buses, would drive straight through beeping their horns. I can only assume they had identity problems and thought they were motorcycles. Cars and buses generally drove along the centre, whereas bicycles and motorbikes zoomed along lanes on the outside. Because they travel on the right hand side, I was never sure which way to look before stepping out onto the road. Then often there would be vehicles going in both directions along the same side of the road.

#

Ouch,' I murmured when he nipped my arm, raising a red welt and bruising the skin. I wasn't expecting that but immediately forgave him when I looked into his soulful round onyx eyes and was captivated by his charms. The black fur patches around them contrasted beautifully with his cream fur, matching his dark ears, legs and shoulders. A keeper spread honey on his arm, and he started licking it before munching on some apple.

Donned in blue overalls and plastic gloves, sitting on a wooden bench, I cuddled this handsome giant panda. Just a baby, at only a year old, he was large and heavy weighing sixteen kilograms. He seemed as content sitting on my lap as I was holding him. Snuggling against his face with my cheek, I could feel the tickle of his coarse coat. The warmth of his body exuded no distinct scent. His claws were blunt, and he wriggled his toes whilst I tickled the dark, smooth sole of his paw.

I wanted to stay with him forever, and I'm sure he reciprocated my feelings because he bleated loudly, in protest, when they took him off my lap. It was difficult to say goodbye. I'd only known him briefly but was dismayed at the thought of never seeing him again. Threatened with extinction, the keeper told me there are fewer than two thousand in the wild, mainly due to reduction in their habitat, which saddened me. I wondered whether pandas had a future in their native environment and hoped that they would survive.

Moments later, I was reminding myself, out loud, over and over again, 'I really held a giant panda,' as my dimples appeared from the smile I couldn't hide. It was amazing to have the opportunity to get close to one of these majestic creatures.

As I danced along the pathway, my eyes were drawn to the sign we passed stating "When one tugs at a single thing in nature, he finds it attached to the rest of the world". I thought how true it was and again how delicate the balance of nature can be. It was an occasion I wouldn't forget.

It wasn't long before my heart was captured again when I cradled an adorable red panda in my arms. Much lighter than the giant panda, he looked like he'd been dipped in a pot of sooty paint because he had thick ebony fur on his legs and underbelly. The russet coat on his back and bushy tail contrasted perfectly with the exquisite markings on his face where cream surrounded his black nose, amber eyes, cheeks and ears. His soft velvet fur had no particular odour and I was grateful he constantly munched on a piece of fruit as his teeth looked sharp. It was an intimate experience to get so close to yet another vulnerable species. Their beauty was part of their downfall, because their pelts are so distinctive.

For such a short stay in China, it was remarkable. I never dreamt that one day I'd hold pandas in my arms. Their plight troubled me, but the conservation breeding programs in place at Chengdu Research Base was a good start. I hoped their remaining habitat could be protected rather than destroyed, so they would be around for many generations to come.

#

My heart stopped beating, just for a moment. All my instincts yelled at me to run, but my feet were stuck firmly to the ground. A fully grown male tiger had left the water and was charging straight at me. He looked resplendent, with his coat of fur rippling in the wind and his massive paws pounding the sand, as his muscular legs carried him forward.

The moment seemed suspended in time until someone broke my concentration, stepping behind me and using me as a shield. I suddenly realized the danger, but at the last moment he turned away.

A helper, waving a stick, chased him up the bank and skilfully guided him back to the rest of the streak.

A friend at work had told me all about the Tiger Temple in Kanchanaburi, in Thailand, having recently been there himself. He knew I'd love it as he knew of my adoration of all wildlife and cats in particular. Nevertheless, before going there, I wanted to be sure that by paying to spend time with the tigers it would be contributing to a good cause and not encouraging mistreatment, as there was much controversy.

I read that some people believe the creatures are drugged, and have had their claws removed so visitors can have their photo taken with them. However, there was no proof, and many people said this wasn't true. I also read that they were allegedly mistreated, which wasn't good either and visitors were not protected properly.

The original cats were rescued from poachers, and I believed that was a good thing because their population in the wild was diminishing rapidly, and if they hadn't been cared for by the monks, then they would most likely have perished.

Buddhists are encouraged to love and practice loving kindness towards all living beings and taught it's not right to take away the life of any living creature, since they all have the right to exist. So I was convinced they wouldn't intentionally harm the animals.

Their brochure explained that they were building a new home for the tigers, on twelve acres, where they would be rehoused and new cubs rehabilitated prior to release back into the forest. This made sense, and although I am not a great lover of zoos or wildlife parks, I do believe they have a role to play in raising awareness and increasing numbers of threatened species.

Tiger parts are used in traditional Chinese medicines and fetch a high price. The Environmental Investigation Agency (EIA) believes at least one tiger is killed daily for this purpose. It makes me so miserable to know people can do this to such an endearing animal.

There were also stories of the cats attacking tourists. Having previously spent time with hand reared cheetah and wild gorillas, I didn't have any concerns about my safety. In the end, I decided we should go and make up our own minds.

Russ and I arrived at the Temple, early in the morning, and we were greeted by an Australian volunteer who asked us to sign a disclaimer. Flashbacks of the disclaimers we'd previously signed for white-water rafting and bungy-jumping came to mind, but I decided this was the sort of risk I was prepared to take for such a special encounter.

Immediately inside the gate, a baby calf had just been born. We walked to the temple and took off our shoes. We were part of a group of six visitors and sat around a mat on the floor. There were four cubs that were only five weeks old on the rug, and we were told to keep them there. When I picked one up, he complained loudly, so I put him down because I didn't want to upset him. Another one was nibbling my knee, which tickled. They were gorgeous, and I was enjoying stroking their backs, tickling their bellies and scrunching their ears.

Whilst playing with them, a monk blessed the food and said prayers before we could eat. Sitting on the ground, with our feet pointed away from the monks and our hands pressed together in prayer, I watched the little ones messing around out of the corner of my eye.

After breakfast, I bottle fed one of the four month olds, holding the bottle up so no air got in and stroking his back at the same time. Then I stood by one of the bigger creatures to have my photo taken. I found it hard to believe this was happening, and I was so close to real tigers.

Next, we walked the four month olds to their bathing pool on a lead.

The guide said, 'Make sure they keep their head in front of you because they have a tendency to bite the back of your legs. Also, make sure you don't let them get close to the person in front of you, or they will nip their calves.'

Walking the cub was an amazing experience, and when he ran, I ran with him. At the pool, we got in the water to play but again had to be careful as they were now off their leads. One nipped the back of Russ' leg when he wasn't looking, but he was quickly able to push him off before he broke the skin. I splashed them with water whilst they rough and tumbled, and played ball together. Afterwards, we washed them with shampoo, and then their keepers hosed them. Once they were tied up, we hand fed them cooked chicken. I thought this an unusual diet but was told they were also given vitamins, and they didn't want them to eat raw food.

One, only five weeks old, was in a large cage, and the volunteer explained, 'I sleep there at night with the four tiny cubs.'

'Is that why you have a big scratch across your cheek?' I asked.

'Yes, but it's a small price to pay for such a great job,' he said.

It was enjoyable watching and interacting with the younger ones, but I couldn't have been more thrilled to spend time with the eight to eighteen month olds that were so much bigger. Whilst walking him to the canyon, so he could swim in the cool water, again I had to make sure his head stayed in front of me. Holding the restraint with both hands meant that should he try to bite me, I could lock the arm holding the lead close to his neck, so he couldn't turn to reach me. That was the theory anyway. My companion kept stopping to sniff things on the way as well as stretching out along the pathway and up trees. He seemed as happy as a puppy going for a walk.

It amused me when the volunteer told us, 'You need to stand in "The Circle of Life",' as he drew a circle in the sand at the side of the canyon.

'Is that from Lion King?' I asked.

'You are the first person to realize I have taken the expression from the movie. It's easier to protect everyone if you are all in one area.'

Each of the eight cats had an individual minder. The eighteen month old kept attacking one of the small trees in the canyon, so they had to keep chasing him away. A few of the others tried to climb out of the canyon, but a guardian chased them back. Then another charged at us. The tigers frolicked in the cool water, chasing each other, jumping off the rocks and playing ball. After an hour or more in the gorge, our time was up. Walking the largest, oldest cat on a lead, he looked so regal and powerful that I was honoured to have the opportunity to do this.

Afterwards, walking through the park, I saw deer, wild boar and horses roaming freely. The leopard was in his impressive new enclosure with green grass, trees and plants.

At the waterfall enclosure, called "The Tiger Falls", a moat surrounded two caves providing hiding places for the tigers and a green grassy area where an older tiger lay sleeping. The sign indicated it housed three tigers, Pa Yu, Saifa and Sangtawan. They were from the oldest generation of tigers in the temple.

By now the park had opened to the general public, so the four month old cubs appeared on leads. A bit later, some of the older tigers were shown, including a five year old. The Abbot walked amongst them, dressed in orange robes, patting their heads and one licked his hand. I then got to walk alongside another cat to the canyon where photos were taken with a fully grown tiger resting his head on my lap.

I could hear tourists saying they must be drugged but having seen them charge around the canyon in and out of the water, they just seemed exhausted from all the exercise they'd had that morning. They still had their claws, and I never saw any of the staff mistreat them, although I did notice one of the volunteers had bruised calves where the cubs had sunk their teeth.

I had such a fantastic time that I didn't want to leave, but our taxi driver had been waiting too long already to give us a ride back to our lodgings. I got into the taxi with wonderful memories etched on my heart.

Today I think differently as it has since been alleged that some of the tigers and their cubs have been bred, so their body parts can be sold for a high price on the black market. I couldn't understand how anyone could be so cruel to these splendid creatures, especially as they are endangered in the wild. It's tragic and my admiration goes out to the organizations that persevered to uncover this illegal trade and stop it from continuing.

#

A few days later, we crossed the Australian funded friendship bridge, from Thailand into Laos, and caught a taxi into town where I'd booked a guesthouse, not far from the banks of the café latte coloured Mekong River. It reminded me of Thailand, twenty years ago, before it was urbanised.

Wandering around town, there were several expensive French bakeries and restaurants, but I was more interested in the Nam Phu water fountain which wasn't running. It was empty. Dirt roads, lined with trees, ran parallel to the river where we walked broken pavements to fascinating wats and peaceful temples full of ancient artefacts and Buddha images. The cast of the last rays, from the sun, ironed the furrows from my brow as I watched the light disappear over the Mekong River whilst my mind transferred to the plump foam cushions around the al fresco dining table.

It was the first scorching hot day we'd experienced and seemed even hotter when we walked to the Patuxai Victory Monument. It resembled the Arc de Triomphe in Paris where, more than twenty years ago, I'd nearly lost my knees when stepping out in front of a car.

The building was built in the sixties with US purchased cement that was supposed to have been used for the construction of a new airport. Instead, they made a memorial for all those who had fought for independence from the French, Japanese and Thai.

It appealed to me that the tower symbolized the five Buddhist principles of amiability, flexibility, honesty, honour and prosperity as I believed they were great ethics.

It was an easy climb, past seven floors and many souvenir shops, to the spiral staircase leading to the observation deck. As usual, my stomach fluttered as I eyed the tapering stairs. My legs wobbled as my feet tried to find support. I made it to the top of the monument for a good view of the city and The Royal Stupa which was coated in gold leaf and glistening in the sun's rays.

I peered down at the water fountains in the grounds below, which were empty. Maybe there was a water shortage in Vientiane, or perhaps they were just temporarily broken down. Possibly they were drying out, ready to be repainted. I'd never know.

#

It wasn't long before we were back in Bangkok for the day. We tried to catch a taxi to Dusit Zoo only to find it was closed for the day. The driver explained it was something to do with people in yellow shirts, but we didn't understand what he meant at that stage.

We travelled on to Phuket, staying in Karon Plaza which is built around a small temple and off the main streets so not too noisy. The rest of the town was extremely commercialised with many flashy restaurants and shops. Nothing like I remembered when we were there nineteen years ago.

We had return train tickets to get us back to Bangkok for our flight home, but that was all disrupted when we discovered the airport was being held under siege by the PAD (The People's Alliance for Democracy), who were wearing yellow shirts. Now I understood what the taxi driver had been trying to explain when we were in Bangkok.

I asked a local shop owner to contact British Airways (BA) in Bangkok for us, but after holding on her mobile phone for forty minutes, she got cut off, and I had to pay two hundred baht for the call. In the meantime, the power went down, so we were unable to use the internet or make phone calls from the guesthouse until at least one o'clock, which didn't help because we were due to leave to travel back to Bangkok before then.

Eventually we found an internet café with a generator, and on searching BA's website, it showed today's flight had been diverted to Singapore. I also discovered there was a branch of the travel company I had booked through, in Phuket. Since I'd booked our flights through this company, the shop owner phoned them for us, only to be told they were at lunch, so she suggested we come back later in the afternoon.

Running out of time, we made the decision to throw away our booked train tickets to get back to Bangkok that afternoon. She rang again for us later, but the travel agent said, because I'd booked our tickets online, they wouldn't help us. Consequently, I tried faxing BA in Bangkok to see if we could get any response that way, but they faxed us back just providing phone numbers in Australia and the UK.

After purchasing a phone card, I rang the Australian number which was toll free, but they turned out to be Qantas. Their representative gave me BA's number in Singapore and then tried to transfer me to BA in Australia. However, it was a recorded message to say they were closed.

Exasperated, I emailed the travel agency in Australia, to see if they could help but got no reply. Having emailed a friend in Australia, who then phoned them, they told her the airport would open later in the day. We knew that couldn't be true as the PAD had now taken over Don Muang and Chang Mai airports as well.

At a loss as to what to do, I emailed the Australian Embassy whose staff couldn't help us either and just referred us to the smart-traveller website. I tried phoning BA in the UK, but the phone number was incorrect. It was all so frustrating, but I had to resolve the problem one way or another if we ever wanted to get home.

It was three in the afternoon by the time power was restored, so I got back on the guesthouse computer and found another number for BA in London. My phone card then decided to play up, and a couple of international phones wouldn't recognise it. I finally got through, but all they could offer me were flights out of Singapore and not for several days. We'd no other choice so took that option. The buses to Singapore were not only a twenty-two hour trip, but there were problems with fundamentalists on the border between Thailand and Malaysia. I didn't want to run into any more problems.

Needing time to think, we went for a two hour walk along Karon beach, an idyllic stretch of white sand that is about three kilometres from end to end. Oblivious to the actions unfolding in Bangkok, sun loungers lined the length of the beach, but it was still relatively quiet with just a handful of water sport facilities. The pale sand squeaked audibly when we walked on it. If we were going to be stranded somewhere, Phuket was a great place for it to happen.

Back at the guesthouse, I checked the internet for flights from Phuket to Singapore. They were extremely expensive, so I looked into flights to Kuala Lumpur instead which would avoid travelling over the Thai/Malaysian border by bus. Asia Air had reasonably priced flights, so I quickly booked on-line because the prices were escalating by the minute.

When the confirmation came through, we noticed we were not allowed more than fifteen kilograms each of luggage. As we checked in leaving Sydney, I am sure we had thirty-four kilograms between us, so we might be in trouble, and it didn't say how much they charged for excess luggage.

Later at the guesthouse, I found a hostel in Kuala Lumpur on the internet, and because we'd committed to go to Singapore, booked to stay there overnight before travelling on by bus. We watched the Australian News about Bangkok airport and heard the Chief of Police had been fired when he refused to clear the airport of protestors.

With our travel plans now sorted, we got up late and caught buses to Cape Panwa. The sun was shining on the sapphire sea when we arrived, and it looked spectacular. We walked along the promenade, up a side road and down a dirt track to a small bay where they were building a massive resort right on the beach. It seemed such a shame to have so much development along the coastline.

Later, we went to the aquarium and were amazed at the tanks of different fish and an underwater travellator. Stingrays and small sharks were in the overhead tunnel. Outside, we followed a nature trail where we saw pens of mainly green turtles and a few olive ridley turtles. Once again, I thought of the tiny turtle I set free in Borneo and wondered where he was now and if he had survived.

On the way back, I hit my head on the rafters on the bus, so hard that it knocked me to the ground. Later in the evening, I had an awful migraine and kept vomiting for hours. I hoped I'd be well enough for our adventure the following morning.

I'd recovered well and was pleased to be driven to Phang Nga Bay which was about an hour's drive from town and then transferred to a long boat to get to James Bond Island which rose dramatically from the sea. On the way there, I got drenched in spray as the boat caused plumes to shoot into the air when it crashed against the waves. It was a hot day, so I dried quickly.

There were many tourist stalls on the island with all the usual souvenirs for sale. James Bond Island found fame through the 1974 Bond film "The Man with the Golden Gun". I thought it was apt for Russ to go there because he was often told by friends that he looked like Pierce Brosnan, who had played James Bond. A girl in Vietnam also told him so, and a waitress in Fiji said he looked like Roger Moore, who starred in this particular film.

On the way back, we went elephant trekking along a creek. Unlike in Africa, we didn't sit on a saddle but on a wooden seat which was tied to the elephant's back. Although comfortable, I thought it took the authenticity away from the experience.

It started to rain, so we put up umbrellas, which looked hilarious and reminded me of old movies set in colonial India. I just wasn't wearing a corset, long skirt and bonnet.

Afterwards in a show, a macaque collected a coconut and then decided to jump on my still sore head with it. I was pleased it didn't try to crack it on my skull, because I couldn't cope with another migraine.

We were up very early, at four-thirty, to catch a taxi to Phuket airport where our luggage was weighed and deemed within our allowance before the Air Asia flight spirited us to Kuala Lumpur. The SkyBus took us to the main bus station, from where we caught the mono rail the four stops to Imbi and then followed detailed instructions to walk to the hostel.

The following day, the yellow bus transported us to Singapore. It was rather flash looking, and the seats on the bus were first class. The arms looked like a walnut dashboard, the seats were wide, reclined and had a leg rest as well as a foot rest. It was going to be a long trip home, but at least we could relax in relative comfort.

From the bus station in central Singapore, we walked down the road to the MRT station, changing trains once to get to the airport where we took the Skytrain to terminal 1 to check-in.

The attendant said, 'There have been some changes to your flight.' I immediately panicked, thinking, what next, were we to be stuck in Singapore? I'd enjoyed the extra few days but now needed to get home. However, he must have meant the changes already made, not that there were new ones, because he checked us in okay.

Although a fantastic trip, as Thailand seems to have continuous civil unrest, I will avoid it where possible rather than risk getting stuck there again. Asia is getting developed so quickly, it's harder and harder to find more untouched areas to visit. I enjoy experiencing the remoteness of places by ourselves rather than sharing with hordes of tourists. I finally felt that having visited a quarter of the countries in Asia, my childhood quest to visit another of the five continents I was taught about at school, had been fulfilled. Now I just hoped to visit the Americas.

CHAPTER SEVENTEEN – ALL THAT GLISTENS ISN'T GOLD
Hawaii, USA, Mexico

It was time to expand my travels and finally include America that fifth continent I'd learnt about in geography classes. I'd left it until last because I hadn't found it quite as alluring as Asia and Africa. Perhaps I'd find a different culture in Hawaii.

When I landed in Oahu, I quickly learnt two Hawaiian words which would prove useful, "Aloha" meaning hello and "Mahalo" being thank you.

We checked into our hotel and carried our backpacks along to our room. I pushed the swipe card into the lock and turned the handle. Nothing happened, it was still locked. I tried again with the card the other way up, but it still didn't open.

'Let me try,' said Russ, taking the card and jabbing it in and out of the slot as fast as he could.

'Perhaps it goes the other way,' I suggested whilst looking at the lock.

He tried it quickly, then in both directions slowly, then pushing with pressure and finally softly. Nothing worked, we were stuck outside our room.

'I'll take it back to reception,' I advised.

'Excuse me, the card won't open our room,' I explained.

'Just a minute, maybe it didn't program properly,' he replied, typing on the computer keyboard.

I waited patiently until he handed back the card advising, 'It should work fine now.'

Back I went to join Russ outside our room, and we started the card dance all over again.

'Let's do it together,' I said cheekily. 'First this way, then that, fast, then slow, gently then harder.' Still nothing worked.

Back at reception, I swallowed clearing the lump in my throat before explaining, 'This swipe doesn't open the door either.'

'Maybe it's faulty,' he replied unapologetically.

After programming another card, I again returned to Russ and followed the swipe dance one more time. On my third attempt the door finally opened and with a spring in my step I left our bags inside whilst we went exploring.

Late in the afternoon, I curiously wondered why a crowd had gathered together on the beach and were looking out to sea.

'Russ what do you think they're looking at?' I asked.

'I don't know. I can't see anything,' he replied, following my gaze.

Although many people filled the beach, it was still peaceful standing barefoot on the soft sand with palm trees growing in a long line and the Diamond Head tuff cones in the distance. A gentle breeze caressed my skin and cooled my brow as I breathed the salty fresh air.

Slowly, as time passed, it became apparent what the crowd was waiting for when the sun set over the ocean emitting a tangerine glow across the sky and a mosaic of colours along the rippling surface of the water.

The next morning, the sun was shining and seared my skin as we walked to the entrance of the volcano. From the start of the trail, I could see the summit ahead and was pleased a handrail snaked along the track, so I could hold on whilst climbing the seventy-four steps. Twenty minutes later, we entered a long dark tunnel, high enough to be able to walk through comfortably without bending over, but a little spooky as it was dimly lit, and my eyes didn't adjust well to the darkness. Because the tunnel curved, no daylight was available until close to the end.

The next ninety-nine steps were steep and exerted my thigh muscles whilst leading to another shorter lit tunnel. I found the narrow spiral staircase even more confronting. Struggling with the tapered stairs, inside an unlit bunker, I placed my feet carefully. Impatient to get to the top, I briskly scaled the last of the trails steps ending at the summit. The refreshing wind cooled my face and the sweat running down my back whilst I absorbed the panoramic 360 degree view. I happily pointed out the tall lighthouse, sailboats in the cobalt bay and the coral reefs to Russ.

On the way down, I noticed that, although the crater was dry, it was littered with grasses, trees and wildflowers including the small yellow-orange official flower of Oahu. The descent of 560 feet to the bottom was much quicker than the ascent.

I relished the time we spent in Oahu, visiting Iolani Palace, Foster Botanical Gardens and USS Arizona Memorial, but it was soon time to move on to the Big Island.

The 2.45 morning wake-up call was to enable us to catch the three o'clock shuttle bus. The receptionist assured us, 'It will be an hour long journey to the airport, and you need to be ready to check in two hours beforehand.'

I guess the journey might have taken an hour in rush hour traffic, but early in the morning, it only took fifteen minutes, and the airport wasn't even open when we arrived. We stood outside in the crisp dawn air until four o'clock when the doors were opened, and we were, at last, able to get our boarding passes.

There was a notice advising to take all film out of checked through baggage because the x-ray machines would process it. I sifted through our backpacks and put it all in our hand luggage, just in case, but was then asked to put that through the x-ray machines along with my shoes, hand-luggage and jewellery. I still set off the alarm when I went through and had to be searched, which Russ found highly amusing.

The customs officer asked him, 'Can you pick up your wife's belongings that have been through the x-ray?'

'No, I don't want to touch her shoes,' he said, holding his nose.

I was self-conscious standing in front of everyone, first lifting each arm and then each leg to be frisked whilst he joked a more detailed search might be required. I do love his sense of humour but not at those crucial moments, in case it's taken literally.

Once we'd landed, a shuttle bus took us to the car rental place where we picked up our hire car.

'Aloha, I have booked a vehicle,' I said.

'You have booked an economy car, but would you like to upgrade to a convertible?' the clerk asked me.

'No thank you, we are happy with what I booked.'

'Perhaps you should upgrade to a bigger more comfortable car.'

'No thank you, may I just pick up what I ordered because it's all we need.'

'We don't have an economy car to give you, so you may have a Pontiac Grand Am, which is an upgrade of four classes free of charge.'

'Mahalo.' I took the keys and we headed towards the car.

It was strange for Russ driving on the right and confusing for me as a passenger.

The first junction we arrived at, he asked me, 'Where do I go, do I take the slip road to the right?'

'Yes, I think so,' I said. Lack of sleep was inhibiting my thought process.

He ended up pulling over at a lookout point after about thirty minutes because we were both too tired to concentrate. After an hour of snoozing, we continued on to Hawaii Volcanoes National Park which was ninety-seven miles from Kailua-Kona.

At the huge reserve, I found the landscape remarkable with masses of smouldering craters, steam vents and cinder cones. I could smell the sulphuric gases whilst viewing the steaming rocks in various hues of yellow and orange.

I was amazed at the oasis amidst the pumice rock and hardened lava of rich green trees, bushes and ferns which attracted birds. I shone my torch as I walked further inside a lava tube beyond the lit area.

Some children were straining to see into the darkness, so Russ shouted loudly, 'I am a troll and coming to get you.' They screamed and ran out of the tunnel.

On the way back, we stopped at Kahalu'u Beach Park, which was the highlight of my trip. Whilst snorkelling, I saw huge schools of large colourful fish with unusual names such as ringtail surgeon fish, lagoon triggerfish, orangeband surgeonfish, raccoon butterflyfish, convict tang, longnose butterflyfish, saddle wrasse, Moorish idol, Christmas wrasse, Picasso triggerfish, yellow tang, stripebelly pufferfish and bullethead parrotfish. I had to pinch myself when a large Hawaiian green sea turtle swam so close to me that I could have touched it.

Swimming alongside, I watched whilst it swam effortlessly through the water. With so many turtle species on the endangered list, I wondered if the turtle I'd released in Borneo was still alive as it had touched my soul.

#

On arrival at LA airport, I had trouble giving my fingerprints at passport control because the machine wouldn't read them properly. I asked myself whether they would let me in. They took my photo and then tried the fingerprint machine again. The index finger on my right hand would not register, so they tried the left and this time it worked. After picking up my backpack, we headed through customs and caught the Flyaway bus to Union Station where the first thing I noticed on our way downtown were the palm trees. They looked out of place on city streets.

'Here is our booking confirmation,' I said to the hotel receptionist whilst handing her our receipt.

'We don't have your booking,' she replied, running her finger down the reservations book.

I looked at Russ with an anguished expression because I'd no idea where to find another hotel at the same sort of price.

'We're not fully booked, so I can fit you in,' she stated, handing me a key.

Whilst we climbed the stairs, I said to Russ, 'At least we don't have to do the swipe dance again.'

Our room had air-conditioning and a coffee percolator. Outside in the corridor, I used the ice dispensing machine. I pressed and held the button as ice clattered into my cup, but then it continued in an avalanche overflowing all over the floor. It looked like a hail storm had whirled along the landing. Oops, I should've just pressed the button once and not held it.

I had a great time in Los Angeles visiting Hollywood, Santa Monica, the Braer Pits and some of the theme parks. At the Hollywood Wax Work Museum, I spotted many famous stars including Captain Jack Sparrow. I was surprised the statues weren't melting like candles as it was the hottest day recorded there. With the second instalment of "Pirates of the Caribbean" only just released, he would have been a popular sight. I could never have anticipated meeting this charismatic pirate many years later, not in America but in Queensland, when the fifth sequel was filmed. I admired his enduring patience with the crowd of well-wishers when Johnny Depp kept in character as Captain Jack Sparrow whilst chatting casually to his fans.

The only celebrity I got to meet in America was in San Diego Zoo whilst spending the day there. Working our way down the hill, I was surprised to spot Mel Gibbon. His black hair stood out against his white cheek patches as he watched over his six offspring. His mate Tina looked quite different, light yellow with a black stripe down the middle of her head. Their crested gibbon babies were the same colour as her and camouflaged amongst her fur.

From LA, we'd caught the local bus to the Greyhound station. It travelled straight along Seventh Street, and when it stopped to let others off, and I could see the Greyhound sign, I too alighted.

'Thank you,' I called to the driver.

'This is not your stop, Ma'am,' he reprimanded me.

When I finally understood what he was saying, I got back on the bus suitably contrite but just for one more stop.

At the station, after some time queuing, I bought return tickets to San Diego. The guard helped me work out which gate to line up behind because the half past eight morning bus didn't arrive until nine o'clock. Surprisingly, not many passengers spoke English as they were mainly Hispanic. It was freezing on the bus, from the air conditioning, but fairly empty. The seats were stuck in various positions of recline, or should I say decline, as they had seen better days. No food or drink was allowed on the bus, and there was no entertainment provided. During the journey, we stopped for a break.

Getting back on the bus, Russ told me, 'The men's toilets don't have doors on them.'

'Never mind,' I replied, not understanding the consequences.

'I'm in shock. It was horrific because they were occupied when I entered.' He laughed in mock anguish.

Arriving in San Diego about midday, we hiked about ten blocks to our accommodation. The hostel was located on a corner above a classy seafood restaurant in the heart of the historic Gaslamp Quarter, in Downtown San Diego. Each night, my mouth would water when I walked passed the diners at outdoor tables eating lobster whilst I headed for the supermarket to see what was on special.

Before dinner, I had a scorching shower. The shower dial indicated it should run cold and the more it turned the hotter it should've got. However, it turned out to be the reverse and because I couldn't work it out, I ended up rinsing the soap off with an empty beer bottle filled from the sink. The water consumption must have been terrible. To get cold, it needed to be turned up high and run for a long time before it was bearable.

The heat was sizzling all day and all night. Our room was a sauna. Although we had an ineffective ceiling fan, there wasn't any air-conditioning. At night-time we would soak our towels in cold water and drape them over our naked bodies to cool down. When they warmed to body temperature, we would run them under the tap once again. I just hoped we wouldn't go mouldy.

The kitchen reminded me of our accommodation in Austria. At three storeys up, I didn't feel safe with the low windows open and only a strip of masking tape across them. I'd no intention of base jumping out of them, on purpose or by accident, so I chose to sit in the centre of the room.

The hostel put on free activities such as guided trips around the park or to Mexico on particular days. We didn't get the chance to go on any, so Russ decided to start his own trip and hand wrote a flyer for a pub crawl. It read, "To go on this guided tour you just have to ply the leader with free beer". I thought it a great idea, but unfortunately he didn't get any takers.

I couldn't resist visiting Mexico because it was less than twenty miles to the south. I'd heard it had a bad reputation for extreme violence between the drug cartels. I wasn't too worried about that, but I was wary of the tales of corrupt police and greedy shopkeepers. Having introduced the world to chocolate and chillies, surely it couldn't be all bad.

Russ and I caught the blue trolley to San Ysidro and then tried to catch the Mexicoach, from the car park to Tijuana, but it never turned up. In the end, we walked across the border with four others who had been waiting with us for the bus to arrive. The Tourist office directed us to a bus station, but a cab driver made us a better deal to travel together to Rosarito Beach. The usual vendors were there trying to sell us jewellery, sarongs and other souvenirs. It was a relief to find they took no for an answer and were not as pushy as those in Bali or Egypt.

Bored of the beach, and with no historical sights nearby, we caught a taxi to Foxploration, a tatty worn out park. Originally built ten years earlier for the filming of Titanic, the complex overlooked the Pacific Ocean just three miles south of Rosarito. Eight films had been made there along with several TV shows, commercials and video productions. The most interesting part was a guided tour through the sets of Titanic. It must have been a majestic ship, in its time, with intricately carved wood work, elegant sculptures, deep piled lush carpets supporting rich velvet fabrics and aromatic smelling leather covering comfortable chairs around a table set with a bottle of champagne and glasses.

Eventually we returned to Tijuana and walked along Avenida Revolucion, at a brisk pace, where hundreds of shops and stalls spilled out onto the pavement stocking blankets, baskets, pottery, hand-carved trinkets and toys. Music carried into the still night air and onto the streets from dance clubs and seedy bars. I didn't want to still be in Mexico after dark, so there wasn't time to stop and browse, but apparently it's the world's most-shopped street.

Safely back in San Diego, a ferry took us to Coronado where the sand sparkled like it had gold glitter in it.

'Look at the sand,' I said to Russ, making grooves in it with my toes.

'Maybe it is gold, and the American's are so rich they cannot be bothered to collect it,' he replied, scooping up a handful.

I laughed. 'I read that it's actually the presence of the mineral mica, also known as sugar sand, which looks like gold, so there is no point in trying to put it in your pocket.'

We paddled in the cold sea while the sun caught the glint of the gold sticking to our feet.

I didn't mind when it was time to leave America, but I struggled with their security. As I went through passport control to the gate, I set off the alarm, even though I'd already taken my bangles off. I got checked over with the hand operated machine, but when they discovered I had a money belt on, they marched me into a room to take it off. They checked there was nothing inside but a few leftover travellers cheques and then patted me down before finally letting me go.

I found it an interesting country with many big flashy parks and zoos such as Disneyland, Universal Studios, Hollywood and SeaWorld. They were bigger and better than anywhere else I'd seen, but somehow I still didn't feel at home.

CHAPTER EIGHTEEN – THE LONG ROAD
St Kitts, Antigua, St Lucia, Barbados, St Vincent

Thinking of travelling to a different part of the Americas, the Caribbean sounded interesting, so I decided to do a little research on which islands to visit. I visualized myself relaxing by palm trees lining white soft sandy beaches, bordering crystal clear blue seas, in a tranquil paradise.

I found out LIAT (Leeway Islands Air Transport) flew to certain islands which would enable us to island hop. They covered twenty-one destinations, and I picked a few independent islands rather than those that were regions of France, municipalities of the Netherlands, territories of England or part of the USA. I decided on Antigua, St Lucia, Barbados, St Vincent, and St Kitts and Nevis.

Once I started researching on the internet, I discovered a darker side to the Caribbean I'd not known about. Murder rates in St Kitts, St Lucia and St Vincent are some of the highest in the world with Antigua and Barbados still much higher than Australia. I wondered if there was a better way to see the islands, and perhaps it would be safer to go on a cruise instead. Nonetheless, on the forums, I read about cruise passengers being robbed at gunpoint and some even murdered on the islands. It certainly didn't sound like paradise to me.

Although a bit dubious about it, I'd never been put off by fear before and wouldn't this time. However, for the second time, I was experiencing problems taking time off work. To take advantage of several travel deals, I ended up organizing flights and accommodation on-line. I then spent several nervous weeks awaiting my leave application approval. I knew if it was declined I'd have to resign and find another job.

It would be a long journey because we had to stop at Miami to get to the islands, changing planes in Los Angeles and Detroit on the way there. I pondered on several occasions whether I'd made the right decision, but it was too late now with either large deposits or full fares paid.

Luckily I was granted my accrued holiday, in the end, so could enjoy the trip without worrying about every penny we spent and knowing I had employment to return to.

We decided to see the Everglades, and since we only had one complete day there, it was easiest to take a tour which was also informative.

When we passed huge areas of ugly looking trees, devoid of life, the stumps stood eerily above the water in silence like a cemetery of trees. I couldn't see or hear any birdlife.

The bus driver explained, 'These are imported Australian melaleuca trees, but because they're eliminating all of the vegetation surrounding them in the Everglades and soaking up too much water, we are trying to eradicate them. Over fifty years, they have spread through hundreds of thousands of acres. To kill the trees, we tried chopping them down to just six inches high, but this inadvertently created another three million seeds which took hold. The only option left was to poison them with herbicides.'

It was heart-breaking to see such destruction. I hoped something had been learnt from the mistake of introducing new species to an area.

He continued, 'Burmese pythons are another imported problem in the Everglades. Once pets, but no longer wanted, snakes had been released into the wild and had multiplied possibly to as many as one hundred and fifty thousand. Because they eat the native birds and mammals and are not indigenous to the Everglades, we are again trying to eradicate them.'

'Wow, nature has an extremely fine balance, and as much as I love reptiles, it's depressing to hear we're still messing it up,' I said to Russ.

'I know, sadly it's happening all over the world,' he replied.

At Gator Park, we got front seats on the airboat for a thirty-five minute ride. We took off slowly when the boat navigated a narrow channel where we spotted birds and alligators. Reaching open waters, I pictured myself as Crockett from the Miami Vice television series when the driver opened the throttle, propelling us forward and spinning the boat creating spray to cool us down. He gave us earplugs to wear because the engine was deafening, and I held on tightly whilst we flew across the water and straight over the saw grass. We spotted a magnificent blue heron standing regally in the water, then travelled slowly back down the channel again, sighting more alligators and a purple gallinule with cute fluffy little chicks.

From Miami, we were able to fly directly to St Kitts and then island hop with LIAT. I'd booked to stay in a guesthouse at Conaree but was surprised to find Conaree Beach had dark, mostly black, sand on the Atlantic side of the island, and it didn't look inviting with litter strewn along it. Where are those palm trees and the white sand? I walked along Half Moon Bay where a brown pelican dived for food. Whilst strolling past Muddy Point, I spotted a vervet monkey and an egret. I thought about taking a photo, but by the time I got my camera out, a swarm of mosquitoes appeared and bit me relentlessly. Not wanting to contract dengue fever, I briskly walked away to escape the blood-suckers and quickly exited the golf course up a steep hill from where I'd a fabulous view of the coastline. We followed the road around and back down to Frigate Bay where I finally found the leafy palm trees on a long bleached beach with only a scattering of people on it.

The following day, the ferry bobbed gently as it cut through the water to the island of Nevis where we discovered the enchanting Botanical Gardens of Nevis with Mount Nevis as a backdrop in the distance. An impressive pair of lion dog statues guarded the entrance, and inside, Hindu statues, including the elephant-headed Ganesh, the Teaching Buddha and Shiva, were set amongst the gardens and ponds. Inside an imposing rainforest glasshouse (which wasn't actually glass but flyscreen mesh), I touched the rough surface of the Amazonian themed statues and a lost temple whilst listening to the friendly parrots in cages. Outside, I strolled around a lovely formal garden with symmetrically set out flower beds growing bromeliads with a water fountain in the centre. The orchid garden was full of colourful blooms along the pathway leading to another fountain, with dolphin sculptures no longer spouting water, perhaps because the electricity had been "outed" until three that afternoon. Well that was the case on St Kitts, but perhaps not on Nevis.

Abruptly, my smooth soled sandals skidded on the loose gravel and when my feet whooshed from underneath me, I found myself sitting on the ground. Russ was laughing heartily but stopped as soon as he saw how quickly my knee was swelling. I twisted it as I fell and now feeling nauseous, struggled to put any weight on it. At least it took my mind off the itchy mosquito bites on my legs.

The cooling sea breeze made the palms dance around us, cloaked in the sultry air. I rested my knee whilst sitting on a cast iron chair in the gazebo, overlooking the glassy still waters of the lily pond. The tweeting of birds filled the air along with the hooting call of a bird, or maybe the sound was from one of the tiny frogs. Small lizards darted between the foliage and basked in the sun which was warming the concrete path.

It was so peaceful and relaxing with only the nagging pain from my knee. I stood and gingerly put weight on it. It was bearable but dreadfully sore. Slowly limping through the fruit trees and passed the cacti and succulent beds, I returned to the entrance. Although reluctant to leave, I knew we needed to be back at the guesthouse before dark because it wasn't safe in Basseterre at night.

LIAT flew us to Antigua where I'd been looking forward to strolling along the beach near our hotel. Antigua is said to have 365 beaches, one for each day of the year, so having dropped off our backpacks, we followed the directions we'd been given. At the back of the hotel, we came to a gate and when we passed through it, were approached by a guard.

'We're just walking to the beach,' I explained.

'You can't come this way. This is now private property and no longer a thoroughfare,' she said, closing her fingers around the handle of her baton.

'How do we get to the beach if we can't access it this way?' I politely asked.

'You need a car because you have to drive the long way around,' she said grumpily.

Without a vehicle, we decided to go to English Harbour instead. One bus took us to St. John's, the capital and largest city of Antigua, from where we caught another. It was at least a forty minute ride to Nelson's Dockyard where we entered the eighteenth century naval base which was full of old buildings converted into shops and a museum for Horatio Nelson. Plaques explained the history of the buildings. The harbour was peaceful. A massive black yacht was anchored with its main sail up, but there wasn't a beach.

After browsing the shops, we walked around to the marina on English Harbour where the sea was a sapphire blue but lacked the white sand normally complementing the water's edge. Feeling tired, I sat and watched the frigate birds flying high in the sky above the ocean. Why were we having so much trouble finding a nice beach?

Back at the hotel, I put cold drinks in the fridge and then went outside where we watched the sun disappear behind the clouds, not quite meeting the water. Humming birds and turtle doves fluttered around the verdant foliage enveloping the deck. Geckos darted in and out of the planks, calling to each other.

'It's so peaceful here and the view over Deep Bay is picturesque,' I said to Russ as I sat relaxing in a chair. 'Look, the deep blue lagoon is separated from the bay by a narrow strip of land covered in tropical palm trees,' I pointed out.

'We must be able to get to one of the beaches on Antigua whilst we're here,' Russ said, sipping on a glass of ice cold beer.

'We only have one more day, but let's try to find one tomorrow,' I replied.

In the morning, we undertook another bus journey, this time alighting before the dockyard to make the steep climb to Shirley Heights. About a mile up the hill, it was good to stop at the air-conditioned interpretation centre to cool down. Back outside, the sun roasted the skin on the back of my neck to a chestnut brown, evaporating the droplets caused from the humidity in the air, sapping my energy and weakening my determination to reach the summit.

When we finally arrived at the lookout at Fort Shirley, I was glowing from exertion and sweat stung my eyes and trickled down my back. A cold drink was refreshing whilst I pulled at my wet t-shirt sticking to my skin. It was a strenuous climb, but already I was mesmerised by the rich royal blue sea stretching across the Caribbean, from the harbour below to the islands of Guadeloupe and Monserrat. The sun danced across the surface sparkling like diamonds.

Determined to find a beach on the way back, we turned off for Galleon Beach, down another steep road. Taking off my sandals, I paddled along the water's edge, the soft sand massaging the soles of my feet, and the sea gently cooling my aching muscles. Beneath the undulating hills, which were covered in tropical foliage, I sat on the wooden jetty dangling my legs in the water whilst watching Russ swim. I sighed, comprehending that this was the only beach on Antigua I was likely to visit as we were leaving early the next morning.

It was pouring with rain when we landed in St Lucia which, reflected my mood when I was told we needed an entry visa at a cost of US$50 each. I started to think that passport control was robbing us before we even made it into the crime-ridden country.

We were shuffled into a room to complete the necessary paperwork and hand over the dough. Russ made a comment about how expensive the three month visa was, considering we were only staying for two days.

'Can we get a refund on the other eighty-eight days when we are leaving?' he enquired cheekily.

The officer obviously had no idea of our tight budget when replying, 'It will be small change to you.'

Once we had the visa stamped in our passports, we cleared customs and caught a taxi to the hotel. On the way there, the driver explained that the resort had changed its name because it had a new owner. Immediately I was worried, as I'd booked and paid in full on the internet. I hoped the new owner would honour our booking.

Russ stayed with the taxi, in case we had to find somewhere else to stay, whilst I checked in. The young lad on reception was so polite and helpful. It was amazing compared to the laid back attitude we'd encountered previously. He checked us into a large room with two king size beds and a lovely view of the coastline from the balcony, overlooking the pool below.

We decided to go for a walk to Gros Islet, the newest town in Saint Lucia having been recently promoted from a village. On the way down the road, rain hosed us down. We took shelter under someone's carport, and when it eased enough, headed back to our room to pick up our raincoats. Heavy showers soaked us a few more times, so we took our cagoules on and off whilst strolling through town. Locals were sitting outside their colourful wooden houses on verandas, or standing chatting on street corners. A steel band at practice brightened up the grey day.

The scenic beach edging the sapphire lagoon called Rodney Bay, was flaxen sand curving around to Pigeon Island, the dense national park at the end of the causeway. I wriggled my feet, burying them under the soft sand whilst I watched a horse and foal frolic together.

In the evening, we explored the hotel roof top where we met the hotel owner, who was Scottish.

'Your receptionist was most helpful and great to deal with,' I told him whilst leaning against the wall.

He explained how difficult it was to get good staff, 'My cleaners don't bother to turn up for the day if it's raining, and when they do, they think it's sufficient to get paid, and they don't actually need to do any work.'

'It must be very frustrating,' I said sympathetically.

On a tour of the island, we drove through tropical rainforest and some spectacular mountain ranges spanning the length of the country. I held a St Lucian Boa constrictor whilst taking in the view of the Grand Bois Forest. I realized how far I'd travelled since holding my first snake in Singapore, over thirty years ago. I was so lucky to have seen so much and experienced many personal encounters with endangered animals. However, I hoped not to cross paths with the venomous fer-de-lance this trip.

On the steep road winding down into Soufriere, meaning "Sulphur in the Air", we drove through the only set of traffic lights in St Lucia which were across a one lane bridge. Frigate birds flew overhead casting shadows on us below.

The van travelled right up to, and through, the crater of Sulphur Springs, the Caribbean's solitary drive-in volcano. It housed fuming pools of dark water and bubbling mud, emitting a pungent aroma of rotten eggs, at temperatures well above boiling point. We weren't allowed to walk over the crater, which was covered in a thin crust, because unfortunately, at one stage, a volcano guide fell in and suffered third degree burns, so we didn't stray passed the fence. The rocks were stained various colours from the mixture of iron, calcium oxide, sulphur, copper oxide, carbon and magnesium.

It was time to move on, and after another short flight, we landed in Barbados. I found it more commercialised than all the other Caribbean islands we visited, although in some ways it made it easier to explore. Staying at St Lawrence, it was only a short walk to Dover

Beach, a picturesque blonde sand beach with crystal clear blue sea. I sat enjoying the view whilst stroking a friendly ginger and white moggy.

The weather was perfect with the sun caressing my skin when we boarded an elegant fifty-seven foot catamaran called Heatwave. The cool breeze blew the vessel across the flat aqua blue sea, occasionally the wind gusted whilst it gently pushed us up the western coastline.

At Paynes Bay, I snorkelled with the sea turtles and fish. A hawksbill surfaced right beside me and startled, quickly ducked back down again. It's beautifully patterned shell, although attractive, also made it vulnerable as poachers sold the tortoiseshell for a high price on the black market. I hoped this critically endangered species could survive as it was much more valuable to be able to watch it gracefully swimming, than to see it as part of somebody's collection.

Several green turtles swam gracefully underneath and around me, occasionally bumping against my limbs with their strong flippers. They ranged in size and age. Mesmerised, I watched them through my snorkel mask, a picture into another world. Even though they were not only endangered from poaching for their eggs, meat and shells but also from habitat destruction, I hoped would live on.

Heatwave ferried us to another bay. Snorkelling over a shipwreck and active reef, I observed a kaleidoscope of fish. The guide tempted them with food, so whole shoals swam around me, and one bit my finger. A slice of bread landed on Russ' back, and the fish had a feeding frenzy, eating it with their fins sticking out of the water like sharks. There were many variegated fish sculptured in different outlines and proportions.

It wasn't long, and we were off to another bay. Peacefully inhaling the wind on my face whilst standing on the front of the starboard bow, I moved with the rhythm of the catamaran as it cut through the waves on the way to Batts Rock Bay. Having anchored in the idyllic cove, I went for a swim with a pool noodle which assisted me in floating on the crystal clear azure water, gently lapping against the almost white soft sandy beach.

'Ahh, this is the life,' I crooned to Russ as I moved with the gentle waves.

'Not quite perfect, watch out for the manchineel tree on the beach. Don't touch it, or the fallen fruit, as it will cause a nasty rash and blisters,' he informed me from the deck.

'I have no intention of leaving the water.' I was chilling out before I had to return to land later that afternoon.

The following morning, crammed into a minibus, listening to the loud music blasting from the front console, I noticed each of the bus stops had its own name like "Samantha" or "Janet". There were advertising plaques for people to adopt a bus stop, so I assume the names were those of their sponsors.

In Bridgetown, we boarded a large comfortable yellow bus to Sturges, travelling through lush countryside to Welchman Hall Gully near the centre of Barbados, in the Parish of St Thomas.

I followed the wet slippery pathway through the unique gully which was fully formed eons ago when the roofs of caves collapsed. A green monkey sat high up in the trees surrounded by flourishing foliage. An abundance of tropical plants, embracing the edge of the pathway, revealed a prolific number of millipedes, making it impossible not to stand on a few.

Occasionally, I ducked underneath the fine roots hanging in mid-air from the bearded fig trees. Stalactite and stalagmite columns hung from the limestone cap, just like inside caves. I cautiously walked beneath the tall slender coconut palms laden with fruit in case it should drop. I thought about the boule that left an egg shaped lump on my head, in Boulogne years earlier, but had read that people have been injured or killed by a falling coconut.

I looked gloomily at the giant African snails because they were accidently introduced to the island, a decade ago, and are now an invasive species. They looked like something from a horror movie, but I wondered what they would be like to eat. I'd only tried snails once before. When I lived in England, I'd bought a tin of them marinated in garlic sauce. They were flavoursome, but the texture was gristly, and I couldn't bring myself to swallow it. I didn't consider them a delicacy, more a slimy repugnant creature to be avoided, especially as these snails were as big as my fist.

From the gully, we plodded on towards the Botanical Gardens Flower Forest. Signposted as only about three kilometres away, we had a pleasant stroll between green fields, stopping now and again to admire the views of the coastline. The tropical air made me quite sticky by the time I reached the entrance. However, the actual gardens were down an endless windy road which I trailed along wearily, a few metres ahead of Russ.

Halfway along the track, a truck of armed men in camouflage uniform overtook me and pulled over to the side of the road. Rifle in hand, one jumped off the back of the truck and walked towards me. We were in the middle of nowhere and extremely vulnerable. Stay calm, I told myself as he approached.

'Get in the truck,' he said, standing close to me.

I didn't even think to decline. As I pulled myself up the steps, Russ followed having caught up.

'We give you a lift to the gardens,' he explained as he climbed in behind us.

I smiled, relieved we weren't in any trouble, but Russ taunted, 'Why didn't you stop when you drove past me? You only stopped for the lady.'

This was a brave statement considering the rangers guns were aimed at his feet. Luckily they laughed, but I was pleased when we pulled up outside the gates and were free to wander at our leisure.

Inside, we set off to explore the flower forest along snaking paths with well set out signs stating "Don's Downhill", "Fritz's Fruits" and "Brown's Bypass" where I slipped on the wet stepping stones with an abrupt bump onto my bottom.

'Ouch,' escaped through my tight lips.

'Are you okay?' Russ laughed loudly.

'My dignity has been hurt more than my derriere.'

Easily distracted, I spotted a couple of mongooses that quickly scurried away into the undergrowth.

'Look in the palm tree, there is a rodent settling down to sleep,' pointed out Russ as I followed his gaze.

'I'm not surprised as it's so peaceful in this meticulously nurtured garden. We have the place to ourselves,' I replied, fanning myself with our map. I hoped the African snail would never reach these gardens, as they would be destroyed.

We meandered through the mature rainforest, majestic palms and colourful tropical blooms, stopping to admire the spectacular vision of the coast, lined with exotic beaches before having to tackle the journey back to St Lawrence.

Another day, we took the usual minibus to Bridgetown and walked to the northbound station. On enquiring how to get to the Barbados Wildlife Reserve, in the parish of St Peter, we found out we needed to catch a blue public bus going to Indian Ground. The buses ran infrequently, so locating the stop, we patiently waited about an hour and a half for the bus to arrive.

'There's the bus,' pointed out Russ when it pulled into the wrong spot.

'Phew, that was close because it certainly didn't stop for long,' I exclaimed, as we clambered on board. 'Thank goodness we didn't miss it, as it would be a long wait for the next one,' I pondered out loud.

It was a comfortable hour's ride, as the bus was almost empty, and then a short uphill walk to the reserve.

Walking to the gate, Russ called out, 'Look, mongooses,' whilst pointing them out before they disappeared into the undergrowth.

'They're cute, but it's such a shame they were introduced to eradicate the rats from the sugar cane fields, because they have now eradicated some species of endemic snakes, instead,' I informed him.

'It reminds me of our cane toads,' he replied as we approached the gate.

Inside the park, tortoises were roaming freely and mating noisily. I wandered through the serene mahogany forest, trying not to frighten the brocket deer which were a bit skittish and a few mara which were resting. Whilst I followed two miles of winding pathways, I discovered caiman in the water, caged snakes, macaws and other birds, endangered Cuban iguanas and baby bunnies.

I heard the Barbados Green Monkeys when feeding time neared, and they clambered over the fence from Grenade Hall Forest.

'Even these monkeys are not endemic,' I informed Russ as we watched their antics.

'They seem quite at home,' he replied, 'Stand beside the juvenile over there, and I will take your photo.'

Memories rushed back of the vervet monkey grabbing my foot at Victoria Falls National Park, in Zimbabwe, when it looked into my eyes and made a grab for my shoelaces.

'No thanks, they're wild, and I'm going to keep my distance.' I, backed away. 'I don't want to get between them and their food.'

When the keeper dumped a barrow load of sliced mangos into the feeding area, he had to pick up each of the tortoises and move them out of the way. The monkeys walked all over them to get to the food and then perched on top of their shells to eat it.

'I'd never have expected the tortoises to make such good seats,' I informed Russ.

Afterwards, we followed the nature trail, through the forest and under the light canopy of trees, to the Grenade Hall Forest and Signal Station and spotted the monkeys returning from the reserve. Several of them had small babies which clung tightly to their mothers as they jumped from tree to tree.

It was time to move on to St Vincent, the last island on our trip. On arrival, we caught a taxi to the guesthouse as it was nestled atop an extremely high hillside in the suburb of Cane Garden.

Nearby, Kingstown was a lively town and although called the City of Arches, wasn't particularly picturesque. The cobbled streets were quaint, but the historic stone buildings seemed cold and grey, perhaps it was because it was raining. Although there was a wharf adding to the noise, there were no waterside cafes or restaurants to tempt us inside.

We walked to the Botanical Gardens, up a steep hill. Immediately inside the gates, a local told us, 'It is compulsory to have a guide to take you around the gardens, and you will need to pay him. Wait here and I will find one for you.'

'We don't need one thank you. We'd just like to walk around on our own,' replied Russ, eager to get away.

'You can't, you must wait for a guide and pay him to give you a tour.'

'But there isn't one here, so we are going to wander by ourselves.' We hurriedly walked off.

We hadn't got far when another man in the park approached us. 'I belong to the park security and will find you a guide.'

'We really don't want one. We'd just like some quiet time to ourselves in the park,' I explained with a smile.

We wandered around the small park and found cages with some almost extinct St Lucian parrots inside. Nature was so fragile with species all over the world declining in numbers. After finding a bench to rest on, the dark moody clouds burst open, so we took cover under a tree until it eased to a drizzle.

The next day, when there was a break in the weather, we decided to walk into town. Up and down some steep hills we climbed until we were halfway down the last huge incline and could see the city. It started to rain heavily, so throwing on our raincoats, we sheltered under a tree as torrents of water rushed down the ascent. When it finally eased to a trickle, we pushed on, only to get caught in another deluge. This time, we could not find anywhere to shield ourselves so just kept walking. It was like a waterfall from the sky as it cascaded down on top of us and raced down the slope, much faster than we could walk. I spotted a small hut at the side of the road and ducked inside. Taking off my joggers and turning them upside down, water streamed out. I rang out my socks but had to put them back on again sodden.

It continued to rain on our last day when we caught a swaying boat to the island of Bequia, nine miles south of St Vincent. The ferry docked in Port Elizabeth, the capital, which is built along the waterfront of Admiralty Bay and into the rising hills surrounding it. We meandered along the Belmont Walkway beside the seaside, weaving our way south, passed restaurants, cafes and the Gingerbread Hotel with its intricate fretwork.

We walked along the coastal road where Caribbean music was blasting and people dancing as if the carnival had already started. A local youth rode by on a bicycle, and I couldn't help but laugh because he wore a bicycle helmet perched right on top of a huge Rasta cap full of dreadlocks. The helmet certainly wouldn't have protected his skull if he fell off but might have saved his hairstyle.

We climbed the steep gradient to Hamilton Fort where the panorama of the harbour and sandy beaches further along the coast was spectacular. Heading back to Port Elizabeth, we walked further around the coast to a small beach where we had a paddle in the refreshing sea before following a track inland. On our way back, I heard a loud crack and looking up, saw a coconut dropping from a lofty palm tree. I froze and watched in slow motion as it whistled by, almost skimming the tip of my nose.

'Did you see that?' I exclaimed loudly to Russ as I stepped back shaking. 'It just missed me. If it had hit my head, it would have cracked it open. What would you have done if I'd been killed?'

'Run away quickly, leaving you by the side of the road,' he replied nonchalantly, grinning at me.

For the rest of the holiday, I avoided sitting under any palm trees as I didn't want to tempt fate.

The Caribbean has beautiful scenery and excellent beaches but so does Australia. At home, the crime rate is a fraction of what it is in these tiny islands. I couldn't imagine living permanently in the Caribbean, although it was brilliant to visit and a relaxing experience.

Even though I live comfortably in Australia, I try not to waste water or electricity and appreciate having food and shelter each day. There are koalas and wallabies in the reserves nearby and sea turtles, dolphins, whales and dugongs in the local bay. They're all endangered by too much development, which makes me sad.

I'm privileged to have seen so much, experienced such wonderful adventures and encountered so many astonishing creatures. Species have become extinct for millions of years, dating back to when dinosaurs perished. However, today it's humans who are endangering species, due to pollution, habitat destruction and greed. I hope we can all be better people and live united with the earth's diverse fauna and flora, without destroying it.

Everyone can help contribute a little to conservation, just by visiting some of these remarkable places to help fund the research and breeding programs as well as encourage preservation.

Having explored a third of the countries in North America, I feel I've fulfilled my childhood dream to explore the five continents I learned about in my geography class at school, many years ago. I've looked for a place to live that I could call home, somewhere with warmth. My love and compassion towards wildlife, especially those vulnerable or endangered, fuels an ache in my chest, as much as my family, whom I miss and have left behind in England, although they will always be close in my heart. Each time I go away, I can return to a warm place that I am happy to call home.

Recently whilst spending time with my niece when she visited Australia, Hannah told me, 'I was taught at school that there are seven continents, Europe, Africa, Asia, Oceania, North America, South America and Antarctica.'

In some countries, they now teach that there are eight continents because Central America is counted separately to North America. So my goal posts have been moved, and I now have two more continents to explore.

Travelling has changed so much over the past five decades. Computer search engines make it easier to find out what there is to see, where to go and whether it's safe. The internet provides the facility to book flights, accommodation and activities, leaving less to chance. I no longer have to worry whether I'll be able to find somewhere to eat or sleep for the night, although I can never be certain the website isn't a scam, nor that I won't miss a flight, pushing all the booked accommodation out of schedule. Modern technology makes keeping in touch by email or video calling applications much simpler than chasing letters and sending postcards. There is less to carry with smaller cameras and music players. Even online stores sell dozens of useful ebook guides in one small package. Does that make it less adventurous? I don't think so. It opens up more of the world to explore.

Some places are becoming endangered, much like animals, and I'd love to visit them and discover more of the world and its precious creatures, so I will continue to travel.

ACKNOWLEDGEMENTS

I would like to thank all those who have supported and encouraged me to write my memoir. In particular my sister, Diana, whose opinion has been invaluable through my latest journey, not just whilst writing but as I tackled the publishing process. Ben, Jade and George who created my cover design. My close friend and writing buddy, Simone, who kept me motivated along with many others at Redwrites, including Celena, Rowena, Geoff and Brian.

My great-grandmother, whom I never met, inspired me to record my stories for future generations, so I dedicate this to my niece, Hannah.

Julia, Ian, Stewie, Michael, John, Ali and Ian, Dee and Bill and my parents (Sheila and Derek) for their company during my travel adventures. I'm grateful for your friendships and have refreshing memories of my time with you all, but especially with Bill and Derek, who can no longer leave footprints in this world. I met many interesting and generous characters along the way, who have helped shape me into the person I am today. However, without my husband Russ, I wouldn't have travelled nearly so far.

I appreciate and admire the conservation groups that are fighting to save our planet, the endangered animals that inhabit it and to wipe out world poverty. Your dedication made my encounters with mountain gorillas, rhino, tigers, pandas and orangutans possible.

Last, and definitely not least, I acknowledge your support if you are reading this.

Printed in Great Britain
by Amazon